In This Land

Jewish Life and Legal Culture in Late Medieval Provence

PINCHAS ROTH

Toronto

PIMS PONTIFICAL INSTITUTE OF MEDIAEVAL STUDIES

Library and Archives Canada Cataloguing in Publication

Title: In this land : Jewish life and legal culture in late medieval Provence / Pinchas Roth.
Names: Roth, Pinchas, author. | Pontifical Institute of Mediaeval Studies, publisher.
Series: Studies and texts (Pontifical Institute of Mediaeval Studies) ; 223.
Description: Series statement: Studies and texts ; 223 | Judaism in the medieval and early modern world ; 1 | Includes bibliographical references and index. | Text in English; appendix in Hebrew.
Identifiers: Canadiana (print) 20200402293 | Canadiana (ebook) 2020040251X | ISBN 9780888442239 (hardcover) | ISBN 9781771104135 (PDF)
Subjects: LCSH: Jews – France – Provence – History – To 1500. | LCSH: Jewish courts – France – Provence – History – To 1500. | LCSH: Jews – France – Provence – Social life and customs. | LCSH: Provence (France) – Social life and customs. | LCSH: Provence (France) – Ethnic relations.
Classification: LCC DS135.F85 P7685 2021 | DDC 944.9004924009/02–dc23

Pontifical Institute of Mediaeval Studies
59 Queen's Park Crescent East
Toronto, Ontario M5S 2C4
Canada
www.pims.ca

PRINTED IN CANADA

Contents

Preface

I owe thanks to many people who taught, guided, corrected and encouraged me and to the institutions that housed and supported me as I studied the rabbinic literature of late medieval Provence and struggled to find the way to share that literature with a wider audience. At the forefront stands my teacher Simcha Emanuel, who supervised my doctoral dissertation and who has continued to share his wisdom, advice and vast knowledge with me over the years.

Two post-doctoral fellowships allowed me to delve deeper into the material and to publish the results of my research in a number of journal articles. I acknowledge the generous support of the New York University Tikvah Center for Law and Jewish Civilization in 2012–2013 and the Goldstein-Goren International Center for Jewish Thought at Ben-Gurion University of the Negev in 2013–2015. I am grateful for the support of the Israel Council for Higher Education, through its Alon Fellowship for Outstanding Young Researchers. Since 2015, I have had the privilege of being a member of the Department of Talmud and Oral Law at Bar-Ilan University. I owe special thanks to the successive chairs, Chaim Milikowsky and Aaron Amit, for placing their trust in me and assisting my work in every way. My colleagues in the department, and particularly Leib Moscovitz and Judah Galinsky, have gone out of their way to be helpful and encouraging, not least by offering valuable advice about the publishing process.

A number of dear friends and mentors read sections and chapters of the book through various iterations and offered incisive comments that I was not always wise enough to heed. I thank Elisheva Baumgarten, Jay Berkovitz, Judah Galinsky, Debra Kaplan, Alexander Kaye, Jennie Rosenfeld and Rebecca Lynn Winer. David Sclar's friendship and frank criticism deserve special mention. Rachel Furst, Judith Kogel, Rami Reiner, Jonathan Rubin and Avi Shmidman were always willing to answer my questions. Menachem Butler secured copies of bibliographic items that were difficult or even nearly impossible to find.

When I was searching for a publisher, it was Judith Olszowy-Schlanger who suggested I approach the Pontifical Institute of Mediaeval Studies. I am honoured that Joanna Weinberg and Piet van Boxel accepted *In This Land* to inaugurate the series Judaism in the Medieval and Early Modern World. The argument and structure of the book are sharper for their exacting standards, and I am grateful for the thought and time they invested, not to mention their patience, in reading multiple versions of the manuscript. The anonymous readers for the press added vital corrections and invaluable suggestions for improvement. Fred Unwalla shepherded me through the publication process with professionalism, scholarly acumen, responsiveness and a rare attention to detail. Possessing both linguistic expertise and her own scholarly familiarity with medieval Provençal Jewry, Jaclyn Piudik did a masterful job of copyediting the book. Atara Snowbell proofread an earlier version of the manuscript and Reuven Soffer produced the beautiful maps. Megan Jones devoted great care to overseeing the production of the volume.

Since completing my dissertation in 2012, I have revisited many of the issues addressed there and encountered texts of which I was unaware at that time. In a number of articles published over the past few years (listed in the bibliography), I have focused on topics in the rabbinic culture of medieval Provence that often intersect with the discussions in this book. Portions of those articles that bear directly on the contents of this book have been incorporated in revised form as follows. Chapter 2 adapts material that first appeared in "Legal Strategy and Legal Culture in Medieval Jewish Courts of Southern France," *AJS Review* 38 (2014): 375–393. Chapter 3 draws on two previously published articles: "Asking Questions: Rabbis and Philosophers in Medieval Provence," *Journal of Jewish Studies* 67 (2016): 1–14 (https://doi.org/10.18647/3255/JJS-2016) as well as "Rabbinic Politics, Royal Conquest and Provençal Jewish Identity," in *Regional Identities and Cultures of Medieval Jews*, ed. Talya Fishman, Ephraim Kanarfogel and Javier Castaño (London, 2018), 173–191. I am grateful to the editors of these publications for permission to reuse them here. That said, my understanding of the medieval rabbinic sources and their context has evolved considerably over the past decade; in the course of writing this book I have revisited the original texts, corrected errors, uncovered new sources and revised my conclusions.

Without Jennie, none of this would have been possible, nor would it have seemed worthwhile. I dedicate this book to our children, with love and hope and with the prayer that Provençal Jews placed in the mouth of God: "Instead of derision, I will give you love. I will show you more kindness and send you my blessing for the year" (from "Shanah be-Shanah," a liturgical poem by Rabbi Yitzhak ha-Seniri included in the Provençal rite for the first day of the Jewish New Year).

Jerusalem
September 2020, Erev Rosh ha-Shanah 5781

Southern France and the Surrounding Region

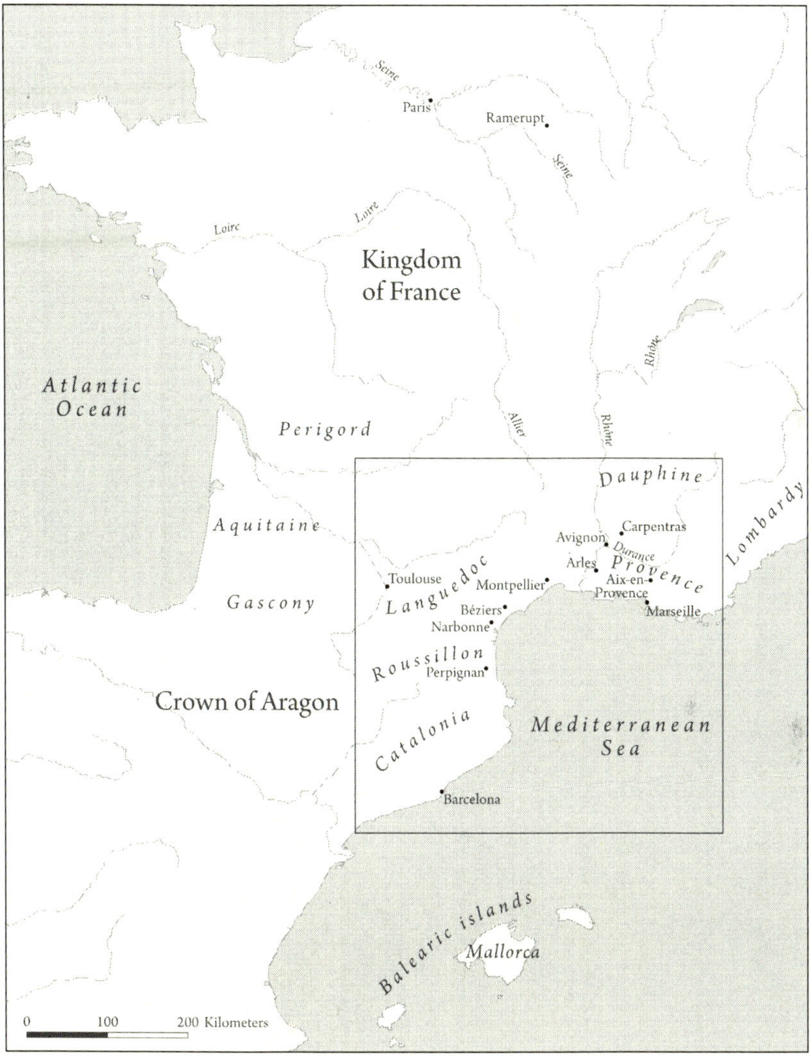

Jewish Communities in Provence Mentioned in the Current Volume

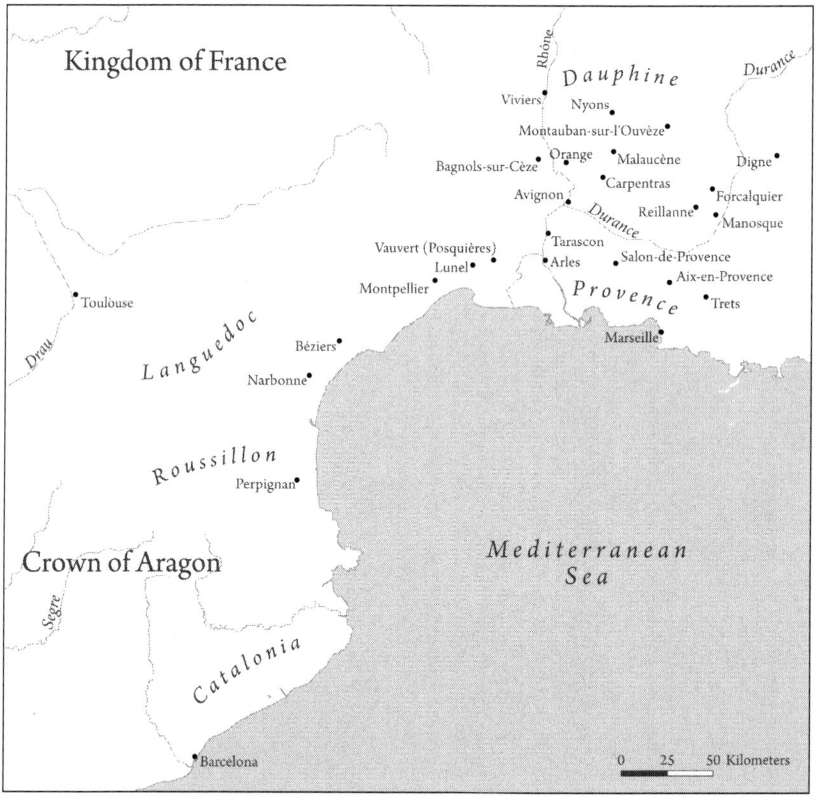

Introduction

A Jewish farmer somewhere in fourteenth-century Provence sat in mourning for a close relative. Remaining at home for the duration of the seven-day *shiv ʿah* period of mourning was more than his fragile economic abilities could sustain. Instructed by someone more learned in Jewish law, the farmer spent three days at home and then returned "to inspect the threshing house and to drive his beast and to carry a load on his shoulder."[1] Some other person wrote to a prominent rabbi named Isaac Kimḥi to ask his opinion about this lenient ruling and Kimḥi responded that there was no foundation for allowing a mourning Jew to work in public.

This brief legal exchange offers a fleeting (and, unfortunately, solitary) glimpse of Jewish agricultural work in southern France – a phenomenon known to have existed but about which little is known.[2] The story also encapsulates many of the questions discussed in this book, the majority of which took place in the cities and towns of medieval Provence, and not in rural settings. The Jewish farmer who could not afford to go without work for seven days is precisely the type of person who eluded mention in many medieval documents.[3] His existence was noted in Kimḥi's *responsum* by virtue of his legal, rather than his economic, status. But his fragility impacted the legal responses he received, first from a sympathetic unnamed scholar and later from an esteemed authority. The farmer did not approach Kimḥi directly, nor was the legal response he received preserved in

1. Paris, Bibliothèque nationale de France, Hébreu 1391, fol. 89v (see Appendix, source 1, pp. 121–122). The Talmud (bMo ʿed Katan 21b) permitted a pauper to work in the privacy of his home after the first three days of mourning.

2. Richard W. Emery, *The Jews of Perpignan in the Thirteenth Century: An Economic Study Based on Notarial Records* (New York, 1959), 21; Salo Baron, *A Social and Religious History of the Jews* (New York, 1952–1993), 12: 37; Michael Toch, *The Economic History of European Jews: Late Antiquity and Early Middle Ages* (Leiden, 2013), 79–87, 215–230. See also Andrew Berns, "The Importance of Agriculture in Medieval Jewish Life: The Case of Crete," *Jewish History* 33 (2020): 275–298.

3. "Because poor people have only a fleeting relationship with possessions, they tend to elude those public records – which predominated in the Middle Ages – that concern the possession, conveyance, and taxation of property." Sharon Farmer, *Surviving Poverty in Medieval Paris: Gender, Ideology, and the Daily Lives of the Poor* (Ithaca, 2005), 2.

its original form. Only when a third party wrote to Kimḥi about the case was the first ruling preserved for posterity, in the form of a *responsum* that undermined it entirely. Who was the person who first told the farmer to go back to work? How were they connected, and who initiated the conversation? Who questioned the first decision by forwarding it to a more recognized rabbi, and why did Kimḥi feel no compunctions about overruling it? I do not know the answers to these questions, but they point the way towards the type of questions that will be tackled here.

Provençal Jewish History

Provence lies at a crossroads between empires and cultures.[4] The Jewish communities of the region, some of which date back to the Roman period, were buffeted and moulded by the shifting cultural currents that swept through their land. Jewish culture is often bifurcated into Ashkenazic (northern European) and Sefardic (Iberian and Middle Eastern) traditions, and drawing distinctions between those two traditions is common practice among writers purporting to explain medieval Jewish culture.[5] Smaller communities, like those of Provence, which were neither Ashkenaz nor Sefarad, were forced to contend with the influence of more robust Jewish cultures. Such smaller communities played a vital and often unappreciated role in the formation of Jewish identity. Medieval Provençal Jews produced a rich and fascinating literary heritage, encompassing poetry and prose, philosophy and science, mysticism and magic, and it was precisely their entanglement with other cultures that fostered the complexity of their own heritage.

A great deal is known and has already been said about Jewish history in medieval Provence. From the 1880s onwards, a stream of studies was devoted to the publication and analysis of documents relating to the Jewish communities of

4. Linda Paterson, *The World of the Troubadours: Medieval Occitan Society, c. 1100–c. 1300* (Cambridge, 1993); Thierry Pécout, *L'invention de la Provence: Raymond Bérenger V (1209–1245)* (Paris, 2004). Jewish historians often refer to all of southern France (including Languedoc and Roussillon) as Provence. In this book, however, I generally use Provence in the more limited sense of the region east of the Rhône while the term "southern France" refers to the area as a whole. That said, the adjective "Provençal" is used here less discriminately to describe aspects common to the entire region.

5. See the recent critical remarks by Talya Fishman, "Introduction," in *Regional Identities and Cultures of Medieval Jews*, ed. Javier Castaño, Talya Fishman and Ephraim Kanarfogel (London, 2018), 1–4.

southern France.[6] Many such articles appeared in a range of French-Jewish periodicals.[7] During the twentieth century, a number of monographs were devoted to the history of individual communities.[8] Based primarily on the rich medieval archives of the cities and towns of Provence, the research of Monique Wernham, Juliette Sibon and others has demonstrated the degree to which Provençal Jews were immersed in the economic activities of the region. Joseph Shatzmiller utilized legal records from Manosque that show Jews bringing and responding to civil suits in the local courtrooms and occasionally standing trial for criminal offenses.[9] Local archives also provide information about Jewish neighbourhoods within the towns of Provence.[10] However, these sources afford very limited insight into the cultural and social dimensions of Jewish life in Provence.[11]

Similarly, the treatises, commentaries, astronomical tables, polemics for and against philosophy, original Hebrew compositions or translations from Arabic and Latin into Hebrew that were produced in southern France constitute a body of literature that has fueled innumerable studies on Jewish intellectual history.[12] Although it is based upon a rich literary corpus, this line of inquiry leaves major aspects of Provençal Jewish culture unexplored and provides very little insight into the lives

6. For surveys of nineteenth and early twentieth-century scholarship, see Danièle Iancu, *Les Juifs en Provence (1475–1501) de l'insertion a l'expulsion* (Marseille, 1981), 11–16.

7. Danièle Iancu-Agou, "Un siècle d'investigation sur les juifs du Midi médiéval dans les revues savantes juives d'expression française," in *Les revues scientifiques d'études juives*, ed. Simone Claude Mimouni and Judith Olszowy-Schlanger (Leuven, 2006), 83–92.

8. Joseph Shatzmiller, *Recherches sur la communauté juive de Manosque au moyen âge: 1241–1329* (Paris, 1973); Monique Wernham, *La communauté juive de Salon-de-Provence d'aprés les actes notaries 1391–1435* (Toronto, 1987); René Moulinas, *Les juifs du pape: Avignon et le Comtat Venaissin* (Paris, 1992); Juliette Sibon, *Les juifs de Marseille au XIVe siècle* (Paris, 2011).

9. See especially Shatzmiller, *Recherches*, 65–118.

10. Danièle Iancu-Agou, *Provincia Judaica: dictionnaire de géographie historique des juifs en Provence médiévale* (Leuven, 2010).

11. Much of this scholarship is synthesized by Ram Ben-Shalom, *The Jews of Provence and Languedoc: Renaissance in the Shadow of the Church* (Raʿananah, 2017), 50–169 (Hebrew).

12. Colette Sirat, *A History of Jewish Philosophy in the Middle Ages* (Cambridge, 1985); Ron Barkaï, *A History of Jewish Gynaecological Texts in the Middle Ages* (Leiden, 1998); Gad Freudenthal, "Arabic and Latin Cultures as Resources for the Hebrew Translation Movement: Comparative Considerations Both Quantitative and Qualitative," in *Science in Medieval Jewish Cultures*, ed. Gad Freudenthal (Cambridge, 2011), 74–105; Moritz Steinschneider, *Hebrew Translations of the Middle Ages and the Jews as Transmitters*, ed. Charles H. Manekin, Y. Tzvi Langermann, Hans Hinrich Biesterfeldt (Dordrecht, 2013); Howard Kreisel, *Judaism as Philosophy: Studies in Maimonides and the Medieval Jewish Philosophers of Provence* (Boston, 2015); Ben-Shalom, *The Jews of Provence and Languedoc*, 413–564.

led by the Jews who produced that culture. Hebrew poems and other literary works from Provence can be persuaded to yield some information about the concerns and hopes of Jews, but the range of topics culled from Hebrew poems is highly limited, as is the depth of historical information they elicit.[13] Precious few sources remain that provide true insight into life as it was lived by Jews in medieval Provence.

Reading Responsa

This book offers a partial solution to the historiographical problem described above by turning to the genre of Hebrew writing known as *responsa* (*she'elot u-teshuvot*, literally: questions and answers) – texts written by rabbinic scholars as answers to questions addressed to them regarding matters of Halakhah (Jewish law).[14] Other genres of rabbinic writings, such as talmudic commentaries or legal codes, are primarily focused on earlier texts or on ideal legal categories, and the imprint of the historical circumstances under which they were composed is often difficult to discern.[15] By contrast, *responsa* were usually written in response to specific legal questions, asked at a particular point in time by one person (or more) to another person (or group of people). Often the question was sparked by a specific, practical situation that some of the people involved felt required the input of a rabbinic scholar. Other questions were crafted by scholars in order to receive feedback from their colleagues, and many questions dealt with purely theoretical issues or with the correct interpretation of classical rabbinic texts. Due to its temporal nature, when read contextually alongside other types of documentation, rabbinic *responsa* literature allows the historian to reveal dimensions of Jewish life that would otherwise remain obscured.[16]

13. Susan Einbinder, *No Place of Rest: Jewish Literature, Expulsion, and the Memory of Medieval France* (Philadelphia, 2009); Uriah Kfir, *A Matter of Geography: A New Perspective on Medieval Hebrew Poetry* (Leiden, 2018), 140–164.

14. Menachem Elon, *Jewish Law: History, Sources, Principles*, trans. Bernard Auerbach and Melvin J. Sykes (Philadelphia, 1994), 1453–1468. An important step towards reading rabbinic texts from Provence as evidence of cultural tensions was taken by Simcha Emanuel, "The Struggle for Provençal Halakhic Independence in the Thirteenth Century," *Hispania Judaica Bulletin* 9 (2013): 5–14.

15. Haym Soloveitchik, "Can Halakhic Texts Talk History?," *AJS Review* 3 (1978): 153–196; revised version in Haym Soloveitchik, *Collected Essays* (Oxford, 2013–2014), I: 169–223.

16. Shatzmiller made judicious use of *responsa* in his studies on the Jews of southern France. See also Shlomo H. Pick, "Jewish Aristocracy in Southern France," *Revue des études juives* 161 (2002): 97–121; Shlomo H. Pick, "Medieval Provençal Jewish self-government," *Trumah* 15 (2005): 105–138.

To be sure, the historical utilization of *responsa* comes with its fair share of methodological challenges.[17] First, as with any type of pre-modern evidence, is the problem of preservation. Without question, many of the *responsa* composed in late medieval Provence are no longer extant. Even if all the *responsa* ever written had been preserved, they would not encompass all of the legal and religious debates that roiled Provençal Jewish society. For these reasons, quantitative analysis of the data is unfeasible.

A second major methodological challenge is reliability. To what degree can the descriptive content of *responsa* be taken as historically accurate? At times, *responsa* have proven to be wholly fictitious. For example, Moses de Leon (or a close contemporary of his with a similar Kabbalistic agenda) forged texts in the names of earlier rabbis and planted them within *responsa* collections.[18] Moses Botarel, who was active in Avignon at the end of the fourteenth century, perpetrated similar frauds.[19] However, such ideologically driven cases – while fascinating in their own right – are rare and do not pose an insurmountable obstacle to historical research.

A different type of *responsa* was written in response to questions that were invented by the respondent himself. Legal discussions of a theoretical nature formulated in question-and-answer format are fairly common, but such texts normally lack the narrative detail of full-blown *responsa*. For example, study texts in the form of questions and answers were used for reviewing the laws of kosher meat preparation, but these have nothing to do with the *responsa* genre.[20] For an author to concoct a fictional story to which he would then compose a response required an audience of likeminded readers who read the story and appreciate its artifice. Such a scenario has been suggested for certain rabbis in fifteenth- and sixteenth-century Central Europe.[21] However, as we will see below, Provençal

17. Haym Soloveitchik, *The Use of Responsa as an Historical Source* (Jerusalem, 1990) (Hebrew).

18. Israel M. Ta-Shma, *Studies in Medieval Rabbinic Literature* (Jerusalem, 2004–2010), 4: 112–129 (Hebrew); Avishai Bar-Asher, "Kabbalah and Minhag: Geonic *Responsa* and the Kabbalist Polemic on Minhagim in the Zohar and Related Texts," *Tarbiz* 84 (2015): 195–263 (Hebrew).

19. Simcha Assaf, "'Teshuvot ha-Ge᾽onim' mitokh genazav shel R. Moshe Botarel ("Geonic *responsa*" from the archives of Moses Botarel)," in *Sefer ha-Yovel: kovets torani mada῾i mugash le-Dr. Binyamin Menashe Lewin*, ed. J.L. ha-Kohen Fishman (Jerusalem, 1940), 1–20; reprinted in Simcha Assaf, *Tekufat ha-Ge᾽onim ve-Sifrutah* (Jerusalem, 1967), 323–340.

20. For a text of this sort from Provence, see New York, Jewish Theological Seminary of America, MS. R34 (8163), fols. 243v–246v.

21. Israel ben Petaḥiah Isserlein's *Terumat ha-Deshen* (Venice, 1519); Shlomo Eidelberg, *Jewish Life in Austria in the XVth Century* (Philadelphia, 1962), 51–52; Yedidya Alter

responsa were preserved only within a very small circle. They never reached a wider audience that would justify fictionalized writing.

There is, however, one type of false *responsum* that existed, or at least was believed to exist, in medieval Provence: a respondent received an ostensibly practical question about real circumstances, when in fact the description had been invented by the questioner. Samuel ben Joseph Mikhtam was asked by Abraham, a wealthy scholar (*ḥakham nadiv*), whether vegetables that had been purchased through the barter of leavened bread shortly before the Passover festival could be consumed during Passover.[22] Before tackling the legal problem, Samuel commented:[23]

> I will answer your question ... although I know that the case about which you inquired was not presented before you [for adjudication] and such a thing never happened in your midst. You invented it, and on a day when you were at leisure from your work you decided to read your books, and perhaps you found a ruling that you had never noticed before.

Even if the question was not entirely fictional, there was a real concern that its factual core had been redacted in order to elicit a specific legal response from the recipient. People often requested rulings in order to add legal weight and prestige to their own positions, which they could then say were supported by prominent rabbis. It may be assumed that the manner in which the question was crafted – the information that was supplied or omitted and the descriptive language used in presenting that information – could influence the response. Often, a question about a court case would be posed by one side in the conflict or by a family relative. A supportive response from an influential rabbinic scholar could be put to great strategic use when produced at the right moment in court. The German rabbi Meir of Rothenburg (d. 1293) maintained a policy of responding only to

Dinari, *The Rabbis of Germany and Austria at the Close of the Middle Ages* (Jerusalem, 1984), 304–309 (Hebrew); Tirza Kelman, "The Use of Ashkenazic Decisors in the Beit Yosef Yore Dea 183–200 as a Case Study," MA thesis (Ben-Gurion University, 2012), 47–49 (Hebrew); Ya'ir Ḥayyim Bacharach, *Havot Ya'ir* (Frankfurt am Main, 1699); Elchanan Reiner, "Ma'ase she-ira be-k.k. Vermaiza ba-ra'ash ha-gadol bi-shenat 396 (A story that happened in the community of Worms at the time of the great earthquake in 1626)," *Haaretz*, 4 October 2006.

22. Oxford, Bodleian Library, Opp. Add. 4°127, fols. 95v–96v; published in *Sefer ha-Mikhtam 'al masekhtot Pesaḥim Sukkah u-Mo'ed Katan*, ed. Moshe Yehudah Blau (New York, 1958), 363–366. Ownership of leavened bread is forbidden from several hours before the Passover festival begins.

23. Bodleian Opp. Add. 4°127, fol. 96r; Blau, *ha-Mikhtam 'al masekhtot Pesaḥim*, 364.

questions sent by the court, and not by parties to the cases.[24] Meir's policy was adopted by scholars in his orbit, but other rabbis did not hesitate to take sides.[25] As we will see in Chapter 2, a rabbinic respondent could be manipulated into providing a response that served the interests of the questioner, but which was at odds with the reality as witnessed by other people involved in the case. When the manipulation came to light, it could severely damage the reputation of a respondent as a disinterested arbiter.

The presence of verifiable details, or of multiple descriptions of a case, diminishes the concern that a question might be fictional and, at the same time, enriches the historical information that can be learned about that question. When the identity of the questioner is known, it can shed important light on the motivations for asking the question. Untangling the skein of personal connections and political affiliations between questioners and respondents can clarify some of the motivations behind the writing of a *responsum*.

Often, *responsa* present a very different type of challenge. Far from containing false or unreliable information, they seem to contain no information at all. To be sure, not every *responsum* is ripe for the historian's picking, and many, if not most, of the *responsa* written over the centuries are better left undisturbed. Yet, if a question was indeed asked – formulated, written out, delivered – and answered at a given moment in history, it must have held some degree of fascination at least for the person who asked it, and probably for those who copied it and preserved it for posterity. That fascination might not be with the content of the question itself but rather in the interaction that it elicited. When the armchair intellectual Abraham asked Samuel Mikhtam a question about bartered vegetables on Passover, he was probably less interested in Samuel's legal conclusion than in his willingness to tackle an obscure issue. It is the question in the *she'elah* that suggests a historical occurrence that requires explanation.

Likewise, in reading the answer, attention to ostensibly technical details such as the prooftexts cited by the respondent can uncover complexity in an otherwise unremarkable *responsum*. For example, if a rabbinic scholar in late medieval Provence based his ruling on the writings of the northern French Tosafists, he could be signaling an affinity for a Talmud-centered non-rationalist approach to Judaism. On the other hand, Halakhists who based themselves extensively on the legal works of Maimonides were usually familiar with his philosophical writ-

24. Meir ben Baruch of Rothenburg, *She'elot u-Teshuvot* (Cremona, 1557), no. 192, fol. 65v.

25. Judah Galinsky, "The Legacy of R. Judah ben Ha-Rosh, Rabbi of Toledo: A Chapter in the Exploration of the *Responsa* Literature of Christian Spain," *Pe'amim* 128 (2011): 175–210, at 178 n11 (Hebrew).

ings as well. The rhetoric of a *responsum* can also be revealing. *Responsa,* like other types of medieval writing, include generic tropes that were introduced almost by rote – the author protests that he is unworthy of the questioner's attention, too young or ignorant to answer the question, too tired and miserable to do it justice. Obviously, they cannot be taken at face value, but, standard as they may be, these protestations are expressed in a unique way by each respondent. More rewarding, though, are the more personal comments, the unguarded turns of phrase that a scholar let slip or intentionally wove into his *responsum* in order to signal his feelings about the questioner, the case or his rabbinic colleagues whose opinions on the case he was critiquing.

In almost every case, both question and answer were penned by Jewish men, and often the questioner was almost as well versed in rabbinic texts as the scholar to whom he addressed his question. Obviously, the homogeneous social profile of the people directly involved in the exchange of *responsa* curtails the efficacy of the genre as a historical source. At the same time, *responsa* are not fundamentally different in this respect from other forms of medieval writing that have been tackled by feminist historians.[26] Even when reported second or third hand, the voices of other people – Jewish women, uneducated men, Gentiles – can often be heard in the *responsa.* Some questions were written by scholarly men on behalf of laypeople. Others, like Isaac Kimḥi's *responsum* about the mourning farmer, respond to legal situations without the direct protagonist necessarily having asked for such a response. Halakhic discussions seeped into the lives of medieval Jews even without their awareness.

Historical study of *responsa* has advanced on two major fronts.[27] First, the biographical and bibliographic investigation of halakhic works and their authors has drawn a great deal of attention. This type of inquiry is indispensable for historians, since it aims to clarify the coordinates of time and place within which a given halakhic statement must be located, but it does not treat Halakhah *per se.*[28] The second front tackles Halakhah head-on, tracking the various iterations of a given legal question over time in search of trends, changes or shifts in legal think-

26. For examples, see *Gendered Voices: Medieval Saints and Their Interpreters,* ed. Catherine M. Mooney (Philadelphia, 1999); J.H. Chajes, "He Said She Said: Hearing the Voices of Pneumatic Early Modern Jewish Women," *Nashim* 10 (2005): 99–125.

27. Jeffrey Woolf, "Methodological Reflections on the Study of Halakhah," *European Association for Jewish Studies Newsletter* 11 (2001): 9–14.

28. Much of my doctoral dissertation was devoted to this type of research. Pinchas Roth, "Later Provençal Sages – Jewish Law (Halakhah) and Rabbis in Southern France, 1215–1348" (PhD diss., Hebrew University, 2012).

ing. Often, historians have pointed to instances in which a halakhic decision or position was crafted under the influence of external factors such as economic pressures, societal forces, philosophical or mystical beliefs, and the desire to either emulate or reject behaviors and beliefs found in the non-Jewish host culture.[29] Although this book will touch upon both of these aspects by tracing the development of legal doctrines and by clarifying when and where the *responsa* were written, its main focus is the social and cultural history embedded within the halakhic texts. This is explored in two directions – by enlisting information from other historical sources in order to illuminate details within the *responsa*, and by recovering historical data from the *responsa* to fill in the blanks left by other sources. By utilizing all of the available resources, it becomes possible to fill in some of the gaps in our understanding of Jewish life in medieval Provence, to feel the texture of its social fabric and to recognize the issues that led Provençal Jews to bicker, debate and litigate.

Textual Sources

Most of the *responsa* discussed in this book were preserved in four collections. The best known, *Teshuvot Ḥakhme Provinẓia (Teshuvot Ḥakhme Provintsya)*, was published from manuscripts by Abraham Sofer (Schreiber) in 1967.[30] The collection was originally collated by a grandson of Mordechai Kimḥi in the late fourteenth or early fifteenth century, and most of the *responsa* were written by Kimḥi, his son Isaac and their contemporaries.[31] The compendium in its original state is partially preserved in a sixteenth-century manuscript that was not used for Sofer's edition, which reveals that the original editor organized his material thematically to follow the order of Jacob ben Asher's *Arba῾ah Turim* (a major halakhic code completed in Toledo in the mid-

29. The pitfalls of such an approach have been noted often by scholars. See especially Soloveitchik, *Collected Essays*, I: 196–199; II: 219–221.

30. *Teshuvot Ḥakhme Provinẓia (Teshuvot Ḥakhme Provintsya)*, ed. Abraham Sofer (Schreiber) (Jerusalem, 1967). The English title page translates the title as *Responsae of the Sages of Provence*. The *responsa* by Mordechai and Isaac Kimḥi in this volume were published in German translation by Hans-Georg von Mutius, *Rechtsentscheide Mordechai Kimchis aus Südfrankreich* (Frankfurt am Main, 1991); Hans-Georg von Mutius, *Rechtsentscheide Isaak Kimchis aus Südfrankreich* (Frankfurt am Main, 1992–1993).

31. The authors of the *responsa* are listed by Sofer, *Teshuvot Ḥakhme Provinẓia (Teshuvot Ḥakhme Provintsya)*, pp. xx–xxii. Thirty-one out of a total of 110 signed *responsa* were written by Mordechai or Isaac Kimḥi. Roth, "Later Provençal Sages," 48–50.

fourteenth century).[32] However, in the pair of manuscripts utilized by Sofer in his edition, the Provençal *responsa* were submerged within a much larger collection of Iberian and North African *responsa*.[33] The extant portions of that larger collection are likewise arranged according to *Arba'ah Turim*, encompassing two of its four section – family law and civil law.[34] While the Provençal portion of the family law section is quite extensive, with eighty-five *responsa*, the second section contains only forty-nine *responsa* from southern France (most of which date to the twelfth century).

Another extensive collection of *responsa* tied to the Kimḥi family remains unpublished.[35] Copied in Provence during the fifteenth century by a scribe named Israel, the manuscript is preserved at the Bibliothèque nationale de France as ms. Hébreu 1391.[36] Israel's exemplar was the personal notebook of Isaac ben Mordechai Kimḥi (d. ca. 1343), as evidenced by marginal comments copied by Israel that were signed "Amitz," an acronym for "*Amar Yitzḥak* (Isaac said)."[37] Of the fifty signed *responsa* in the manuscript, twenty-eight bear the name of Isaac Kimḥi, and he probably also wrote many of the unsigned *responsa* in the collection.[38]

32. Paris, Alliance Israelite Universelle, ms. H 135 A. The manuscript is described by Isidore Loeb, "Le procès de Samuel ibn Tibbon," *Revue des études juives* 15 (1887): 70–79, at 70. A fragment of this manuscript (or another manuscript much like it), now lost, was described by Samuel Poznanski, "Sur un fragment d'une collection de consultations rabbiniques du XIVe siècle," *Revue des études juives* 40 (1900): 91–94.

33. Oxford, Bodleian Library, Opp. Add., fol. 70 (Neubauer cat. no. 2550); London, British Library, Add. 22089. The two manuscripts were copied by the same scribe, a Sefardic Jew living in Italy, during the fifteenth century. Benjamin Richler, "Hebrew Manuscripts that were Separated," *Asufot* 1 (1987): 105–158, at 141–142 (Hebrew).

34. Bodleian Opp. Add., fol. 70 covers family law (*Even ha-Ezer*) and BL Add. 22089 contains the *responsa* on civil law (*Ḥoshen Mishpat*).

35. The manuscript was purchased by the French library from Nissim Elisha Eliyahoo Zechariah, minister of the Iraqi "Keneseth Eliyahoo" synagogue in Mumbai during the late nineteenth century. Extracts from the manuscript were published and discussed in a serial article by Israel Lévi, "Un recueil de consultations inédites de rabbins de la France méridionale," *Revue des études juives* 38 (1899): 103–122; 39 (1899): 76–84, 226–241; 43 (1901): 237–258; 44 (1902): 73–86. Sofer occasionally cited variants from this manuscript in his edition of *Teshuvot Ḥakhme Provinzia (Teshuvot Ḥakhme Provintsya)*.

36. The scribe disclosed his name by marking the word "Israel" when it occurred in the text he was transcribing. See e.g. BnF Héb. 1391, fols. 6v, 49v, 170r. The manuscript also contains marginal annotations by Menaḥem de Lonzano, a seventeenth-century Mediterranean polymath with an abiding interest in medieval Provençal rabbinic texts. Jordan S. Penkower, *Masorah and Text Criticism in the Early Modern Mediterranean: Moses ibn Zabara and Menahem de Lonzano* (Jerusalem, 2014), 78–79.

37. BnF Héb. 1391, fols. 103v–105v, noted by Lévi, "Un recueil," *Revue des études juives* 43 (1901): 239.

38. Roth, "Later Provençal Sages," 53.

Several *responsa* from late medieval Provence were preserved by Isaac ben Immanuel de Lattes, who was born in the Comtat Venaissin towards the beginning of the sixteenth century and migrated in 1539 to Italy, where he served as rabbi in different communities until his death in 1570.[39] De Lattes evidently carried medieval manuscripts with him when he left his ancestral home. When he prepared a clean copy of the *responsa* that he had written himself over the course of his rabbinic career, he incorporated copies of the Provençal *responsa* into the volume:[40]

> Behold, I found this in a notebook... and I decided to include it along with my own decisions and others that are in my possession, so that they should not be lost and they will add to the volume and increase the glory of my notebook.

The medieval materials preserved by de Lattes include *responsa* by Mordechai and Isaac Kimḥi and by Isaac of Manosque, among the central figures in this book.[41]

Finally, the massive corpus of *responsa* by Solomon ben Abraham ibn Adret (Barcelona, ca. 1220–1310) contains crucial information about Provençal halakhic culture.[42] Ibn Adret was the foremost rabbinic authority of his time, and

39. David Fränkel, "Biographie des R. Isaac di Lattes," *Alim: A Periodical for Bibliography and History of the Jews* 3 (1937): 27–33 (Hebrew); Robert Bonfil, *Rabbis and Jewish Communities in Renaissance Italy*, trans. Jonathan Chipman (Oxford, 1990), 102–103; Simon Schwarzfuchs, "Rabbi Isaac Joshua ben Immanuel of Lattes and the Jews of the Apostolic States," *Italia Judaica* 6 (1998): 66–79; Bernard Dov Cooperman, "Political Discourse in a Kabbalistic Register: Isaac de Lattes' Plea for Stronger Communal Government," in *Be'erot Yitzhak: Studies in Memory of Isadore Twersky*, ed. Jay M. Harris (Cambridge, MA, 2005), 47–68; Bernard Dov Cooperman, "Organizing Knowledge for the Jewish Market: An Editor/Printer in Sixteenth-Century Rome," in *Perspectives on the Hebraic Book: The Myron M. Weinstein Memorial Lectures at the Library of Congress*, ed. P.K. Pearlstein (Washington, DC, 2012), 79–129.

40. Isaac ben Immanuel de Lattes, *She'elot u-Teshuvot*, ed. Mordechai Tzvi (Max Hermann) Friedländer (Vienna, 1860), 26.

41. The medieval *responsa* appear in de Lattes, *She'elot u-Teshuvot*, 26–34 (Abraham ben David of Posquières), 34–45 (a series of *responsa* concerning Isaac of Manosque), 51–53 (Isaac of Manosque), 87–97 (a different case involving Isaac of Manosque), 97–111 (*responsa* from Aragon about a divorce in Marseilles, 1386) and 127–138, on which see Pinchas Roth, "'My precious books and instruments': Jewish Divorce Strategies and Self-fashioning in Medieval Catalonia," *Journal of Medieval History* 43 (2017): 548–561, at 554–555.

42. Joseph Perles, *R. Salomo b. Abraham b. Adereth: Sein Leben und seine Schriften* (Breslau, 1863); Isidore Epstein, *The Responsa of Rabbi Solomon ben Adreth of Barcelona as a Source of the History of Spain* (London, 1925); Elka Klein, *Jews, Christian Society, and Royal Power in Medieval Barcelona* (Ann Arbor, 2006), 159–161.

he fielded questions from across the Jewish world.[43] The Jews of Provence and Languedoc had a particularly enthusiastic relationship with him, as attested by almost one hundred *responsa* addressed to the region.[44] As a rule, at the head of each *responsum* Solomon ibn Adret named the community to which it was addressed. Regrettably, these superscriptions were often removed, and sometimes mangled, when the *responsa* were published.[45] However, Simcha Emanuel has demonstrated that specific manuscripts preserve original clusters of ibn Adret's correspondence, enabling researchers to piece together *responsa* on different topics sent to a single recipient.[46] As a result, it is possible to identify more of ibn Adret's responses to Provence and to restore the original context in which they were framed.

In addition to these collections of *responsa*, one fascinating text that sheds light on the personalities of many rabbinic scholars of the period is the "Minor Epistle of Apology" composed by Kalonymos ben Kalonymos.[47] In 1305 or 1306, as a young man, Kalonymos left his home, his wife and his young children in Arles and travelled to Barcelona to study Talmud under Solomon ibn Adret. Recognizing the need to defend his actions to his brother, who was left to support the abandoned family, Kalonymos explained in detail why none of the rabbis closer to home were suited to the task of teaching him. Kalonymos went on to become one of the most distinguished translators of his day as well as a skilled satirist, and his literary skill and sharp wit are evident in his Apology.[48] His sketches of the rabbis of his day provide rare glimpses of the human beings behind the *responsa*.

43. Simcha Emanuel, "Halakhic Questions of Thirteenth-Century Acre Scholars as a Historical Source," *Crusades* 17 (2019): 115–130.

44. Pinchas Roth, "Regional Boundaries and Medieval Halakhah: Rabbinic *Responsa* from Catalonia to Southern France in the Thirteenth and Fourteenth Centuries," *Jewish Quarterly Review* 105 (2015): 72–98.

45. Seven volumes of *responsa* were printed between 1480 and 1868. A cumulative edition by Aharon Zaleznik, *She'elot u-Teshuvot* (Jerusalem, 1997–2005), includes an eighth volume of previously unpublished *responsa*.

46. Simcha Emanuel, "'From Where the Sun Rises to Where It Sets': The *Responsa* by Rashba to the Sages of Acre," *Tarbiz* 83 (2015): 465–489 (Hebrew); Simcha Emanuel, "Additional *Responsa* by Rabbi Shlomo ben Aderet," in *Professor Meir Benayahu Memorial Volume*, ed. Moshe Bar-Asher, Yehuda Liebes, Moshe Assis and Yosef Kaplan (Jerusalem, 2019), 1: 329–339 (Hebrew).

47. Joseph Shatzmiller, "Minor Epistle of Apology of Rabbi Kalonymos ben Kalonymos," *Sefunot* 10 (1966): 7–52 (Hebrew).

48. Theodor Dunkelgrün, "Dating the Even Bohan of Qalonymos ben Qalonymos of Arles: A Microhistory of Scholarship," *European Journal of Jewish Studies* 7 (2013): 39–74 (with references to earlier literature at n5).

Structure of This Book

The first chapter of this book provides the background for the chapters that follow by defining the term "halakhic culture" while exploring its social and intellectual context in medieval Provence. As rabbinic study became more firmly established in southern France during the twelfth century, a localized tradition began to emerge. (The cities, towns and rivers mentioned in the *responsa* are depicted in the maps prepared for this book; see pp. ix–x.) That tradition was complicated and overshadowed by more dominant rabbinic schools of thought from the south – the rabbinic academies of Sefarad – and from the north, by the Tosafists. From the end of the thirteenth century onwards, the writings of Maimonides exerted a powerful new influence on the region – a development which led, in turn, to the growing significance of rationalist philosophy for Provençal Jewish intellectuals. The new intellectuals challenged local traditions and shifted the balance of religious authority within the community.

Each of the following chapters revolves around a particular rabbinic figure and, through him, focuses on a particular theme in Provençal Jewish culture. The men whose writings form the foundation for Chapters 2–5 lived during the late thirteenth and early fourteenth centuries. Their involvement in legal debates led to interactions and direct exchanges between them all, so that each of these men represents a node in the social network that dominated halakhic discourse in this period. An understanding of their biographical details provides a firmer grasp on the nuances of their *responsa*. This book focuses on those details not for their own sake, but in order to peer through the *responsa* as an aperture onto wider Jewish society in late medieval Provence.

Chapter 2 explores the Jewish courts in Provence as they changed towards the end of the thirteenth century through the experience of Mordechai Kimḥi, who served as a judge in Narbonne and Carpentras. Jewish courts functioned in Provence and Languedoc throughout the High Middle Ages and played a crucial function in Jewish society. Staffed by rabbinic scholars, their clients came from all walks of life. As the spread of Roman law changed the culture of courts throughout Provence and Languedoc, Jewish courts changed as well, along with the expectations that Jews held about their courts. Some of the rabbinic judges who staffed those courts faced the changing landscape with equanimity, while Mordechai Kimḥi struggled and protested against what he perceived as the manipulation of a divinely ordained system.

During the thirteenth and fourteenth centuries, as French encroachment from the north grew steadily stronger, the entire Midi was forced to clarify its distinctive identity. Provençal Jews found themselves in an increasingly diverse environment that included not only French royal officials and bureaucrats but also migrant Jews from northern France. They developed a form of autochthonous pride that resisted and chafed against new people and norms from northern France. Isaac Kimḥi, the central figure discussed in Chapter 3, was himself a fierce local advocate who battled the growing influence of foreign Jewish traditions. Yet his *responsa* also reveal a policy of tolerance that respected difference and invited understanding between French and Provençal Jews, and also between Jews, Christians and Muslims.

The French Jews who migrated south to Provence settled in ethnically distinct clusters. Fights within the migrant French community sometimes spilled over and led to the involvement of the Provençal community as well. Their experience offers vivid glimpses of a transplanted Jewish community whose tensions with locals presaged the fraught encounter of Sefardic Jews exiled from Spain in 1492 with communities in North Africa and the Ottoman Empire. Chapter 4 explores the tensions roused by this population, primarily by focusing on Rabbi Isaac of Manosque, one of the leading rabbinic figures in the migrant French community. A respected leader and a volatile lightning rod, Isaac of Manosque's writings expose the central and destabilizing role played by ethnic tensions in fourteenth-century halakhic discourse in Provence.

Jewish intellectual life in southern France was marked by bitter ideological polemics. The potentially subversive and allegedly corrosive influence of Moses Maimonides and his rationalist followers led to simmering tensions that erupted on several occasions into public controversy. Chapter 5 is devoted to Abba Mari of Lunel, who instigated the controversy over rational philosophy and allegory that engulfed southern French and Catalonian Jewry in 1304–1305. While his role in the controversy is relatively well known, modern scholars have never considered Abba Mari's halakhic writings. These date from two periods – during his anti-philosophical campaign, and after the 1306 Expulsion from France – and reflect the complicated place that zealotry played in Jewish religious life.

The first five chapters of the book present interlocking perspectives on a single timespan, from the late-thirteenth century until the 1340s. The same names and the same historical events, encountered repeatedly from disparate perspectives, underscore the dense mutual influences exerted by the cultural factors explored in each of the chapters. The final chapter turns to the second half of the fourteenth century, picking up the shards of communal identity that survived disaster.

The Black Death reached Provence in late 1347 and ravaged local society in recurrent waves over the following decades. Jacob ben Moses of Bagnols served as a teacher and rabbi in Avignon and Carpentras during the Black Death. He is virtually the only Provençal rabbi from the mid-fourteenth century whose writings survive. Preserved in a single manuscript copied by Jacob himself, they provide a bleak picture of a community that was rapidly losing the tools to understand its own heritage. Jacob gave particularly rich descriptions of local rulings and customs relating to child marriage. These acquired a new resonance in a time when social and familial ties were being stretched and severed.

CHAPTER ONE

Jewish Culture and Religious Life in Southern France

Around the year 1304, a fierce debate engulfed the Jewish communities of southern France.[1] The controversy over the legitimacy of rationalist philosophy entered a new phase of intensity in the summer of 1305 when Solomon ben Abraham ibn Adret of Barcelona pronounced a *ḥerem* (excommunication) against people voicing opinions he deemed heretical. One of the most eloquent and respectful responses issued by the rationalist camp was an "apology" (in fact, a full-throated defense) by Yedaiah ha-Penini, a Hebrew poet and philosopher.[2] At stake was not simply an intellectual dustup over how best to interpret biblical stories, but the cultural identity of an entire community:[3]

> Go and ask the first generation of sages and rabbis in this land whether they thought and believed in the ideas that are being spread around today. Their lips will speak from the grave on behalf of their persecuted children. Would our ancestors have agreed with you and with the French rabbis regarding the secrets of belief, or would they have fought against them? Why do you say that our faith today is death and destruction, any more than the faith of our teachers in Narbonne and Béziers and Lunel and Montpellier and the other communities of Provence and Venaissin all the way to Marseille, that you have singled out these regions for evil and derision?

In this short passage, Yedaiah invoked several of the key elements that defined his community's identity – the memory of venerated scholars in earlier generations, the fear of encroachment by rabbis outside local borders and a complicated def-

1. Gregg Stern, *Philosophy and Rabbinic Culture: Jewish Interpretation and Controversy in Medieval Languedoc* (London, 2009); Tamar Ron Marvin, "A Heretic from a Good Family? A New Look at Why Levi b. Abraham b. Hayim was Hounded," *AJS Review* 41 (2017): 175–201.

2. Abraham S. Halkin, "Yedaiah Bedershi's Apology," in *Jewish Medieval and Renaissance Studies*, ed. Alexander Altman (Cambridge, MA, 1967), 165–184.

3. Solomon ben Abraham ibn Adret, *She'elot u-Teshuvot*, 1: no. 418, ed. Aharon Zaleznik (Jerusalem, 1997–2005), 1: 207.

inition of those geographic borders. "The first generation of sages and rabbis" was not named – perhaps because the names of those early scholars had been entirely forgotten – but its existence was assumed and lent legitimacy to the generation living in the present. That legitimacy was now being questioned by "French rabbis" and by ibn Adret himself, living in Barcelona. Although Yedaiah's sense of those inside and outside the community was sharply defined, it could only be expressed by listing a chain of cities and towns stretching from Narbonne in western Languedoc, along the Mediterranean coast "until Marseille." This was his land.

Throughout the Middle Ages, the southern part of modern-day France remained a patchwork of diverse and intertwined political entities. Despite these divisions, inhabitants of the region and its modern historians concurred with Yedaiah ha-Penini that they possessed a unifying cultural foundation, and they struggled to find an apt name to signify that unity.[4] Local Jews during the Middle Ages found a solution by referring to it simply as "this land."[5]

Ignoring the finer details of local political history, for our purposes it is sufficient to speak of three regions – Roussillon in the west formed a part of the Crown of Aragon, Provence in the east was an independent county until the end of the fifteenth century, and Languedoc, between Roussillon and Provence, was annexed to the French kingdom during the mid-thirteenth century. Avignon and the Comtat Venaissin were enclaves within Provence that became part of the Papal states.[6] By the thirteenth century, Jewish communities existed in all of these regions.[7]

4. Joseph R. Strayer, *The Albigensian Crusades* (New York, 1971), 10–11; Pierre Bonnassie, "L'Occitanie, un état manqué?," *L'histoire* 14 (1979): 31–40; Andrew Roach, "Occitania Past and Present: Southern Consciousness in Medieval and Modern French Politics," *History Workshop Journal* 43 (1997): 1–22; Linda M. Paterson, "Was there an Occitan Identity in the Middle Ages?," in Linda M. Paterson, *Culture and Society in Medieval Occitania* (Farnham, 2011), chapter 1.

5. For some examples, see Paris, Bibliothèque nationale de France, Hébreu 1391, fol. 85r: "the custom of the women in this land"; BnF Héb 1391, fol. 154r: "all of the sages that lived in this land." See also Stern, *Philosophy and Rabbinic Culture*, xiii: "Note on geographic terms"; Uriah Kfir, *A Matter of Geography: A New Perspective on Medieval Hebrew Poetry* (Leiden, 2018), 140, n1.

6. William Chester Jordan, "The Jews and the Transition to Papal Rule in the Comtat-Venaissin," *Michael* 12 (1991): 213–232.

7. The most comprehensive survey of these medieval communities remains Henri Gross, *Gallia Judaica* (Paris, 1897), based primarily on Hebrew sources. Since then, a host of archival studies have greatly enriched our understanding of certain local communities. See Danièle Iancu-Agou, "Un siècle d'investigation sur les juifs du Midi médiéval dans les revues savantes juives d'expression française," in *Les revues scientifiques d'études juives*, ed. Simone

Jewish life in Languedoc came to an abrupt halt in the summer of 1306, when King Philip IV (the Fair) imprisoned and then expelled all the Jews in his kingdom.[8] By then Languedoc was part of France, and its Jews were expelled along with their brethren from Paris, Normandy and Champagne. Officially, the expulsion was short-lived, since Philip's son King Louis X readmitted the Jews in 1315, but Jewish life in France and particularly rabbinic learning never returned to its pre-1306 strength.[9] The community in the county of Provence persevered until it was absorbed into the French kingdom and the Jews were expelled in 1501.[10] Small pockets of Jewish presence remained even after that, confined to ghettos within the Papal cities of Comtat Venaissin and Avignon, until the French Revolution when they were granted full civil rights.[11]

Many historians have been drawn to the Jewish communities of Provence. They glean rich information, primarily about economic aspects of Jewish life, from the extensive municipal archives of the region.[12] They show Jews deeply embedded in the economic fabric of Provençal society, working as tradesmen, merchants, doctors, and also as moneylenders.[13] The coral trade was an area with a particu-

---

Claude Mimouni and Judith Olszowy-Schlanger (Louvain, 2006), 83–92; Danièle Iancu-Agou, *Provincia Judaica: Dictionnaire de géographie historique des juifs en Provence medieval* (Leuven, 2010).

8. William Chester Jordan, *The French Monarchy and the Jews: From Philip Augustus to the Last Capetians* (Philadelphia, 1989), 200–213; William Chester Jordan, "Administering Expulsion in 1306," *Jewish Studies Quarterly* 15 (2008): 241–250; Céline Balasse, *1306: L'expulsion des juifs du royaume de France* (Bruxelles, 2008); Susan Einbinder, *No Place of Rest: Jewish Literature, Expulsion, and the Memory of Medieval France* (Philadelphia, 2009), 1–4; Gérard Nahon, "Le figuier du Seigneur: relations hébraïques méridionales des exiles de 1306," in *Philippe le Bel et les juifs du royaume de France (1306)*, ed. Danièle Iancu-Agou (Paris, 2012), 211–241; Abraham David, "L'expulsion des juifs français à la lumière des sources hébraïques," in *Philippe le Bel et les juifs du royaume de France*, 243–252.

9. William Chester Jordan, "Home Again: The Jews in the Kingdom of France, 1315–1322," in *The Stranger in Medieval Society*, ed. F.R.P. Akehurst and Stephanie Cain Van D'Elden (Minneapolis, 1997), 27–45.

10. Danièle Iancu, *Les Juifs en Provence (1475–1501): de l'insertion a l'expulsion* (Marseilles, 1981).

11. René Moulinas, *Les juifs du pape: Avignon et le Comtat Venaissin* (Paris, 1992); Marianne Calmann, *The Carrière of Carpentras* (Oxford, 1984).

12. Iancu-Agou, *Provincia Judaica;* Danièle Iancu-Agou, "Provence: Jewish Settlement, Mobility and Culture," in *The Jews of Europe in the Middle Ages (Tenth to Fifteenth Centuries)*, ed. Christoph Cluse (Turnhout, 2004), 175–189.

13. Judith Olszowy-Schlanger, "Binding Accounts: A Ledger of a Jewish Pawn Broker from 14th Century Southern France (Ms. Krakow, BJ Przyb/163/92)," in *Books within Books: New Discoveries in Old Book Bindings*, ed. Andreas Lehnardt and Judith Olszowy-Schlanger (Leiden, 2014), 97–147; Julie Mell, *The Myth of the Medieval Jewish Moneylender* (New York, 2017–2018), 2: 113–146.

larly high concentration of Jews.[14] At least one Jewish family ran a toll station.[15] Most Jews dwelt in cities, and some two dozen fragments from medieval Hebrew inscriptions – tombstones and synagogue dedications – have been recorded in Aix, Arles, Carpentras and Tarascon.[16] At the same time, local documents reveal Jews living in towns and small villages.[17] Such documents sometimes contain information about the physical institutions of Jewish life, such as synagogues and ritual bathhouses, or about its political leadership.[18] However, for information about what happened within the homes and synagogues, for the texture of Jewish existence in medieval Provence, we must turn to rabbinic sources.

When the rabbinic sources are read against the backdrop of their historical context as reconstructed from the notarial documents, royal policies and other Latin or vernacular documents, the result is mutually enriching. Individuals named in the *responsa* can sometimes be cross-referenced with names mentioned in document-based studies to reveal biographical information that deepens our understanding of the rabbinic text.[19] The disappearance of a prominent Jew from the Latin documents was explained by his murder, discussed at some length in a series of *responsa* but left unmentioned by the notaries.[20] Unexplained facts and puzzling details in one corpus are often illuminated by information in the other. For example, in her study on the Jews of Salon-de-Provence, Monique Wernham noticed that Jews never purchased pressed grapes from Christians, even though such sales were generally very common in Provence.[21] Anticipating the

14. Meritxell Blasco Orellana, José Ramón Magdalena Nom de Déu and Juliette Sibon, "Le *pinqas* (carnet personnel) de Mordacays Joseph (1374–1375), corailleur juif de Marseille," *Revue des études juives* 175 (2016): 251–307.

15. William D. Paden, *Two Medieval Occitan Toll Registers from Tarascon* (Toronto, 2016), 4.

16. Gérard Nahon, *Inscriptions hébraïques et juives de France médiévale* (Paris, 1986), 366–384.

17. Édouard Baratier, *La démographie Provençale du XIIe au XVIe siècle* (Paris, 1961), 69–72. Town-dwelling Jews often conducted business in the villages. John Drendel, "Jews, Villagers and the Count in Haute Provence: Marginality and Mediation," *Provence historique* 49 (1999): 217–231.

18. Iancu-Agou, *Provincia Judaica*, 3–6; Joseph Shatzmiller, "Community and Super-Community in Provence in the Middle Ages," in *Judenverteibungen in Mittelalter und früher Neuzeit*, ed. Friedhelm Burgard, Alfred Haverkamp and Gerd Mentgen (Hannover, 1999), 441–448.

19. The identification of Isaac of Trets, discussed in Chapter 2, is a striking example.

20. Gérard E. Weil, "Symilon de Lambesc Courrier du Dauphin, Symilon d'Hyeres Assassiné au Conil du Castelet en 1340 & les rabbins de Haute-Provence," in *Les juifs dans la Méditerranée* (Nice, 1986), 25–52.

21. Monique Wernham, *La communauté juive de Salon-de-Provence d'aprés les actes notariés 1391–1435* (Toronto, 1987), 99–100.

explanation that grapes pressed by Christians were not kosher and therefore Jews did not buy them, Wernham noted that the French Tosafists had explicitly permitted such grapes, which suggests that the behaviour of Jews in Salon could not have been due to halakhic considerations. However, a recently published Hebrew text from thirteenth-century Narbonne reveals that the Tosafist position permitting grapes pressed by non-Jews was strongly opposed by some rabbis in Languedoc. Reading the halakhic text in light of the documents from Salon, it emerges that the French permissive ruling was ignored and the stringent ruling by southern rabbis was adopted by a sizable proportion of the Jewish population.[22] The rabbinic text clarifies a pattern in the Latin documents, which confirm in their turn that the rabbinic text was put into practice.

To some degree, the twin lenses of Latin and Hebrew sources correspond to bifurcated aspects of Jewish life in Provence. Many Jewish men used two different names – a Hebrew name for use in ritual contexts and a vernacular name deployed in everyday life.[23] This was true even of noted rabbis and even when they were mentioned in Hebrew texts. The liturgical poems of Isaac Kimḥi, one of the central figures in this book, were attributed in prayerbooks to "Maestri Petit de Nyons, of blessed memory."[24] When Isaac's father Mordechai Kimḥi addressed a learned letter to Abba Mari ben Moses, he referred to him by his Occitan name: Sen Astruc de Lunel.[25] This bilingual and bicultural duality found other expressions in Provençal Jewish life. At their weddings, Jewish couples would sign a *ketubah*, the Aramaic wedding contract required by talmudic law, but also a Latin contract drafted by a notary. The Latin document was referred to as a "Christian *ketubah*," and its legally binding status was upheld in a *responsum* by Isaac Kimḥi.[26] Medieval Provençal Jews lived in "Hebrew" and "Latin" spheres, and the record of their lives is preserved in both languages.

22. Pinchas Roth, "Halakhah and Criticism in Southern France: R. David ben Saul on the Laws of Wine Made by Gentiles," *Tarbiz* 83 (2015): 439–463, at 449–452 (Hebrew).

23. Juliette Sibon, *Les juifs de Marseille au XIVe siècle* (Paris, 2011), 227–267. On the naming patterns of medieval Jewish women, see Chapter 4.

24. *Mahzor Carpentras le-shalosh regalim*, ed. Avraham Montil (Amsterdam, 1759), fol. 98a.

25. *Teshuvot Ḥakhme Provinzia (Teshuvot Ḥakhme Provintsya)*, (*Responsa* of the Sages of Provence), no. 64, ed. Abraham Sofer (Schreiber) (Jerusalem, 1967), 222.

26. Roth, "Regional Boundaries and Medieval Halakhah: Rabbinic *Responsa* from Catalonia to Southern France in the Thirteenth and Fourteenth Centuries," *Jewish Quarterly Review* 105 (2015): 72–98, at 91–95.

Axis of Rabbinic Creativity

In order to appreciate late medieval *responsa* from Provence, it is necessary to identify their roots in earlier medieval rabbinic writings. The earliest surviving rabbinic texts written in Languedoc date from the first half of the twelfth century, while Jewish centers in other regions such as the Rhineland and Muslim Spain had already created a durable literary heritage a century earlier. Scholars are divided whether this time-lag should be explained away with the assumption that there was significant rabbinic activity in southern France during the eleventh century which has simply vanished, or whether local scholars were too mediocre to produce any written works.[27] In any case, Abraham ben Isaac of Narbonne, who died in 1158, is the earliest author whose halakhic writings have been extensively preserved.[28] Abraham travelled from Narbonne to Barcelona, where he studied with Judah ben Barzilai, a scholar whose work was deeply suffused with the traditions of the Babylonian Geʾonim. Abraham of Narbonne's halakhic work, *Sefer ha-Eshkol,* is an epitome of Judah of Barcelona's (largely lost) *Sefer ha-Ittim* and therefore a reflection of his teacher's thought rather than of his own.

Later in life, Abraham of Narbonne became aware of the work being done by Rashi of Troyes (d. 1105), his grandson Samuel ben Meir (d. after 1158) and the Tosafist movement coalescing around them in northern France.[29] The Tosafists were developing a new methodology for studying the Talmud, a methodology that very quickly revolutionized the rabbinic academies of France, Germany and beyond.[30] Solomon Luria, a sixteenth-century Polish rabbi put it best when he described "the French rabbis, the Tosafists, who turned [the Talmud] into a ball... turning and rolling it from place to place until it appears to us as one, without contradictions or ruptures."[31] Like Gratian's *Concordia discordantium canonum,*

27. Ram Ben-Shalom, *The Jews of Provence and Languedoc: Renaissance in the Shadow of the Church* (Raʿananah, 2017), 351–352 summarizes the opinions of Binyamin Zeʾev Benedikt (d. 2002), who believed in an early literature that has been lost, and Israel Ta-Shma (d. 2004), who dismissed that belief.

28. Abraham ben Isaac of Narbonne, *Sefer ha-Eshkol,* ed. Shalom Albeck and Ḥanokh Albeck (Jerusalem, 1935–1938); Israel M.Ta-Shma, *Rabbi Zeraḥiah ha-Levi ba ʿal ha-Ma ʾor u-vene ḥugo: Le-toldot ha-sifrut ha-rabanit be-Provans* (Jerusalem, 1992), 7–10, 38–50.

29. Avraham (Rami) Reiner, "From France to Provence: The Assimilation of the Tosafists' Innovations in the Provençal Talmudic Tradition," *Journal of Jewish Studies* 65 (2014): 77–87.

30. Ephraim Elimelech Urbach, *The Tosaphists: Their History, Writings and Methods* (Jerusalem, 1980) (Hebrew); Haym Soloveitchik, *Collected Essays* (Oxford, 2013–2014), 1: 3–30.

31. Solomon Luria, *Yam shel Shelomoh: ʿal masekhet Bava Kama* (Prague, 1618), 2r.

the Tosafists turned the identification and resolution of textual contradictions with the talmudic corpus into an art form. *Tosafot* – the glosses produced by the Tosafists – would come to dominate Talmud study for generations and by the end of the Middle Ages manuscript copies of various *Tosafot* editions were found throughout southern France.[32] Abraham of Narbonne was fascinated by the innovative approach of the northern French Tosafists, but he also viewed it with suspicion and reserve, unwilling to let it replace the traditional approach to Talmud study that he had received from his master in Barcelona.

Abraham of Narbonne's ambivalence towards the *Tosafot* crystallized a problem of geo-cultural orientation that faced the rabbinic community of southern France from the twelfth century, and perhaps even earlier.[33] Would their primary commitment be to the academies of Sefarad (al-Andalus, or Muslim Spain) and Barcelona, and, still further back, to the Ge᾿onim of Babylonia who had flourished until the eleventh century?[34] Was the revolution of Tosafist dialectic emerging from northern France a legitimate alternative to the Sefardic tradition? From the time of Abraham of Narbonne onwards, it fell to individual scholars to navigate their way among these disparate rabbinic influences.

After Narbonne, the second major centre of rabbinic learning in southern France was Lunel, which housed an academy led by Meshulam ben Jacob (d. 1170).[35] Meshulam and his son Asher played a crucial role in persuading Judah ibn Tibbon to turn his linguistic skills towards translating Judeo-Arabic works of religious philosophy into Hebrew, thereby inaugurating the multi-generational process of Tibbonide translations in southern France.[36]

The greatest of Meshulam of Lunel's students was Abraham ben David, known as Rabad of Posquières (d. 1198).[37] Rabad married Abraham ben Isaac of

32. Pinchas Roth, "Manuscript Fragments of Early Tosafot in Perpignan," *European Journal of Jewish Studies* 14 (2020): 117–136.

33. Binyamin Ze᾿ev Benedikt, *Merkaz ha-Torah be-Provans* (The Torah Center in Provence) (Jerusalem, 1985), 8–12; Yaacov Sussmann, "Rabad on Shekalim? A Bibliographical and Historical Riddle," in *Me᾿ah She῾arim: Studies in Medieval Jewish Spiritual Life in Memory of Isadore Twersky*, ed. Ezra Fleischer et al. (Jerusalem, 2001), 131–170, at 150–161 (Hebrew).

34. Robert Brody, *The Geonim of Babylonia and the Shaping of Medieval Jewish Culture* (New Haven, 1998).

35. Gross, *Gallia Judaica*, 279.

36. Gad Freudenthal, "Abraham Ibn Ezra and Judah Ibn Tibbon as Cultural Intermediaries: Early Stages in the Introduction of Non-Rabbinic Learning into Provence in the Mid-Twelfth Century," in *Exchange and Transmission across Cultural Boundaries: Philosophy, Mysticism and Science in the Mediterranean World*, ed. Haggai Ben-Shammai, Shaul Shaked and Sarah Stroumsa (Jerusalem, 2013), 52–81.

37. Isadore Twersky, *Rabad of Posquières: A Twelfth-Century Talmudist* (Cambridge, MA, 1962; 2nd ed., Philadelphia, 1980).

Narbonne's daughter. Father-in-law (known by the acronym Rabi) and son-in-law (Rabad) were often conflated or confused by later generations due to their similar names, yet the two men were quite different from each other in background and personality. As we have seen, Abraham of Narbonne was a devoted follower of his master Judah of Barcelona. His talmudic commentaries, to the extent that they can be reconstructed, covered the tractates traditionally studied in *yeshivot* – the sections of the Talmud that deal with Sabbath and festivals, family law and civil law.[38] In contrast, Abraham of Posquières was a fiercely independent scholar, and although he too commented on many of the traditional tractates, he also sought out the more obscure sections about purity laws and Temple sacrifices as targets for exegesis precisely because they had escaped the attention of earlier commentators.[39] For later generations, Rabad marked the high point of local Provençal rabbinic achievement. As Isaac Kimḥi described him in the fourteenth century:[40]

> The greatest men of every generation drank from his water – the rabbis of Lunel and Montpellier and Narbonne and Barcelona, all the way to Sefarad. All of Israel in these lands said of them: "Ho, all who are thirsty, come for water" (Isaiah 55:1).

This lineage – Abraham of Narbonne, Meshulam of Lunel and above all Rabad of Posquières – served as proof that Provençal rabbis could achieve greatness. In terms of breadth and practical guidance, though, their literary corpus could not answer the full range of questions in Jewish law that arose daily. Provençal Jews were never halakhically self-sufficient. They had to contend with three major sources of influence on their rabbinic culture – the Ge'onic-Sefardic tradition, the Tosafists of northern France and local scholarship. The apparently overwhelming task of weighing these conflicting approaches drove one local scholar to ask the heavenly angels for guidance.[41] The more conventional response, though, was to turn back to the Talmud. A long series of works was composed in Languedoc and Provence during the thirteenth century, cri-

38. Shalem Yahalom, *Between Gerona and Narbonne: Nahmanides' Literary Sources* (Jerusalem, 2012), 11–36 (Hebrew).

39. Haym Soloveitchik, "Rabad of Posquieres: A Programmatic Essay," in *Studies in the History of Jewish Society in the Middle Ages and in the Modern Period*, ed. Immanuel Etkes and Yosef Salmon (Jerusalem, 1980), 7–40.

40. BnF Héb. 1391, fol. 69r.

41. Israel M. Ta-Shma, *Studies in Medieval Rabbinic Literature* (Jerusalem, 2004–2010), 4: 112–129 (Hebrew); Pinchas Roth, "*Responsa* from Heaven: Fragments of a New Manuscript of 'She'elot u-Teshuvot min ha-Shamayim' from Gerona," *Materia Guidaica* 15–16 (2010–2011): 555–564.

tiquing medieval codes in light of the Talmud itself.[42] Yet the Talmud was a difficult steed to tame, and the conundrum of striking a balance between indeterminate talmudic discussions, conflicting rabbinic traditions and shape-shifting local customs continued to baffle the scholars of Provence and Languedoc for centuries.

The Maimonidean Revolution and Non-Rabbinic Jewish Intellectuals

The last years of the twelfth century saw a sea-change in southern French rabbinic culture with the arrival of Moses Maimonides' *Mishneh Torah*.[43] Maimonides had purposely written his legal code in Hebrew, unlike his other writings which were all originally composed in Judeo-Arabic, so that it would transcend the confines of the Islamicate world in which he lived. It was a revolutionary work in the annals of rabbinic writing because it offered a new, rational structure of the law that was not linked to the order of the talmudic tractates. Equally revolutionary, it went beyond existing halakhic codes that were confined to a limited number of topics by covering the entire range of Jewish law (even subjects like Temple sacrifices that were not immediately applicable in any way). Finally, Maimonides made his Code more accessible by stating only the bottom line and dispensing with the intricate back-and-forth of the talmudic discussion.[44]

Eased by its linguistic and structural accessibility, *Mishneh Torah* became an instant success in Languedoc. The sages of Lunel read the work quickly but carefully. Rabad of Posquières jotted down marginal comments, several of which

42. Commentaries on Isaac Alfasi's code *Halakhot Rabbati;* Meshulam ben Moses of Béziers, *Sefer ha-Hashlamah*, ed. Judah Lubetzky (Paris, 1881) and ed. Avraham Ḥafuta (Tel Aviv, 1961–1975); David ben Levi of Narbonne, *Sefer ha-Mikhtam,* ed. Yosef Hillel (Jerusalem, 2015–2017); Commentaries on Maimonides' code *Mishneh Torah* – Samuel ben Mordechai of Apt, *Perush* in *Mishneh Torah,* vol. 1b (*Sefer Ahavah*), ed. Shabse Frankel (Jerusalem, 1975–2003); Manoaḥ of Narbonne, *Sefer ha-Menuḥah,* ed. Elazar Hurvitz (Jerusalem, 1970); David ben Samuel Kokhavi of Avignon, *Sefer ha-Batim ʿal ha-Rambam*, ed. Moshe Blau (New York, 1978–1979).

43. It is unclear when exactly *Mishneh Torah* arrived in southern France – before 1194, or only in 1195.Twersky, *Rabad of Posquières*, 125; Itzhak Shailat, *The Letters and Essays of Moses Maimonides* (Maʿaleh Adumim, 1995), 474–475 (Hebrew); Shlomo Sela, "Queries on Astrology Sent from Southern France to Maimonides: Critical Edition of the Hebrew Text, Translation and Commentary," *Aleph* 4 (2004): 89–190, at 126. A medieval Hebrew chronicle recorded that *Mishneh Torah* reached Lunel only in 1198. Abraham David, "Sarid mikhronikah Ivrit (Fragments from a Hebrew Chronicle)," *Alei Sefer* 6–7 (1979): 198–200.

44. Isadore Twersky, *Introduction to the Code of Maimonides (Mishneh Torah)* (New Haven, 1980).

were sharply worded.[45] His colleagues, led by Jonathan ha-Kohen of Lunel, mailed a series of questions to the author in Egypt. Maimonides' response, when it eventually arrived, was respectful and warm, and the trans-Mediterranean relationship blossomed. When they became aware that in addition to his legal code Maimonides had also written a work of theology (the *Guide of the Perplexed*) in Judeo-Arabic, the Lunel scholars commissioned Samuel ibn Tibbon to prepare a Hebrew translation. The *Guide*, when it became available to non-Arabic readers, was revolutionary. In its own right, and through the library of Greco-Arabic philosophy and science it introduced to Provençal savants, the *Guide* turned southern France into a hotbed of rationalism for centuries.

The first translations from Arabic into Hebrew executed in Languedoc by Judah ibn Tibbon and other Andalusian migrants from 1160 onwards were devoted mostly to works by Arabic-speaking Jewish authors – theological treatises, such as Baḥya ibn Pakuda's *Ḥovot ha-Levavot* and Judah ha-Levi's *Kuzari*, or books on Hebrew grammar by Jonah ibn Janaḥ. As such, they did not stray far from the existing body of Provençal Jewish knowledge. However, a confluence of factors towards the end of the twelfth century – not least among them, the glimpses into the world of Greco-Arabic learning provided by Maimonides' *Guide of the Perplexed* – pushed some Jews to expand their horizons and to begin to translate and study works of science and philosophy by Galen, Averroes and others.[46] Over time, the thirst for foreign knowledge expanded to include translations of Latin works, particularly in areas of practical use for Jews who worked as doctors or astronomers.[47]

45. Although they were not written as a systematic composition, these glosses are the work by which Rabad was best remembered in the history of rabbinic literature. Soloveitchik, "Rabad of Posquieres: A Programmatic Essay"; Shalem Yahalom, "On the Place of Hasagot ha-Rabad in the Literature of the Rishonim," in *Ta Shma: Studies in Judaica in Memory of Israel M. Ta-Shma*, ed. Avraham (Rami) Reiner et al. (Alon Shevut, 2011), 443–465 (Hebrew).

46. For the argument that Christian polemics against Judaism played a crucial role as well, see Gad Freudenthal, "Arabic into Hebrew: The Emergence of the Translation Movement in Twelfth-Century Provence and Jewish-Christian Polemic," in *Beyond Religious Borders: Interaction and Intellectual Exchange in the Medieval Islamic World*, ed. David M. Freidenreich and Miriam Goldstein (Philadelphia, 2012), 124–143.

47. Gad Freudenthal and Resianne Fontaine, "Philosophy and Medicine in Jewish Provence, *anno* 1199: Samuel ibn Tibbon and Doeg the Edomite Translating Galen's *Tegni*," *Arabic Sciences and Philosophy* 26 (2016): 1–26; Gad Freudenthal, "The Brighter Side of Medieval Christian-Jewish Polemical Encounters: Transfer of Medical Knowledge in the Midi (Twelfth-Fourteenth Centuries)," *Medieval Encounters* 24 (2018): 29–61. On the medieval Hebrew translation project as a whole, see Moritz Steinschneider, *The Hebrew Translations of the Middle Ages and the Jews as Transmitters*, ed. Charles H. Manekin, Y. Tzvi Langermann and Hans Hinrich Biesterfeldt (Dordrecht, 2013). A highly useful resource was prepared by

The social prestige that adhered to experts in these new bodies of knowledge marked a new class of Jewish scholars – men distinguished and respected not by virtue of their rabbinic learning but rather by their scientific and philosophical knowledge. From the heights of their newfound respect, rationalist scholars could critique and question rabbinic rulings in ways that would have been unthinkable before the thirteenth century.[48] The rise of non-rabbinic intellectuals[49] in Languedoc and Provence was a precursor of the crisis in rabbinic authority that would arise in other parts of Europe during the late Middle Ages and early Modern period.[50]

Precocious Multiculturalism

Provençal Jewish society was ahead of its time in another respect, in a problem it faced that combined the intellectual and the demographic. Jews who left France (and England) and migrated south from the late 1280s onwards arrived in Provence to find existing Jewish communities with a full array of traditions, customs, rituals and leaders. Discovering a Judaism that differed in so many ways, minor though those differences might appear to an outside observer, must have been jarring for the new arrivals. They were faced with the choice between assimilating into local Jewish culture and preserving their distinct and separate identity, and more often than not they chose to assert themselves as French and not Provençal.

Two factors aided in developing and maintaining their distinct ethnic identity: a pre-existing sense of "Frenchness" and the concentration of significant numbers of French Jews in only a few towns. Within those towns, they created new social networks that strengthened their group cohesion, maintained ties with communities and leaders still in France (until the expulsion in 1306), and asserted their difference from Provençal Jewry. Their "Frenchness" rested upon

---

Mauro Zonta, "Medieval Hebrew Translations of Philosophical and Scientific Texts: A Chronological Table," in *Science in Medieval Jewish Cultures*, ed. Gad Freudenthal (Cambridge, 2011), 17–73.

48. Pinchas Roth, "Asking Questions: Rabbis and Philosophers in Medieval Provence," *Journal of Jewish Studies* 67 (2016): 1–14.

49. Akin to the rise of "anti-intellectual intellectuals" described by Ian P. Wei, *Intellectual Culture in Medieval Paris: Theologians and the University, c. 1100–1330* (Cambridge, 2012), 356–414.

50. Jacob Katz, *Out of the Ghetto: The Social Background of Jewish Emancipation, 1770–1870* (New York, 1978), 148–149; Jacob Katz, *Tradition and Crisis: Jewish Society at the End of the Middle Ages*, trans. Bernard Dov Cooperman (New York, 1993), 195–201.

the great prestige of the Tosafists, two centuries worth of rabbinic scholars whose writings and rulings were known and respected by the rabbis of Provence. Even the least knowledgeable French laypeople were happy to bask in the glory of the French rabbis. Presumably, the growing power of the French monarchy in the south played a role in this as well. The result was a community within a community, a close-knit Jewish ethnic and cultural minority that held itself above the indigenous Jews.

A situation like this was almost unprecedented in Jewish history. In the past, migrating Jews had travelled in small numbers, joining an existing community upon arrival or creating a new one if none was to be found. It would, however, become a rampant and burning problem during the early modern period.[51] Many of the Jews who were exiled *en masse* from Spain in 1492 fled to North Africa, Italy and the eastern Mediterranean – all regions that had been settled by Jews for centuries before the arrival of the Sefardim. A cacophony of problems ensued, including marriage disputes, fights in the synagogue and commercial rivalries. Boasting numerical superiority over many of the old communities, the new arrivals from Spain declared openly that their customs and legal traditions ought to prevail over any others, because they were "Spanish" and therefore more prestigious. Within a century, the Sefardim succeeded for the most part in wresting control of the community in their new habitats from the original population and in reconstituting themselves as a Spanish diaspora.

The scale of French migration to Provence was much smaller than the exodus of Iberian Jewry in 1492. The social and cultural tensions that their migration from France raised, for themselves and for their hosts, anticipated the much more acute problems that would arise in the wake of the Sefardic exodus. Shared spaces – synagogues, *yeshivot*, marital homes – served as hothouses in which cultural and legal differences could fester and eventually erupt into verbal and physical violence.

Jewish Laity and Halakhic Culture

The crisis of identity experienced by French and Provençal Jews as they intermingled in the villages of Provence affected laypeople as well as rabbinic scholars. Similarly, the intellectual shift from a strictly rabbinic curriculum to the Graeco-Arabic corpus of knowledge had ramifications that were felt beyond the

51. Jonathan Ray, *After Expulsion: 1492 and the Making of Sephardic Jewry* (New York, 2013); David B. Ruderman, *Early Modern Jewry: A New Cultural History* (Princeton, 2010), 27–29.

rarified confines of scholarly circles. Some of the new intellectuals made a concerted effort to popularize the central ideas and values of the rationalist approach to Judaism.[52] One prominent example was *Malmad ha-Talmidim,* a collection of sermons on the weekly Torah reading composed by Jacob Anatoli, who was himself a noted translator.[53] Another was *Livyat Ḥen,* a massive encyclopedia compiled by Levi ben Abraham of Villefranche and epitomized by its author in a shorter verse form, which attempted to summarize every aspect of the rationalist corpus.[54] The rationalist sermons and poems were aimed at audiences that would never consume Aristotelian philosophy in unadulterated form. Neither would those audiences have immersed themselves in the Talmud or perused rabbinic *responsa.* Yet Jewish laypeople were inexorably affected by changes to elite Jewish culture because they were, in their way, embedded within that same culture.

Laity is a term that requires some adaptation to be applied helpfully to Jewish society. The stark legal and religious divisions between clergy and laypeople in medieval Christianity never existed to the same extent within Judaism. In order to appreciate the place of Jewish laity, it is necessary to first clarify the institutional context of the rabbinic elite from which it is being distinguished here. The Hebrew terms *yeshivah* or *bet midrash* (translated here as academy or study hall) can refer to a range of different educational institutions.[55] At times, they refer to a kind of sec-

52. James T. Robinson, "Secondary Forms of Philosphy: On the Teaching and Transmission of Philosophy in Non-Philosophical Literary Genres," in *Vehicles of Transmission, Translation, and Transformation in Medieval Textual Culture,* ed. Robert Wisnovsky, Faith Wallis, Famie C. Fumo and Carlos Fraenkel (Turnhout, 2011), 235–248; James T. Robinson, "Al-Farabi, Avicenna, and Averroes in Hebrew: Remarks on the Indirect Transmission of Arabic-Islamic Philosophy in Medieval Judaism," in *The Judeo-Christian-Islamic Heritage: Philosophical and Theological Perspectives,* ed. Richard C. Taylor and Irfan A. Omar (Milwaukee, 2012), 59–87.

53. Marc Saperstein, *Jewish Preaching 1200–1800: An Anthology* (New Haven, 1989), 15–16; Renate Smithius, "Preaching to his Daughter: Jacob Anatoli's Goad for Students (Malmad ha-talmidim)," in *Jewish Education from Antiquity to the Middle Ages: Studies in Honour of Philip S. Alexander,* ed. George J. Brooke and Renate Smithius (Leiden, 2017), 341–397.

54. Warren Zev Harvey, "Levi ben Abraham of Villefranche's Controversial Encyclopedia," in *The Medieval Hebrew Encyclopedias of Science and Philosophy* (Dordrecht, 2000), 171–188.

55. For a general overview, see Jacob Katz, "Jewish Civilization as Reflected in the Yeshivot – Jewish Centers of Higher Learning," *Cahiers d'histoire mondiale* 10 (1966–1967): 674–704. A wealth of sources, from a vast range of places and time periods, was assembled by Mordechai Breuer, *Oholei Torah (The Tents of Torah): The Yeshiva, Its Structure and History* (Jerusalem, 2003) (Hebrew). On Jewish educational institutions in medieval Languedoc and Provence, see Ben-Shalom, *The Jews of Provence and Languedoc,* 372–377; Ephraim Kanarfogel, "Schools and Education," in *The Cambridge History of Judaism, vol. VI: The Middle Ages: The Christian World,* ed. Robert Chazan (Cambridge, 2018), 393–415, at 400–403.

ondary school, educating teenage boys. Jacob ben Moses of Bagnols, the late-fourteenth century scholar discussed in Chapter 6, ran such a school where he recalled celebrating the weddings of his thirteen-year-old students. More typically, though, a *yeshivah* was an institution of higher learning catering to men ranging from their late teens into adulthood. The richest description of such a *yeshivah* in southern France was written by Isaac ben Yedaiah, recounting his experiences in the academy of Rabbi Meshulam ben Moses in Béziers in the early thirteenth century:[56]

> When I reached his study hall (*bet midrasho*), "the royal palace," I was a young boy of fifteen among many fellows older than myself ... and it was difficult for me to absorb the discussion and the questions and the answers and the additions (*tosafot*) that he added on his own, piles and piles on every letter, and my heart was unable to take them all in when I was young.

Isaac ben Yedaiah's account emphasizes that the *yeshivah* in which he studied was centered around the personality of a single rabbi. When Meshulam of Béziers died, "no person from the *yeshivah* arose to take his place ... and all the students returned to their homes."[57] Other study halls were corporate bodies that gathered all of the local scholars, often under the leadership of one dominant figure. Meshulam's grandfather, Meshulam ben Jacob, headed such an institution in Lunel that was described by Benjamin of Tudela in the twelfth century:[58]

> There [in Lunel] is Rabbi Meshulam, the great rabbi, and his five sons – great sages, and wealthy... and Rabbi Moses their brother-in-law,[59] and Rabbi Samuel the Elder and Rabbi Olsarno and Rabbi Solomon the Kohen and Rabbi Judah the physician ben Tibbon the Sefaradi. Whoever comes from a distant land to study Torah, they support him and teach him and find food and clothing for him from the community for the entire period that they spend in the study hall (*bet ha-midrash*).

Although the Lunel study hall was clearly centered around "the great rabbi" Meshulam, it housed a number of other notable figures, not least of whom was

56. El Escorial, Real Biblioteca del Monasterio de San Lorenzo, G.IV.3, fol. 12r; published by Ad[olph] Neubauer, "Yedaya de Béziers," *Revue des études juives* 20 (1890): 244–248, at 247. On Isaac ben Yedaiah, see Marc Saperstein, *Decoding the Rabbis: A Thirteenth-Century Commentary on the Aggadah* (Cambridge, MA, 1980).

57. Neubauer, "Yedaya," 248.

58. Benjamin ben Jonah of Tudela, *The Itinerary of Benjamin of Tudela*, ed. Marcus Nathan Adler (London, 1907), Hebrew section, 4 (my translation).

59. The father of Meshulam ben Moses of Béziers.

Judah ibn Tibbon, recently arrived from Granada. Ibn Tibbon's contribution to the intellectual agenda in Lunel was a crucial one, since he introduced his companions to the ethical and philosophical achievements of Andalusian Jewry. The broader intellectual horizons ushered in by ibn Tibbon introduced a new variable into the profile of southern French *yeshivot*: were they henceforth dedicated solely to the study of classic rabbinic texts, or did their curriculum also include a component of "Greek wisdom?" According to Isaac ben Yedaiah, Meshulam of Béziers taught "the disputations of Abaye and Rava and the work of the chariot and the wheels of the wagon" – apparently referring to a combination of talmudic and metaphysical studies.[60] It would seem that "*yeshivot ḥokhmot ḥiẓoniyot*" (academies of the external sciences), institutions devoted entirely to the study of science and philosophy whose existence in late medieval Castile and Portugal, were not found in southern France.[61] Those studies were often pursued by individuals whose only companions were their books.[62] Yet there were circles of Jewish students who pursued philosophical study under the tutelage of a teacher.[63] What type of institutional framework housed those circles, and how they related to other local educational structures, remains unclear.

The size of *yeshivot* is also difficult to ascertain. Mordechai Breuer claimed that the medieval academies of Ashkenaz could not have held more than fifteen students at any time, while Ephraim Kanarfogel raised that number to twenty-five.[64] The only clear indication regarding the size of a study hall in southern France is provided by Isaac of Manosque, who referred to "his entire study circle, twenty-five wise men."[65] It is hard to extrapolate from a single instance – par-

60. Neubauer, "Yedaya," 247; Saperstein, *Decoding the Rabbis*, 179.

61. Colette Sirat and Marc Geoffrey, "The Modena Manuscript and the Teaching of Philosophy in Fourteenth and Fifteenth Century Spain," in *Study and Knowledge in Jewish Thought*, ed. Howard Kreisel (Be᾽er-Sheva, 2006), 185–202; Colette Sirat, "Studia of Philosophy as Scribal Centers in Fifteenth-Century Iberia," in *The Late Medieval Hebrew Book in the Western Mediterranean: Hebrew Manuscripts and Incunabula in Context*, ed. Javier del Barco (Leiden, 2015), 46–69; Yoel Marciano, *Sages of Spain in the Eye of the Storm: Jewish Scholars of Late Medieval Spain* (Jerusalem, 2019) (Hebrew).

62. Colette Sirat, "Entering the Field of Philosophy: Provence, Mid-Fourteenth Century," in *Jewish Education from Antiquity to the Middle Ages: Studies in Honour of Philip S. Alexander*, ed. George J. Brooke and Renate Smithius (Leiden, 2017), 398–411.

63. Lawrence V. Berman, "A Manuscript Entitled Shoshan Limudim and the Group of Me῾aynim in Provence," *Kiryat Sefer* 53 (1978): 368–372 (Hebrew); Ruth Glasner, "Levi ben Gershom and the Study of Ibn Rushd in the Fourteenth Century," *Jewish Quarterly Review* 86 (1995): 51–90; Dov Schwartz, *Central Problems of Medieval Jewish Philosophy* (Leiden, 2005), 223–248.

64. Ephraim Kanarfogel, *Jewish Education and Society in the High Middle Ages* (Detroit, 1992), 66–67.

65. Ibn Adret, *She᾽elot u-Teshuvot* 1: no. 460, ed. Zaleznik, 1: 242. See below, Chapter 4.

ticularly from the example of Manosque, where many of the Jews originated in northern France – but perhaps this indicates that the Provençal *yeshivot* resembled those of northern Europe in size.

In short, the precise dimensions of the *yeshivah* in southern France were not uniform and cannot always be delineated. Its significance as an intellectual hothouse for local scholars and international students emerges with clarity and radiated outwards onto the entire community, but its denizens lacked any degree of real authority outside the confines of the academy itself. As we will see, the judges who sat on the Jewish courts of Southern France were often rabbinic scholars, but in many communities the courts were composed of prominent local businessmen.[66] Community rabbis, hired by contract and empowered by local authority, did not exist until the mid-fourteenth century.[67] Several of the documents discussed in this book were signed by a series of four, five or more men, whose signatures denote no formal position as rabbis or judges, but simply the fact that they were the leading members of the community. In short, it is difficult to draw an institutional line between rabbis and laypeople.

Neither could lay Jews be defined by their illiteracy, as medieval lay Christians sometimes were, since many Jewish men (and, to a more limited extent, women) possessed basic Jewish literacy.[68] It seems best to define Jewish laypeople as whoever was not counted among those "whose profession it was to think and to share their thoughts."[69] This definition has important social ramifications. Sharing thoughts – or legal rulings – among likeminded men was an important component in the social interaction of medieval rabbinic scholars. Time and again in this book, we will find rabbinic figures of varying stature reaching out to a wider circle of scholars, seeking their approbation and support. That process created and reinforced a social network of scholars. Experts in non-rabbinic scholarship, such as the philosopher Hillel of Verona, could easily join such discussions.[70] Those who remained outside the rabbinic network –who lacked the

66. See Chapter 2.

67. Katz, *Tradition and Crisis*, 142; Mordechai Breuer, "The Ashkenazi Semikha," *Zion* 33 (1968): 15–46 (Hebrew); Jonathan Ray, *The Sephardic Frontier: The Reconquista and the Jewish Community in Medieval Iberia* (Ithaca, 2006), 113–116.

68. Kanarfogel, "Schools and Education," 393–415. On the equation of laity with illiteracy, see Ruedi Imbach and Catherine König-Pralong, *Le défi laïque: Existe-t-il une philosophie de laïcs au moyen âge?* (Paris, 2013), 41–45.

69. Jacques Le Goff, *Intellectuals in the Middle Ages*, trans. Teresa Lavender Fagan (Cambridge, MA, 1993), 1.

70. Pinchas Roth, "Legal Strategy and Legal Culture in Medieval Jewish Courts of Southern France," *AJS Review* 38 (2014): 375–393, at 383.

Hebrew eloquence, higher rabbinic training or simply the time and inclination – were the Jewish laity.[71]

The degree to which medieval Jewish laypeople upheld every stricture of Jewish law in the manner dictated by the rabbinic scholars of their region has been debated by historians.[72] I have argued elsewhere that Provençal communities as a whole upheld certain standards of kosher wine.[73] It is difficult to make a similar assertion about other aspects of Jewish law. But observance of Halakhah, or lack thereof, does not determine the social significance of halakhic culture, a term I use along the lines of Jennifer Hendry's definition of legal culture:[74]

> Employment of the concept of legal culture, it could be argued, involves acknowledgement of and engagement with the compound nature of law, which is to say, with the social norms, socio-political constellations, historical underpinnings, institutional arrangements, societal practices and population dynamics that inform the law's social context, within a jurisdiction or legal "space."

Halakhic discourse was a vehicle for expressing a range of influences, concerns and deliberations about Jewish life and culture, about how Jews lived with one another and in the midst of non-Jewish society. Although the authors of halakhic literature were, assuredly, members of a cultural elite of highly educated men with familial and social ties to a network of other rabbis, the language of Halakhah was (to some degree) understood, utilized and manipulated by much wider circles of Jewish society.[75] Women, non-rabbinic intellectuals, merchants and agri-

71. Cf. the description of "a caste of men of learning" and its implications for the wider populace in Jacques Verger, *Men of Learning in Europe at the End of the Middle Ages*, trans. Lisa Neal and Steven Rendall (Notre Dame, 2000), 34–37.

72. Ephraim Kanarfogel, "Rabbinic Attitudes Toward Nonobservance in the Medieval Period," in *Jewish Tradition and the Nontraditional Jew*, ed. Jacob J. Schacter (Northvale, NJ, 1992), 3–35; David Malkiel, *Reconstructing Ashkenaz: The Human Face of Franco-German Jewry, 1000–1250* (Stanford, 2009), 148–199; Soloveitchik, *Collected Essays*, 1: 283–293. See also Elisheva Baumgarten, *Practicing Piety in Medieval Ashkenaz: Men, Women, and Everyday Religious Observance* (Philadelphia, 2014), 11.

73. Pinchas Roth, "Kosher Wine in Medieval Provence and Languedoc – Production and Commerce," *Revue des études juives* 178 (2019): 59–78 and see above, p. 20.

74. Jennifer Hendry, "Existing in the Hyphen: On Relational Legal Culture," in *Culture in the Domains of Law*, ed. René Provost (Cambridge, 2017), 179–190, at 184. See also Zachary Chitwood, *Byzantine Legal Culture and the Roman Legal Tradition, 867–1056* (Cambridge, 2017), 4–7 ("Legal Culture as a Heuristic Paradigm").

75. Moshe Rosman, *How Jewish is Jewish History?* (Oxford, 2007), 148–149; Baumgarten, *Practicing Piety*, 2.

cultural laborers – all possessed some degree of familiarity with basic halakhic concepts. Those concepts provided a vocabulary with which they lived their lives – the language with which they married, divorced, formed and enforced business deals, fought and cursed, envied and respected each other.[76] Not simply the words they used, but the entire range of their behaviour, "the more significant norms by which we live to the point where they become second nature,"[77] was drawn from (among other sources) the norms, rituals and texts of Halakhah.[78] The cultural position of Halakhah was not a function of the proportion of Jewish society that upheld and performed the ritual and legal demands of Halakhah, but of the extent to which the vocabulary of Halakhah pervaded that society.[79] One of the most important arenas in which Jewish laypeople deployed their halakhic vocabulary was in the courtroom, where legal knowledge could be translated directly into tangible power.

76. Phillip Ackerman-Lieberman, *The Business of Identity: Jews, Muslims, and Economic Life in Medieval Egypt* (Stanford, 2014); Rachel Furst, "Marriage Before the Bench: Divorce Law and Litigation Strategies in Thirteenth-Century Ashkenaz," *Jewish History* 31 (2017): 7–30. See also Thomas Kuehn, *Law, Family, and Women: Toward a Legal Anthropology of Renaissance Italy* (Chicago, 1991), 1–2: "Law's formative influence was not merely occasional ... it informed most levels of activity and discourse."

77. Paul R. Hyams, "Was There Really Such a Thing as Feud in the High Middle Ages?," in *Vengeance in the Middle Ages: Emotion, Religion and Feud*, ed. Susanna A. Throop and Paul R. Hyams (Farnham, 2010), 151–176, at 171.

78. Tom Johnson, *Law in Common: Legal Cultures in Late-Medieval England* (Oxford, 2020), 8: "[T]hese were not merely 'social' actions. They were careful, deliberative, and often legalistic performances, that explicitly appealed to legal forms."

79. "Objectively 'regulated' and 'regular' without being in any way the product of obedience to rules." Pierre Bourdieu, *The Logic of Practice*, trans. Richard Nice (Stanford, 1990), 53.

CHAPTER TWO

Jewish Courts and Legal Culture

The courtroom is a space of performance, a formal public reenactment of events that were originally more private and spontaneous. Every one of the participants in the drama – plaintiffs and defendants, witnesses and judges, spectators and outside officials – realizes that what is at stake extends beyond the disputed details and legal doctrines into the realm of social reputation. For some, a legal procedure shakes the bedrock of their identity.

The pulsating emotions encoded in records of legal proceedings are welcome grist for the mills of historians. Unfortunately, very few documents record the proceedings of Jewish courts in medieval Europe.[1] Some insight can be recovered from the *responsa* about medieval court cases – either opinions by leading rabbinic scholars penned in response to requests for help from Jewish judges or, more rarely, edited versions of the court's ruling composed after the fact by one of the judges for circulation among other rabbinic scholars. The *responsa* provide a particularly rabbinic perspective on the activity of the courts, but they do not obscure the fact that many of those courts did not include any rabbis or scholars among their personnel.

The presence of recognized experts in Jewish law on the bench of a court was usually considered to be a good thing, but it was by no means the norm during the Middle Ages. A court composed of three adult Jewish men was legitimate so long as its authority was accepted by both sides of the case. The judges' erudition and expertise were not directly linked to the permanence of their court. In Iberia and other regions, Jewish courts were staffed by career judges most of whom had never acquired advanced talmudic training. Far more common were ad hoc courts of prominent community members convened to address a specific

1. An exception is the Jewish court of twelfth-century Fustat (Old Cairo), whose work is partially preserved in the fragments of court diaries preserved in the Genizah. Eve Krakowski, *Coming of Age in Medieval Egypt: Female Adolescence, Jewish Law, and Ordinary Culture* (Princeton, 2018), 100–101. The state of early modern Jewish court records is comparatively much richer. Edward Fram, *A Window on Their World: The Court Diary of Rabbi Hayyim Gundersheim, Frankfurt am Main, 1773–1794* (Cincinnati, 2012), 20; Jay R. Berkovitz, *Protocols of Justice: The Pinkas of the Metz Rabbinic Court, 1771–1789* (Leiden, 2014), 3.

problem. However, in some places and at some times, the three judges might include one or even two full-fledged rabbinic scholars. In twelfth-century Narbonne, some court rulings were issued by a panel of five prominent rabbis.[2] During the thirteenth century as well, Narbonne possessed a professional court staffed by rabbinic scholars, one of whom was Mordechai Kimḥi.

Bits and pieces of information about the Jewish courts of thirteenth-century Provence and Languedoc can be scraped together from various sources, but the most revealing accounts of what happened inside those courts are found in the *responsa* of Mordechai Kimḥi. The *responsa* shed light on the legal conflicts that brought Jews into Jewish courts and on the strategies employed by Jewish plaintiffs inside those courts, but they also offer particularly significant insight into the differing responses to those strategies by Kimḥi and other Jewish judges.

The Kimḥi family was among the most prestigious intellectual dynasties in medieval Languedoc. The family's connection to the region began with the arrival of Joseph Kimḥi as a refugee fleeing the Almohade invasion of Muslim Spain around 1148.[3] Mordechai Kimḥi's father Isaac was the son of David ben Joseph Kimḥi (d. ca. 1235), whose biblical commentaries and Hebrew lexicon made him the most famous member of the family.[4] Like his grandfather, Mordechai was born (probably before 1240) in Narbonne, where he studied Talmud with the rabbinic scholar David ben Saul and, in due time, became a teacher in his own right.[5]

2. Binyamin Ze᾿ev Benedikt, *Merkaz ha-Torah be-Provans* (The Torah Center in Provence) (Jerusalem, 1985), 3–4, 28–29.

3. [Pinkus Fritz] Frankl, "Die Familie Kimchi in ihrer Ausbreitung nach Ländern und zeiten," *Monatsschrift für Geschichte und Wissenschaft des Judenthums* 33 (1884): 552–561; Frank Talmage, *David Kimhi: The Man and the Commentaries* (Cambridge, MA, 1975), 1–7; Mordechai Z. Cohen, "The Qimhi Family," in *Hebrew Bible/ Old Testament: The History of its Interpretation*, ed. Magne Saebø (Göttingen, 1996–2015), I:2, 388–415.

4. His line of descent can be reconstructed on the basis of a colophon written by Isaac ben Joseph ben Shlomo ben Mordechai ben Isaac ben David Kimḥi in 1391 in Arles. The colophon was found in a now-lost copy of Shem Tov Falaquera's *Epistle of the Debate*. The manuscript was owned by Solomon Dubno (1738–1813) and is described briefly in the sale catalogue of his library, *Reshimah mi-sefarim rabim va-ḥashuvim* (List of many important books) (Amsterdam, 1814), 40 (octavo manuscripts, no. 5). Its present location is unknown – Benjamin Richler, *Guide to Hebrew Manuscript Collections* (Jerusalem, 2014), 63. The colophon was transcribed by Matityahu Strashun, "Mikhtav al devar R. Shem Tov ba῾al ha-᾿emunot" (Letter about Rabbi Shem Tov, author of Sefer ha-Emunot), *Pirḥe Zafun* 1 (1841): 46–48.

5. On his studies with David ben Saul, see Pinchas Roth, "Halakhah and Criticism in Southern France: R. David ben Saul on the Laws of Wine Made by Gentiles," *Tarbiz* 83 (2015): 439–463 (Hebrew), esp. 440 n7. Evidence of Kimḥi's students in Narbonne is provided by Menaḥem de Lonzano, *Shete Yadot* (Venice, 1618), fol. 25b: "I found the following

Kimḥi joined the bench of the rabbinic court in Narbonne, where he sometimes presided alongside David ben Levi Mikhtam, another noted scholar.[6] His judicial work was not confined to Narbonne; he could also be found in Toulouse and other, unidentified, locales.[7] At some point before the end of the thirteenth century, Mordechai Kimḥi left Languedoc and moved east, crossing the Rhône River into Provence and settling near Carpentras, where he resided until his death shortly after 1310.[8] He became an occasional member of the court in Carpentras alongside another recent arrival from Languedoc named Abraham ben Isaac of Montpellier (*min ha-Har*). The two men shared a similar cultural profile – both were recognized rabbinic scholars and their attitude towards philosophical rationalism was similarly moderate.[9] Yet they held very different beliefs about the law and its place in society.

---

statement in the novellae on [tractate] Megilah by a sage from Narbonne, a disciple of Rabbi Mordechai of blessed memory." See also Jordan Penkower, *Masorah and Text Criticism in the Early Modern Mediterranean: Moses ibn Zabara and Menahem de Lonzano* (Jerusalem, 2014), 78 n206.

6. *Teshuvot Ḥakhme Provinẓia (Teshuvot Ḥakhme Provintsya)* (*Responsa* of the Sages of Provence), no. 18, ed. Abraham Sofer (Schreiber) (Jerusalem, 1967), 91: "[The woman] was permitted [to marry] by the court of Rabbi Mordechai and his circle ... also Rabbi David agreed with him." See also *Teshuvot Ḥakhme Provinẓia (Teshuvot Ḥakhme Provintsya)*, nos. 7 and 9, ed. Sofer, 35–54. On David ben Levi see my introduction to *Sefer ha-Mikhtam*, ed. Yosef Hillel (Jerusalem, 2015), 9–18 (Hebrew).

7. Toulouse: Solomon ben Abraham ibn Adret, *Teshuvot ha-Rashba ha-hadashot*, no. 230 [vol. 8 of *She'elot u-Teshuvot*, ed. Aharon Zaleznik (Jerusalem, 2005), 158; Paris, Bibliothèque nationale de France, Hébreu 1391, fol. 45r]. He may possibly be identified with "Mordosays filius quondam Ysaac" who was head of the Toulouse community in 1281. Gustave Saige, *Les Juifs du Languedoc antérieurement au XIVe siècle* (Paris, 1881), 208–210; Yves Dossat, "Les juifs à Toulouse: Un demi-siècle d'histoire communautaire," *Cahiers de Fanjeaux* 12 (1977): 117–139, at 129. For his judicial work elsewhere (possibly outside Languedoc) see *Teshuvot Ḥakhme Provinẓia (Teshuvot Ḥakhme Provintsya)*, nos. 49 and 62, ed. Sofer, 150–162 and 211–215.

8. According to one source, he settled in Malaucène. Joseph Shatzmiller, "Minor Epistle of Apology of Rabbi Kalonymos ben Kalonymos," *Sefunot* 10 (1966): 7–52, at 38; Isidore Loeb, "Les Juifs de Malaucène," *Revue des études juives* 6 (1882): 270–272.

9. Their responses to Abba Mari de Lunel appear consecutively and take a similar stance. Abba Mari ben Moses of Lunel, *Minḥat Kena'ot*, chapters 111–112, in Solomon ben Abraham ibn Adret, *Teshuvot ha-Rashba*, ed. Haim Zalman Dimitrovsky (Jerusalem, 1990), 2: 786–803. Kimḥi urged Abba Mari to "beat your swords into the plowshares of faith and your spears into pruning hooks of sincerity" by abandoning his campaign against the rationalists, and Abraham begged him "to withdraw from the controversy, seek and pursue the peace of the renowned city, because in its peace will come peace for you and for us" (*Minḥat Kena'ot*, in *Teshuvot ha-Rashba*, ed. Dimitrovsky, 2: 799, 803). "The renowned city" is probably Montpellier, Abraham's hometown where Abba Mari resided until 1306.

One of the cases heard in Carpentras by Mordechai Kimḥi and Abraham of Montpellier opened with a man who appeared in court, ostensibly seeking guidance. He told the judges:[10]

> You should know that my wife has committed adultery, and I know this, and it is utterly clear to me. Those who heard and saw this have no doubt about it. Therefore, I ask you to tell me which way to turn. Based on this, is my wife forbidden to me or permitted?

The judges were disinclined to believe the husband's claim, both on principle ("it is a great sin to defame Jewish women") and on the basis of prior knowledge about the couple ("Perhaps you are concerned because of the story we heard about, with the governor?"[11]). The following day, after he was subjected to a battery of questions, the husband declared:[12]

> You should know that I am not saying this because of the affair with the lord (*sar*), but because I saw it with my own eyes so that I truly believe she has committed adultery. Also know that I warned her several times not to ensconce herself with so-and-so and so-and-so, and I have discovered that she violated my warning several times. You, my rabbis, also know that she is rude and is suspected of many types of shameful activity. Perhaps you remain doubtful, but to me it is clear.

Even after two days in court, the husband's claims remained muddled. After originally claiming to have heard reports of his wife's infidelity from others, on the second day he claimed to have witnessed the adultery himself. Then, shifting from direct charges of sexual content, he focused on the warning he had issued to his wife to avoid spending time in private with specific men, using words taken almost verbatim from the Mishnah's description of the Sotah ritual in the Temple (an ordeal based on Numbers 5:11–31 to test a wife suspected of adultery).[13]

10. *Teshuvot Ḥakhme Provinẓia (Teshuvot Ḥakhme Provintsya)*, no. 50, ed. Sofer, 162. The third judge on the bench, Simon ben Meir, is not known from other sources.

11. No further information is offered about this earlier incident with the governor (*moshel*), besides the husband's reply just below, which refers to him as a lord.

12. *Teshuvot Ḥakhme Provinẓia (Teshuvot Ḥakhme Provintsya)*, no. 50, ed. Sofer, 162–163.

13. mSotah 1:2; Ishay Rosen-Zvi, *The Mishnaic Sotah Ritual: Temple, Gender and Midrash*, trans. Orr Scharf (Leiden, 2012), 22–37. This textual echo may have been inserted by the judge or court secretary writing up an account of the case and translating the husband's testimony into Hebrew, but the claim that he had warned his wife before witnesses surely came from the husband himself.

To wrap things up, he alluded to his wife's negative *fama* in the city.[14] The court, choosing its words carefully, informed him that "according to Heavenly law, whoever believes these things about his wife must divorce her"; "Heavenly Law" is an extra-legal category of Jewish law, implying an unenforceable moral obligation.[15] Its invocation in this context was meant to absolve the terrestrial court of responsibility for the husband's ensuing actions. A court-imposed divorce would have deprived the wife of the cash payment promised in her *ketubah* (marriage contract). Instead of ordering a divorce, however, the judges simply reflected the husband's words back to him, explaining that he personally could not remain in the marriage due to his concerns but that his wife would not lose any of her rights. Undeterred by the court's reticence, the husband requested a record of the ruling, written and signed, as if it were an enforceable court order.

The lengthy court proceedings that led to the signed ruling had been a charade, and all of its participants had been aware of that fact. The judges knew from the outset that the claim of infidelity – even if it was factually accurate – was not the real issue. Along with the rest of the Jews in Carpentras, they knew the woman's reputation, but they were equally aware that her husband had not complained about her in the past. Dredging up old gossip was simply an excuse for threatening her with divorce, the explanation for which lay elsewhere.

The Jewish communities of southern France maintained a ban on no-fault divorce.[16] Depriving husbands of their prerogative (according to statutory Jewish law) to divorce their wives at will was a communal initiative to protect women from the threat of abandonment. This husband was attempting to regain his leverage against his wife with the aid of an official-looking document that mentioned divorce. He had hoped that, when she saw the document and realized that divorce was a real possibility, she would acquiesce to whatever demands her husband was making of her. Once he had managed to procure such a document, with its unenforceability obscured by legal terminology, he returned home. The document achieved its desired effect and, once used, was no longer necessary:

14. Thelma Fenster and Daniel Lord Smail, "Introduction," in *Fama: The Politics of Talk and Reputation in Medieval Europe*, ed. Thelma Fenster and Daniel Lord Smail (Ithaca, 2003), 1–4.

15. Aaron Kirschenbaum, *Equity in Jewish Law: Beyond Equity: Halakhic Aspirationism in Jewish Civil Law* (New York, 1991), 137–177; Levi Yitzhak Cooper, "Liability According to the Laws of Heaven" (LLM thesis, Bar Ilan University, 2001) (Hebrew); Shoval Shafat, "The Interface of Divine and Human Punishment in Rabbinic Thought" (PhD diss., Ben Gurion University of the Negev, 2011) (Hebrew).

16. Shlomo H. Pick, "Medieval Provençal Jewish Self-Government," *Trumah* 15 (2005): 105–138, at 123–124.

> A few days later, regret arose in his heart and he missed his wife,[17] and he asked one of the sages whether he could retract his statement, and he was told that he could, and he asked the sages about this.[18]

This was the point at which a disagreement erupted between two of the judges. Abraham of Montpellier was happy to accept the husband's revised statement that his earlier accusation had been false and to void its legal ramifications.[19] Mordechai Kimḥi did not disagree with this version of the story, but he took umbrage at the husband's flagrant manipulation of the court. Realizing that his arguments would not sway his fellow judges, Kimḥi disassociated himself from the case:[20]

> I do not see any way of allowing this man to remain with his wife. I took a similar stance almost twenty-five years ago when I sat alongside great judges, and they adopted my opinion. But [your] intellect is greater than mine. If, out of a sense of piety and modesty, you request my permission – because of our joint ruling forbidding this marriage – then permission is granted on condition that my name is not included in the ruling.

Kimḥi saw no way to participate in a judicial process that had become unmoored from truth. The husband's revised version of his story was clearly fabricated, but it was no less true than his original account before the court – it was simply more brazen. Applying the law stringently in this case by barring the husband from reuniting with his wife would not achieve justice, but it might force the husband and others like him to think twice before manipulating the court. In contrast, Abraham of Montpellier did not see the husband's behaviour as manipulation. The husband was simply using the court for his own purposes. As long as the court followed the letter of the law, it need not be concerned with the motivations of the people standing before it. As long as Jews continued to use the Jewish court, whether innocently or through calculated self-interest, Jewish law would maintain a presence in their lives.

17. In the original iteration of this quote from the Tanakh (Hebrew Bible): "He remembered Vashti and what was decreed against her" (Esther 2:1).

18. *Teshuvot Ḥakhme Provinẓia (Teshuvot Ḥakhme Provintsya)*, no. 50, ed. Sofer, 163.

19. *Teshuvot Ḥakhme Provinẓia (Teshuvot Ḥakhme Provintsya)*, no. 50, ed. Sofer, 163–166. Abraham of Montpellier's lenient position on this issue is also expressed in his commentary on Kiddushin (published in the margins of the Romm edition of the Babylonian Talmud [Vilna, 1881–1898], vol. 11, under the erroneous title *Tosafot Ri ha-Zaken*), fol. 66a, s.v. *ke-be tre*.

20. *Teshuvot Ḥakhme Provinẓia (Teshuvot Ḥakhme Provintsya)*, no. 51, ed. Sofer, 166–170.

The deep differences between the two judges did not go unnoticed by the Jewish populace. Among his thumbnail portraits of Provençal rabbis in his time, Kalonymos ben Kalonymos described Mordechai Kimḥi and Abraham of Montpellier as "a famous pair of rabbis who guard the Torah."[21] Kimḥi emerges from his description as an obscure and unapproachable figure: "I have never seen him, or known him even from afar, nor had any interaction with him." Abraham, by marked contrast, is described as a judge "troubled by the problems of the masses from all directions, for he gives judgement in ritual and civil law,[22] and his work in the court takes priority over his study." What characterized Abraham as a judge was "his attempt to create peace in the land between man and his fellow ... for in his wisdom he knows how to find the root of every disagreement and blemish." Abraham's reputation as a savvy judge of human foibles made him a popular arbiter, while Kimḥi's insistence on the court's integrity isolated him from the community.

Mordechai Kimḥi's reputation as a learned, unbending and socially isolated judicial authority made him, paradoxically, a prime target for just the type of legal manipulation he abhorred. One of Kimḥi's *responsa* begins with the description of a man in Marseilles suffering from "the black madness" (a condition also known in the Middle Ages as melancholy).[23] His sickness manifested in voices in his belly urging him to abstain from meat and wine and from sleeping in a bed, while in other ways the man was described as being perfectly rational. Since according to Jewish law a man possessed by a frenzy or by demons could not issue a divorce for his wife, the questioner suggested that this man was incapable of granting a divorce.[24] The Talmud (bHagigah 3b) listed three indications of mental deficiency – "he that goes out alone at night, and he that spends the night in a cemetery, and he that tears his garments." Their absence in this case could have affirmed the husband's legal competency.[25] However, Kimḥi understood that talmudic passage as relevant only for obligation in religious commandments. In legal matters such as divorce, even the slight hint of confusion or strange

21. Shatzmiller, "Minor Epistle," 38.

22. Literally, "between blood and blood, between law and law" (Deut. 17:8).

23. *Teshuvot Ḥakhme Provinẓia (Teshuvot Ḥakhme Provintsya)*, no. 57, ed. Sofer, 195–196. The case was discussed briefly by Ephraim Shoham-Steiner, *On the Margins of a Minority: Leprosy, Madness, and Disability among the Jews of Medieval Europe*, trans. Haim Watzman (Detroit, 2014), 102–103.

24. mGittin 7:1; Julius Preuss, *Biblical and Talmudic Medicine*, trans. Fred Rosner (Northvale, 1993), 320–321.

25. This was, in fact, the position taken by Abraham of Montpellier in his Talmud commentary. Avraham min ha-Har, *Perush*, ed. Moshe Yehudah Blau (New York, 1962–1975), 3: 196.

behavior was enough to disqualify a man's competency. The husband could divorce his wife only if it were proved that he was fully healed of his ailment, and any divorce that had already been issued must be disqualified retroactively.[26]

Kimḥi's stringent ruling elicited an impassioned response from leading members of the Jewish community in Aix-en-Provence.[27] It was their local court that had approved the divorce, and the sages of Marseilles had supported the decision. Through no fault of his own, they explained, Kimḥi had been misled by an unscrupulous character trying to undermine their authority. That character was Isaac of Trets, a physician and a highly educated individual. Isaac of Trets had no business writing to Kimḥi about a legal case over which he had no authority, and he had abused his position as a medical practitioner by describing the Marseilles husband as unstable.[28] Contrary to Isaac's report, the men of Aix had in fact examined the husband carefully over time and had concluded that he was fully recovered from his melancholy. Crucially, the behaviour that was taken by Mordechai Kimḥi as symptoms of the disease was in fact a rational decision meant to prevent its recurrence. "His thoughts, along with what he heard from some doctors and in accordance with what he learned from experience, led him to avoid meat and wine because their heat would harm him. In order to dispel the hallucinations that visited him particularly while he slept, he avoided lying in a bed."[29]

There was little consensus among thirteenth-century doctors on the etiology and treatment of melancholy.[30] Isaac of Trets may have sincerely believed that the man from Marseilles was in the grips of mental disease, although he may also

26. Mordechai's son Isaac Kimḥi endorsed his father's position in an almost identical *responsum, Teshuvot Ḥakhme Provinẓia (Teshuvot Ḥakhme Provintsya)*, no. 58, ed. Sofer, 197–198.

27. *Teshuvot Ḥakhme Provinẓia (Teshuvot Ḥakhme Provintsya)*, no. 59, ed. Sofer, 198–200. They included at least two scholars who penned their own legal *responsa* on other occasions – Abraham ben Joseph Baruch ben Neriah and Yekutiel ben Samuel ha-Cohen.

28. Isaac of Trets the doctor, who died in 1307, appears in Latin and Hebrew documents. Henri Gross, *Gallia Judaica* (Paris, 1897), 59; Fred Menkes, "Une communauté juive en Provence au XIVe siècle: Étude d'un groupe sociale," *Le Moyen Age* 77 (1971): 277–303, at 278–279; Joseph Shatzmiller, *Justice et injustice au début du XIVe siècle* (Rome, 1999), 131–132.

29. *Teshuvot Ḥakhme Provinẓia (Teshuvot Ḥakhme Provintsya)*, no. 59, ed. Sofer, 200.

30. Raymond Klibansky, Erwin Panofsky and Fritz Saxl, *Saturn and Melancholy: Studies in the History of Natural Philosophy, Religion and Art* (London, 1964); Peter E. Pormann, "Melancholy in the Medieval World: The Christian, Jewish, and Muslim Tradition," in *Rufus of Ephesus: On Melancholy*, ed. Peter E. Pormann (Tübingen, 2008), 179–196; Iona McCleery, "Both 'Illness and temptation of the enemy': Melancholy, the Medieval Patient and the Writings of King Duarte of Portugal (r. 1433–1438)," *Journal of Medieval Iberian Studies* 1 (2009): 163–178.

have had some vested interest in derailing the divorce. Once the divorce had already been granted, Isaac could not easily find a rabbi to invalidate it, since as a rule even internationally-recognized rabbis avoided overturning divorces that had already been finalized by a Jewish court.[31] Mordechai Kimḥi's reputation as an unbending and isolated figure respected for his scholarship and integrity (and perhaps also known for his less than great respect for other rabbis in Provence) made him the perfect instrument for the doctor's ploy. Isaac of Trets realized that, if he fed Kimḥi information suggesting that the divorce was invalid, Kimḥi would not hesitate to renounce the Aix court's ruling. The uninformed public would be impressed by Kimḥi's reputation as a fearless judge and would henceforth lose its respect for the local judges in Aix and Marseilles. This case demonstrated how easy it was, for a person with sufficient grasp of the legal, medical and political dimensions of a given situation, to play rabbis against each other.

After receiving the letter from Aix, Kimḥi must have realized that he had been manipulated. His mounting frustration with the misuse of his court led him to eventually foreswear judicial work altogether. A case that occurred shortly after 1306 forced him out of retirement and pushed him to his limits. A married man named Mordechai ben Moses (or, by his vernacular name, Pancho of Viviers) approached Kimḥi and explained that he had sworn an oath barring his wife from any benefit that she might derive from him.[32] Such an oath would preclude the couple from engaging in sexual relations and was considered by rabbinic law to be grounds for divorce.[33] Mordechai/Pancho hoped to elicit a court order of divorce so that he could claim to have no choice but to comply by granting the divorce. His wife insisted that she did not want a divorce and was willing to sustain the marriage even under the terms of the oath. Realizing that Pancho was simply trying to circumvent the community's ban on no-fault divorce, Kimḥi refused to even hear the case and hoped that would put an end to the matter.

Kimḥi underestimated Pancho's determination and political connections. Kimḥi found himself being dragged before a series of civil authorities, who probably had no jurisdiction over the case but who wielded irresistible power over the Jews of the city:

31. See, for example, *Teshuvot Ḥakhme Provinẓia (Teshuvot Ḥakhme Provintsya)*, nos. 18–24, ed. Sofer, 91–95, where a series of rabbis in France, Germany and Languedoc reversed their earlier position upon learning that Mordechai Kimḥi's local court in Narbonne had already ruled on the case. This exchange dates to the late thirteenth century.

32. *Teshuvot Ḥakhme Provinẓia (Teshuvot Ḥakhme Provintsya)*, no. 63, ed. Sofer, 215–219. The husband's vernacular name appears in a version of the *responsum* found in BnF Héb. 1391, fol. 159v, cited in *Teshuvot Ḥakhme Provinẓia (Teshuvot Ḥakhme Provintsya)*, ed. Sofer, 216 n62.

33. mKetubbot 5:6.

> They called me before our lord, his highness the bishop (*ha-hegmon*) twice.[34] When he saw that I refused to hear the case, he was gracious to me and released me. I eluded them and then they called me before the judge (*ha-dayan*), and I escaped by [providing] sufficient explanations. Then they called me before the consul (*ha-shoter*),[35] and he pressured me, forcing me to answer his questions one by one.[36]

The five questions Kimḥi was forced to answer evince a fairly high, if limited, degree of Jewish legal knowledge.[37] Pancho may have formulated the questions himself, or he may have received legal counsel from someone else. The questions add further detail to the story by referring to multiple attempts made by Pancho's wife and her relatives to placate him and to preserve the marriage. They were willing to allow him to marry a second wife while maintaining his first. Alternatively, they offered to place witnesses within the marital home to prevent the couple from having sex in violation of the oath. Her family also took the active step of removing the wife from Pancho's home in order to loosen his control over her.

In his coerced response, Mordechai Kimḥi explained that his sympathies lay entirely with the wife. If she were to request a divorce, he would comply without hesitation by issuing a court order compelling the husband to divorce her. However, it was her prerogative to accept Pancho as her husband without the benefit of sexual relations for as long as she was willing, and the court would not intervene in that case. Kimḥi described the communal ordinances that were designed to prevent unilateral divorces which was, he argued, precisely what Pancho was trying to engineer.

Shaken by the experience, Mordechai Kimḥi drafted a letter setting out the facts of the case and the answers he had given to the questions. The letter was sent to Abba Mari ben Moses (Sen Astruc de Lunel), whose response was

34. Bérenger de Mazan was bishop of Carpentras during the years 1294–1318, and this case certainly took place during that period. Jules de Terris, *Les évêques de Carpentras: Étude historique* (Avignon, 1886), 145–154.

35. For *shoter* as a translation of consul, see Joseph Shatzmiller, "Terminologie politique en hébreu médiéval: Jalons pour un glossaire," *Revue des études juives* 142 (1983): 133–140, at 134–135. Relations between the bishop and the civic leadership of Carpentras were strained at the beginning of the fourteenth century, and Pancho may have taken advantage of that tension by encouraging the consul to overrule the bishop. Valérie Theis, *Le gouvernement pontifical du Comtat Venaissin* (Rome, 2012), 539–541.

36. *Teshuvot Ḥakhme Provinẓia (Teshuvot Ḥakhme Provintsya)*, no. 63, ed. Sofer, 217.

37. For some flaws in the legal reasoning behind the questions, see Roth, "Legal Strategy and Legal Culture in Medieval Jewish Courts of Southern France," *AJS Review* 38 (2014): 375–393, at 379.

decidedly unsupportive.[38] Abba Mari faulted Kimḥi for lacking the courage to stand up for his principles, and then switched sides by suggesting that Pancho's behavior was an entirely reasonable way for a man to escape a marriage. He passed Kimḥi's letter on to an unnamed rabbi who did not even know who Kimḥi was, although he did endorse the content of Kimḥi's ruling and the urgent need to uphold judicial authority.[39] No other rabbis are known to have responded.

Unlike the physician Isaac of Trets, who hoodwinked Mordechai Kimḥi through deft control of the information that he fed him, Pancho of Viviers used naked threats to pressure Kimḥi into doing his bidding. Pancho's onslaught was not successful, and Kimḥi emerged from it heroically, in his own eyes. Yet his heroism struck no chord with his rabbinic peers. His legal knowledge and personal stature were never in question, but Mordechai Kimḥi's opposition to the legal culture of his age left him completely isolated.

Civil Law

A crucial component in the Jewish legal culture of late-medieval southern France was the plurality of legal forums. Jews in Provence and Languedoc availed themselves of the local civil (non-Jewish) courts, even in cases involving only Jews.[40] They routinely utilized local notaries to formalize the financial aspects of their marriage agreements.[41] Some court documents from the fourteenth century also preserve Jewish domestic fights over marriage and divorce brought before local

38. *Teshuvot Ḥakhme Provinẓia (Teshuvot Ḥakhme Provintsya)*, no. 64, ed. Sofer, 219–222. On Abba Mari, and on his response to this question, see Chapter 5.

39. *Teshuvot Ḥakhme Provinẓia (Teshuvot Ḥakhme Provintsya)*, no. 65, ed. Sofer, 222–225, is an unsigned *responsum* supporting Kimḥi's ruling, but it was written by someone who appears not to have known Kimḥi directly and received a copy of Kimḥi's letter from Abba Mari.

40. Joseph Shatzmiller, *Recherches sur la communauté juive de Manosque au moyen âge: 1241–1329* (Paris, 1973), 84–92. See also Rena N. Lauer, "Jewish Law and Litigation in the Secular Courts of the Late Medieval Mediterranean," *Critical Analysis of Law* 3 (2016): 114–132; Rena N. Lauer, *Colonial Justice and the Jews of Venetian Crete* (Philadelphia, 2019), 102–125.

41. Simcha Emanuel, "The Struggle for Provençal Halakhic Independence in the Thirteenth Century," *Hispania Judaica Bulletin* 9 (2013): 5–14; Colette Sirat, "Paléographie hébraïque médiévale," *Annuaire de l'École Pratique des Hautes Études* (1971/1972): 399–409, at 399; Robert I. Burns, *Jews in Notarial Culture: Latinate Wills in Mediterranean Spain, 1250–1350* (Berkeley, 1996), 211 n3.

gentile judges instead of Jewish ones.[42] As a general rule, however, Jews used the civil courts for monetary disputes and brought cases of marital law, like those discussed in this chapter, before Jewish courts.

This had not always been the case. During the twelfth century, rabbinic courts in Languedoc dealt with the full gamut of legal issues. No records exist that would allow quantitative analysis, but the *responsa* of Abraham of Narbonne (d. 1158) and Abraham ben David (Rabad, d. 1198) mention monetary disputes that were clearly heard and decided in rabbinic courts.[43] When asked about an aspect of inheritance law, Abraham of Narbonne declared that "this is how the sages and great men of our town would rule, and we follow them and have ruled that way almost on a daily basis."[44] In the context of another ruling about inheritance, Rabad himself was referred to as "the greatest of the judges in the land."[45] Yet, when we turn to the *responsa* on civil law that were preserved in *Teshuvot Ḥakhme Provinẓia (Teshuvot Ḥakhme Provintsya)*, we find only four cases from thirteenth- or fourteenth-century Provence, debated in nineteen *responsa*.[46] Not one of these *responsa* was written by Mordechai Kimḥi.

One of the factors that caused this precipitous drop in the activity of Jewish civil courts was the arrival of Roman law in Provence and Languedoc during the twelfth and thirteenth centuries.[47] First came codices of Roman law, newly dis-

42. Monique Wernham, *La communauté juive de Salon-de-Provence d'aprés les actes notaries 1391–1435* (Toronto, 1987), 191–205; Francine Michaud, *Un signe des temps: Accroisement des crises familiales autour du patrimoine à Marseille à la fin du XIIIe siècle* (Toronto, 1994), 28–29; Juliette Sibon, *Les juifs de Marseille au XIVe siècle* (Paris, 2011), 279–283. There is no evidence to suggest that non-Jewish courts in Provence attempted to decide cases involving Jews in accordance with Jewish law. On this phenomenon elsewhere in Christian Europe, see Lauer, *Colonial Justice and the Jews of Venetian Crete*, 129–146.

43. Abraham ben Isaac of Narbonne, *She'elot u-Teshuvot*, no. 112, ed. Yosef Kafaḥ (Jerusalem, 1962), 88 (splitting a partnership): "we exempted them both from the obligation of an oath and ban"; Abraham ben Isaac of Narbonne, *She'elot u-Teshuvot*, no. 119, ed. Kafaḥ, 96: "Teach us, our teacher – two plaintiffs who have sued each other in many suits, over wheat and barley and money"; Abraham ben David of Posquières, *Teshuvot u-Fesakim*, no. 174, ed. Yosef Kafaḥ (Jerusalem, 1964), 222: "whether he can swear in court that he does not possess anything belonging to Simeon"; no. 183, 225: "Regarding the custom, that someone who holds a debt contract against his fellow, and he is afraid it will get lost, goes to court where they transcribe it word for word and keep a copy in the court."

44. Abraham of Narbonne, *She'elot u-Teshuvot*, no. 114, ed. Kafaḥ, 91.

45. Abraham of Posquières, *Teshuvot u-Fesakim* no. 168, ed. Kafaḥ, 118.

46. *Teshuvot Ḥakhme Provinẓia (Teshuvot Ḥakhme Provintsya)*, ed. Sofer, part II, nos. 1–2, 321–323 and nos. 8–20, 332–377 address a single case. The three other cases are no. 23, 380–386, no. 47, 413–416 and nos. 48–49, 416–429.

47. André Gouron, "Les étapes de la penetration du droit romain au XIIe siècle dans l'ancienne Septimanie," *Annales du Midi* 69 (1957): 103–120; André Gouron, "Diffusion des

covered in Italy and fast becoming the basis for academic legal studies.[48] Towards the end of the thirteenth century, the newly established law faculties at Montpellier, Avignon and Toulouse created a cadre of men looking to put their studies into practice.[49] Some served in official capacities, as judges or as legal advisors to various rulers and urban leaders.[50] Others joined the growing ranks of notaries, who created a wide range of legal documents for their customers.[51] A third option for graduates of the law faculties was the emerging profession of lawyering.[52] These developments most directly affected the existing practitioners of civil law,

---

consulats méridionaux et expansion du droit romain aux XIIe et XIIIe siècles," *Bibliothèque de l'école des chartes* 121 (1963): 26–76, reprinted in André Gouron, *La science du droit dans le Midi de la France au moyen âge* (London, 1984), I.

48. On the process of rediscovery, see Charles M. Radding and Antonio Ciaralli, *The Corpus Iuris Civilis in the Middle Ages: Manuscripts and Transmission from the Sixth Century to the Juristic Revival* (Leiden, 2006), 67–109; Anders Winroth, "The Legal Revolution of the Twelfth Century," in *European Transformations: The Long Twelfth Century*, ed. Thomas F.X. Noble and John Van Engen (Notre Dame, 2011), 338–353.

49. André Gouron, "Note sur les origines de l'université d'Avignon," in *Études offertes à Jean Macqueron* (Aix-en-Provence, 1970), 361–366, reprinted in André Gouron, *La science du droit dans le Midi*, II; André Gouron, "Les juristes de l'école de Montpellier," *Ius Romanum Medii Aevi* IV, 3a (1970): 3–35; Jan Rogoziński, *Power, Caste, and Law: Social Conflict in Fourteenth-Century Montpellier* (Cambridge, MA, 1982), 162–164. In general, see Antonio García y García, "The Faculties of Law," in *A History of the University in Europe*, vol. 1: *Universities in the Middle Ages*, ed. Hilde de Ridder-Symoens and Walter Rüegg (Cambridge, 1992), 388–408; Harold J. Berman, *Law and Revolution: The Formation of the Western Legal Tradition* (Cambridge, MA, 1983), 120–164; James A. Brundage, *The Medieval Origins of the Legal Profession: Canonists, Civilians, and Courts* (Chicago, 2008), 219–282.

50. Joseph Strayer, *Les gens de justice du Languedoc sous Philippe le Bel* (Toulouse, 1970); André Gouron, "Le role social des juristes dans les villes méridionales au *moyen âge*," *Annales de la Faculté des Lettres et Sciences Humaines de Nice* 9–10 (1969): 55–67, reprinted in Gouron, *La science du droit dans le Midi*, III; Jan Rogoziński, "Ordinary and Major Judges," *Studia Gratiana* 15 (1972): 589–611.

51. John H. Pryor, *Business Contracts of Medieval Provence: Selected Notulae from the Cartulary of Giraud Amalric of Marseilles, 1248* (Toronto, 1981); Maïté Lesné-Ferret, "The Notariate in the Consular Towns of Septimanian Languedoc (Late Twelfth-Thirteenth Centuries)," in *Urban and Rural Communities in Medieval France: Provence and Languedoc, 1000–1500*, ed. Kathryn Reyerson and John Drendel (Leiden, 1998), 3–21 (and other chapters in that volume); *Medieval Notaries and their Acts: The 1327–1328 Register of Jean Holanie*, ed. Kathryn L. Reyerson and Debra A. Salata (Kalamazoo, 2004).

52. André Gouron, "The Training of Southern French Lawyers during the Thirteenth and Fourteenth Centuries," *Studia Gratiana* XV (1972): 219–227, reprinted in Gouron, *La science du droit dans le Midi*, IV; and generally: Brundage, *The Medieval Origins of the Legal Profession*.

who had no choice but to incorporate the new principles.[53] They also triggered deep changes in the ways that the general population related to the legal system.[54]

Rabbinic scholars of southern France were intensely aware of these developments from the very beginning, as evidenced by doctrinal changes within Jewish law made explicitly or implicitly due to the arrival of Roman law during the late twelfth century.[55] By the mid-thirteenth century, the Jewish laity embraced the new legal culture by turning in decisive numbers to non-Jewish notaries and courts for their contracts and commercial disputes. The advantages that the developing legal system offered to Jewish merchants were extensive: it followed rules that could be learned and predicted, that were applied equally to Christians and Jews, that were almost identical throughout the region and in the port cities of the western Mediterranean, and it was linked to an extensive network of notaries whose records provided durable and trustworthy documentation for all types of transactions. Jewish communities may have felt positively inclined even towards the enforcement of criminal law, which was becoming more rational and less arbitrary.[56] But the mental shift, the entire attitude towards what law was and the role it could play in life, was also felt in areas of law that remained within the jurisdiction of Jewish courts, such as marriage and divorce.

One of the most revealing changes was the rise of lawyers who represented clients in the Jewish courts of Provence and prepared sophisticated legal arguments on their behalf.[57] This was not simply an innovation in Jewish court procedure copied from the civil courts. It was one manifestation of a new Jewish legal culture that repositioned the plaintiff as a consumer and the rabbinic court as a resource to be exploited.[58] Previously, a Jew would have appeared in court and told a story before the judges, who then endeavoured to unravel truth from

53. Marie-Louise Carlin, *La penetration du droit romain dans les actes de la pratique Provençale (XIe–XIIIe siècle)* (Paris, 1967); Pryor, *Business Contracts*, 22–24, with extensive references to previous literature.

54. Daniel Lord Smail, *The Consumption of Justice: Emotions, Publicity, and Legal Culture in Marseille, 1264–1423* (Ithaca, 2003).

55. Haym Soloveitchik, "A Note on the Penetration of Roman Law in Provence," *Tijdschrift voor Rechtsgeschiednis* 40 (1972): 227–229; Haym Soloveitchik, "Jewish and Provençal Law: A Study in Interaction," in *Mélanges Roger Aubenas* (Montpellier, 1974), 711–723.

56. Pinchas Roth, "Mourning Murderers in Medieval Jewish Law," in *Medieval and Early Modern Murder: Legal, Literary and Historical Contexts*, ed. Larissa Tracy (Woodbridge, 2018), 77–95.

57. Roth, "Legal Strategy," 389–391.

58. My thoughts on this topic are deeply influenced by Smail, *The Consumption of Justice*.

lie and to translate the facts into a legal ruling. In late medieval Provence, that Jew would arrive, not with a story but with a legal argument. Culled from popular understandings of the law or honed by a professional legal advisor, that argument was supposed to achieve an anticipated result in the courtroom.

Mordechai Kimḥi was horrified by this shift. To his eyes, it represented a reversal of roles that undermined the foundations of Jewish society: "Their tongue wags throughout the land: 'Who is our lord, and who will summon us to judgement, and who can decide better than us?'"[59]

Abraham of Montpellier and Kimḥi's other colleagues did not share his horror. From their perspective, if Jewish courts continued to function in accordance with the form and substance of rabbinic law, no harm was done. Jewish courts could be no more and no less than a reflection of Jewish culture.

59. *Teshuvot Ḥakhme Provinzia (Teshuvot Ḥakhme Provintsya)*, no. 63, ed. Sofer, 215.

CHAPTER THREE

Patriotism and Tolerance in the Study Hall

The changes in Jewish legal culture that drove Mordechai Kimḥi out of the courtroom may have been among the factors that led his son Isaac Kimḥi to spend the bulk of his rabbinic career in the study hall. Talmud study is possibly the most insular and emblematic element of Jewish culture. Confined to a highly educated male elite and pursued within the institutional context of *yeshivot*, this realm of rabbinic knowledge might appear to have been cut off from the geopolitical context in which it took place. Certainly, not every political tremor was felt inside the rabbinic academy, but questions of local identity and regional rivalry were sometimes played out through the parries and prooftexts of rabbinic writing.

Isaac Kimḥi was born and raised, like his father, in Narbonne. He may have been born as early as 1270 or as late as 1290,[1] and was still living in the early 1340s, when he wrote his last datable *responsum*.[2] Unlike Mordechai, whose primary occupation was as a judge and whose surviving writings were almost all composed in that context, Isaac Kimḥi was a teacher. He taught at *yeshivot* in Salon-de-Provence,[3] Orange,[4] Montauban-sur-l'Ouvèze,[5] and Nyons in the

1. Henri Gross, *Gallia Judaica* (Paris, 1897), 385, gives the earlier year based on Leopold Zunz's report of a liturgical manuscript from 1290 containing Isaac's works. Leopold Zunz, *Gesammelte Schriften* (Berlin, 1876), 34; Zunz, *Zur Geschichte und Literatur* (Berlin, 1845), 466. However, this manuscript has not been identified to date and, in the absence of any other supporting evidence, cannot be relied upon. No mention of this manuscript appears where it might have been expected in Zunz's other writings: *Namen der Juden* (Leipzig, 1837), 59–60; "Ritus der Synagoge von Avignon," *Allgemeine Zeitung fur Judentums* 1839, 679–680; *Literaturgeschichte der synagogalen poesie* (Berlin, 1865), 505.

2. Gérard E. Weil, "Symilon de Lambesc Courrier du Dauphin, Symilon d'Hyeres Assassiné au Conil du Castelet en 1340 & les rabbins de Haute-Provence," in *Les juifs dans la Méditerranée: médiévale et moderne* (Nice, 1986), 25–52.

3. Gross, *Gallia Judaica*, 655.

4. Paris, Bibliothèque nationale de France, Hébreu 1391, fol. 50r.

5. Amsterdam, Portugees Israëlitisch Seminarium Ets Haim, ms. EH 47 A 31, fourth foliation, fol 39v.

Dauphiné.[6] The legal questions addressed to Kimḥi arose out of the cultural anxieties that concerned many segments of Provençal Jewry in his time – the truth-claims of religion in a scientific age, the reliability of the Provençal rabbinic tradition and the place of Jewish ritual observance in a religiously pluralistic society. Through explicit statements and subtle terminological choices, Kimḥi struck a balance between pride in his own tradition and tolerance of others.

The tension between rationalist philosophy and traditional religion was one of the defining features of Provençal Jewry. Many rabbis subscribed to an intermediate position that accorded respect to secular wisdom while advocating fidelity to the Talmud and Halakhah. Recent scholarship has demonstrated the ways in which this moderate approach found expression in theoretical halakhic works by Menaḥem ha-Me'iri and others.[7] What remains less clear is the impact that Graeco-Arabic wisdom had on applied Jewish law and on the *yeshivot* themselves.

For Isaac Kimḥi, the meeting of cultures was personal since he counted the famed philosopher and astronomer Gersonides (Levi ben Gershom) as a personal friend.[8] More concretely, Kimḥi frequently employed technical scientific terminology in his *responsa*. Often this was a purely rhetorical flourish, as if Kimḥi wanted to show that he knew the current jargon. For example, one of his *responsa* makes its customary apology for the author's unworthiness with a chain of optometric terms:[9]

> Would the viewers of images (*mabite ha-temunot*), the healthy speculators (*beri'e ha-'iyyun*), look to someone suffering from eye ailments (*'alule ha-'enayim*), whose pain is clouded (*ne'ekhar*)?

The rhetorical meaning is straightforward – Kimḥi could not perceive the matter at hand as clearly as his questioners did, so why should they ask him for help? But the words he used to create this metaphor were deeply embedded in scien-

6. Gross, *Gallia Judaica*, 384–387; Frédéric Chartrain, "Die Siedlung der Juden in der Dauphiné während des Mittelalters," in *Geschichte der Juden im Mittelalter von der Nordsee bis zu den Südalpen*, ed. Jörg R. Müller (Hannover, 2002), 1: 167.

7. Moshe Halbertal, *Between Torah and Wisdom: Rabbi Menachem ha-Meiri and the Maimonidean Halakhists in Provence* (Jerusalem, 2001), 50–79, 181–216 (Hebrew); Gabriel Hanuka, "The Philosophy and Halakhic Theory of R. David d'Estelle" (PhD diss., Bar Ilan University, 2013) (Hebrew).

8. Pinchas Roth, "The *Responsa* of Gersonides and their Reception," *Gersonides' Afterlife: Studies on the Reception of Levi ben Gerson's Philosophical, Halakhic and Scientific Oeuvre in the 14th through 20th Centuries*, ed. Ofer Elior, Gad Freudenthal and David Wirmer (Leiden, 2020), 311–340.

9. *Teshuvot Ḥakhme Provinẓia (Teshuvot Ḥakhme Provintsya)* (*Responsa* of the Sages of Provence), no. 53, ed. Abraham Sofer (Schreiber) (Jerusalem, 1967), 176.

tific Hebrew. *Temunah* connotes image, but it was also used to translate the logical concept of figure, just as *ʿiyyun* was the technical term for philosophical speculation.[10] *ʿAlul* was a medieval neologism to translate the Latin *vitium* (ailment, blemish).[11] *ʿAkhur* is found in an ophthalmological context in Gershom ben Solomon of Arles' *Shaʿar ha-Shamayim*.[12] These terms are far more specialized than the more vaguely philosophical expressions found in other medieval rabbinic writings.[13]

The deployment of scientific terminology served a polemical purpose in Kimḥi's writing. On a number of occasions, non-rabbinic intellectuals challenged his legal rulings on the basis of scientific knowledge that, they claimed, the rabbi lacked. As one such character wrote to him, "Even if the books are in your possession, all of the logical distinctions (*dikduke ha-yeshar*) are not in your possession, for you have left room for the nation's chosen ones to distinguish themselves."[14] This challenger acknowledged the *yeshivah*'s preeminence in the realm of traditional Jewish learning ("the books") but claimed that his ignorance of logic and other branches of secular learning undermined Kimḥi's ability to reach proper conclusions even in matters of Jewish law – a task that must be conceded to "the nation's chosen ones," the new Jewish intellectuals. Kimḥi responded to this challenge directly, writing that his interlocutor's claims were themselves tainted by logical fallacies:[15]

10. The online database of PESHAT: Philosophic and Scientific Hebrew Terminology (https://peshat.gwiss.uni-hamburg.de/) has been invaluable in finding the precise meanings of such words in Kimḥi's writings. A glossary of Hebrew logical terms is found in Charles Manekin, *The Logic of Gersonides* (Dordrecht, 1992), 313–323.

11. Gerrit Bos, *Novel Medical and General Hebrew Terminology from the 13th Century* (Oxford, 2011–2016), 1: 34, 2: 71.

12. Gershom ben Solomon, *The Gate of Heaven (Shaʿar ha-Shamayim)*, ed. and trans. F.S. Bodenheimer (Jerusalem, 1953), 253: "The reason for seeing far, but not from nearby, is that the spirit is clouded (*ʿakhur*) and thick when it goes out, and it becomes cleaner and purified whilst it spreads beyond the eye into the air."

13. A more typical example is the expression "I will expand the apertures of the traceries," which was coined by Maimonides in his *Guide of the Perplexed* and subsequently entered the vocabularies of many medieval authors. Shraga Abramson, "Agav keriah (Reading notes)," *Leshonenu* 42 (1978): 314–316; Frank Talmage, *Apples of Gold in Settings of Silver: Studies in Medieval Jewish Exegesis and Polemics*, ed. Barry Dov Walfish (Toronto, 1999), 108–113. Kimḥi uses the phrase in *Teshuvot Ḥakhme Provinẓia (Teshuvot Ḥakhme Provintsya)* ed. Sofer, 377 and BnF Héb.1391, fol. 89r.

14. S.E. Stern, "Be-din ha-notel yadav lo yekadesh (On the law that a person who washes his hands should not recite the blessing)," in *Sefer Zikaron Ner Shaʾul* (Jerusalem, 2009), 28–42, at 37.

15. Stern, "Be-din ha-notel," 37.

> He thought that we know nothing about the rules of contradiction. But in fact, the contradictions and fallacies in his own words are so obvious that even a newborn chick whose eyes have not yet opened would see them.

On another occasion, Kimḥi received a letter asserting that a ruling by Maimonides about kosher meat was based on faulty science. Kimḥi responded that it was actually the questioner's science that was wrong, and Maimonides was correct:[16]

> The liver has, among its other veins, a large vein – the great surgeons called it the gate of the liver[17] or the opening of the liver – branching from its curved surface,[18] as mentioned by the greatest sage:[19] "and from the curve of the liver grows a large vein called the gate of the liver" ... This vein, the gate of the liver, is what the rabbi (Maimonides) called the great tube and the main vein in its center, through which food enters the liver – by which he meant *chyle* nutrition. You already understand this term, *chyle,* which [was transmitted] from Greek to Arabic and [from Arabic] to our language by the translators, and this was discussed long ago.

In a virtuoso performance, Kimḥi demonstrated his own command of scientific literature, his challenger's ignorance and the enduring relevance of the halakhic canon even in an age of new knowledge.

Ethnic Pride

Another front on which Isaac Kimḥi struggled to defend his particular strain of Provençal Halakhah was regional identity. Kimḥi's tradition was founded upon the bedrock of Spanish and Provençal decisors, a foundation he felt was being

16. BnF Héb.1391, fol. 48r–48v; published: Pinchas Roth, "A Responsum by Rabbi Isaac ben Mordechai Kimhi about a Needle in an Animal's Liver," *Yeshurun* 29 (2013): 28–32, at 32 (Hebrew).

17. Galen, *On the Usefulness of the Parts of the Body,* 4.2, trans. Margaret Tallmadge May (Ithaca, 1968), 1: 205.

18. On the term *kibuv* (convex surface) in the Hebrew of medieval translators, see Eliezer Ben-Yehudah, *A Complete Dictionary of Ancient and Modern Hebrew* (New York, 1959), p. 5672 (Hebrew); Israel Efros, *Philosophical Terms in the Moreh Nebukhim* (New York, 1924), 105.

19. Probably a reference to Aristotle, *Parts of Animals* 3.7 (670a), trans. A.L. Peck (Cambridge, MA, 1937), 263.

eroded by halakhic innovations imported from northern France. This concern was not unrelated to the issue of rationalist philosophy. For almost a century, since the Maimonidean Controversy of the 1230s, French and Provençal Jews had traded insults. Jewish writers in the south ridiculed French Jews for their lack of cultural and philosophical sophistication.[20] The French, for their part, claimed superiority by virtue of their (that is, their rabbinic scholars') command of rabbinic texts, a point that many Provençal Jews were willing to concede. But when he entered the fray, Isaac Kimḥi argued vociferously that Provençal rabbinic expertise outshone even the most brilliant Tosafists of northern France.

An opportunity to clearly express his opposition to the French Tosafists and their influence in his homeland came when Kimḥi was asked to express his opinion on a component of liturgy, the famous *Kol Nidre*:[21]

> You asked me, exalted officer – may God increase your honour and raise your station – about the version of *Kol Nidre* which is found in some of the prayer books, whether it is proper to recite it on the eve of *Yom Kippur* (Day of Atonement) or not. And to explain whether it is an absolution of vows made "from the previous *Yom Kippur* to this *Yom Kippur*" or a condition cancelling any vows made in the future, "from this *Yom Kippur* to the next *Yom Kippur*."

Kol Nidre ("all oaths"), the opening prayer of the Day of Atonement in the Ashkenazic rite, purports to free those who recite it from the obligations of any vows they may have pronounced over the preceding year. According to biblical and talmudic law, the absolution of a vow required a thorough investigation by a sage, who would ascertain whether the vow contained formal flaws or whether it had been made on the basis of erroneous assumptions.[22] The *Kol Nidre* prayer rendered this procedure obsolete by giving laypeople the power to cancel their own

20. Joseph Shatzmiller, "Les tossafistes et la première controverse maimonidienne," in *Rashi et la culture juive en France du nord au moyen âge*, ed. Gilbert Dahan, Gérard Nahon and Elie Nicolas (Paris, 1997), 57–82; Adena Tanenbaum, "Arrogance, Bad Form, and Curricular Narrowness: Belletristic Critiques of Rabbinic Culture from Medieval Spain and Provence," in *Rabbinic Culture and Its Critics: Jewish Authority, Dissent, and Heresy in Medieval and Early Modern Times*, ed. Daniel Frank and Matt Goldish (Detroit, 2008), 57–81.

21. BnF Héb. 1391, fols. 48v–49r; Shemu'el Eli'ezer Stern, *Me'orot ha-Rishonim* (Jerusalem, 2002), 118–122. For a *responsum* by Gersonides written in response to the same question, see Charles Touati, "Le problème du Kol Nidrey et le responsum inédit de Gersonide (Lévi ben Gershom)," *Revue des études juives* 154 (1995): 327–342.

22. Moshe Benovitz, *Kol Nidre: Studies in the Development of Rabbinic Votive Institutions* (Atlanta, 1998).

vows once a year, but it had aroused the opposition of rabbis since it first appeared in the ninth century. Amram Gaʾon (Babylonia, d. ca. 875) wrote in his prayer book that it was "a foolish custom and one is forbidden to do so."[23] European communities with a strong allegiance to the Babylonian geʾonim, such as those in Andalusia and southern France, resisted the incorporation of *Kol Nidre* into their liturgy, but in northern France it became an integral component of the Yom Kippur service.[24] A textual emendation, often identified with Rabbi Jacob Tam of Ramerupt (d. 1171), attempted to neutralize the problem.[25] Instead of cancelling vows made in the previous year, the prayer would focus on the future by pre-emptively cancelling any vows that the congregant might make over the course of the following year.

Kimḥi presented *Kol Nidre* as a liturgical misadventure that was initiated by "some of the Frenchmen."[26]

> This custom, whichever version is chosen, is not a custom but an error, according to the straightforward tradition of the geʾonim of Babylonia and Sefarad, whose words guide us and whose practices we follow. That is why this custom was not mentioned by the Fathers of the World, Alfasi and Maimonides, in their works – because it goes against the roots of tradition. Today this custom has been eradicated in most places where there are great and learned sages ... In the days of my late father (Mordecai Kimḥi) I never saw anyone who even thought of reciting *Kol Nidre* in his presence – neither in Narbonne nor in any other place – and I have followed his example.

Notwithstanding Kimḥi's boast about the eradication of the custom, the question itself makes it clear that the French prayer was making major inroads in Provence. In fact, other sources confirm that the practice of reciting *Kol Nidre* was already well established in Languedoc and Provence by the end of the

23. *Seder Rav ʿAmram Gaʾon*, ed. Daniel Goldschmidt (Jerusalem, 1971), 163.

24. Shlomo Deshen, "The Kol Nidre Enigma: An Anthropological View of the Day of Atonement Liturgy," *Ethnology* 18 (1979): 121–133; Shlomo Deshen, "The Enigma of Kol Nidre: An Anthropological and Historical Investigation," in *Studies in the History of Jewish Society in the Middle Ages and in the Modern Period*, ed. Immanuel Etkes and Yosef Salmon (Jerusalem, 1980), 136–153 (Hebrew).

25. Naphtali Wieder, *The Formation of Jewish Liturgy in the East and the West: A Collection of Essays* (Jerusalem, 1998), 372–381 (Hebrew); Richard C. Steiner, "Kol Nidre: Past, Present and Future," *Jewish Studies Internet Journal* 12 (2013): 1–46. The emendation was originally suggested by Jacob's father, Meir ben Samuel of Ramerupt.

26. Stern, *Meʾorot ha-Rishonim*, 121–122.

twelfth century.[27] Moreover, the prayer itself did not truly originate in France and it was just as old as the custom not to recite it. Kimḥi's portrayal of Provençal Jews aping French practices by reciting *Kol Nidre* was inaccurate and tendentious, marginalizing a custom that was already widespread. By creating a historic narrative about the supremacy of the Iberian-Provençal halakhic tradition, Kimḥi attempted to strengthen local Jewish pride by stemming the tide of French influence in Provence.

Ethnic Tolerance

By Kimḥi's time, the tension between French and Provençal Jews was not simply a matter for literary debate – it was a demographic reality. Large numbers of Jews from northern France had begun emigrating to the County of Provence, and especially to its sparsely populated hinterland, where they lived in close proximity to indigenous Provençal Jews. Kimḥi was acutely aware of this delicate situation, which will be explored in greater length in Chapter 4. Outspoken in his defense of local halakhic traditions, Kimḥi resisted the urge to reject and denigrate French rabbinic culture as a whole. His nuanced position, almost unique in medieval rabbinic thought for its tolerance of religious difference, emerges from several of his *responsa*. As we will see, there is no reason to assume that Kimḥi developed any ideology or philosophy of religious tolerance, but his rulings may reflect a stance that resembles a particular strand in medieval thought.

One *responsum* was written to a questioner who pointed explicitly to the tensions between local Provençal Jews and French immigrants:[28]

> You wrote to me, my brother, about a certain French rabbi who did not want to eat the bread of Jews and instructed [his followers] to purchase from the non-Jewish baker. You begged me to explain the matter to you, if I could.
>
> You should know, my brother, that this ruling was issued some years ago by a few French rabbis ... Since it is the habit of the women of this land, when they put aside part of the dough in order to make sourdough, to do so only after removing the priestly portion (*ḥallah*) from the dough. Therefore, [the entire batch of dough] is now exempt from the priestly portion, and when [part of it] is used as starter for a fresh batch of dough, this creates a

27. Yehiel Goldhaber, "Amirat Kol Nidre (Recitation of Kol Nidre)," *Bet Aharon ve-Yisrael* 17:1 (2001): 91–105, at 97 (Hebrew), citing the twelfth-century sages Isaac ben Abba Mari of Marseilles and Abraham ben Nathan of Lunel.

28. BnF Héb. 1391, fols. 84v–85r (see Appendix, source 2, pp. 122–123).

> mixture of exempt and non-exempt parts ... Another reason is that the women nowadays are not careful to make the oven kosher. Thus, [the French rabbis] say that there is no [Jewish] baker since, in their opinion, the Jewish bread is not baked properly. Therefore, they buy from a non-Jewish baker.

The French rabbi's ruling, as described by the questioner, was extremely provocative. The talmudic prohibition on bread baked by non-Jews was part of an array of laws designed to reinforce the social barriers between Jews and others, but even during talmudic times it was often flaunted.[29] The Babylonian Talmud permitted the consumption of non-Jewish bread in locales where there was no Jewish baker.[30] In this (unnamed) Provençal town there were a number of Jewish bakers, including local women who baked bread for their own households and for sale. By spurning their wares and buying from Christians in their stead, the French rabbi was ignoring the very existence of the local Jewish community ("there is no baker"). The only Jews he saw were Jews who, like him, had emigrated from France and they, apparently, were not involved in bread-baking.

Kimḥi offered more charitable explanations for the French rabbi's ruling. According to one, the manner in which the local Jewish women were accustomed to remove the priestly portion (*ḥallah*) from the dough was effective only according to some rabbinic opinions but not others.[31] This portion was to be removed after the dough was mixed and before it was baked; if it was not removed then the bread was forbidden for consumption.[32] The bread of a non-Jew, however, did not require *ḥallah* at all and was therefore acceptable according to all opinions.[33] Another explanation was that "the women nowadays are not careful to make the oven kosher," by which he meant that they had not adopted the practice of tossing a twig into a communal furnace. This practice was intended to avoid the problem of non-Jewish bread by providing a token Jewish participation in stoking the oven. It had been rejected by Provençal Jews for both legal and practical reasons and had already been called a "French" custom by local rabbis in the twelfth cen-

29. David M. Freidenreich, "Contextualizing Bread: An Analysis of Talmudic Discourse in Light of Christian and Islamic Counterparts," *Journal of the American Academy of Religion* 80 (2012): 411–433.

30. bAvodah Zarah 35b.

31. Aharon ha-Kohen of Narbonne (Lunel), *Sefer Orhot Hayyim*, ed. Moses Schlesinger (Berlin, 1902), 2: 202.

32. Maimonides, *Mishneh Torah*, ed. Shabse Frankel (Jerusalem, 1975–2003), Laws of First Fruits, chapters 5–7.

33. *Mishneh Torah*, Laws of First Fruits 6:8.

tury.[34] According to Provençal Halakhah, the twig was useless; according to French Halakhah it was essential.

The questioner, with his first-hand knowledge of the town and its inhabitants, was fully aware of the ethnic tensions that motivated the French rabbi's choice of bakery. By framing the issue as a difference of legal opinion rather than identity politics, Kimḥi may have hoped to promote mutual respect between the two Jewish ethnic groups sharing space in Provence.

Interreligious Tolerance

One of Kimḥi's rulings relates to public mourning, an important but largely unrecognized field of medieval Jewish-Christian interaction.[35] Jewish law prescribes a number of practices performed by relatives of the deceased which demonstrated to themselves and to others that they were in mourning. These practices could arouse the suspicion and derision of non-Jewish onlookers, and in a number of cases Halakhists decided to eliminate those practices altogether because of the negative reactions they aroused among Gentiles. For example, according to the Talmud, a mourner must cover his head and face with a scarf in what is described as "the custom of the Ishmaelites."[36] Rashi explained that "many people do not follow this practice because the Gentiles laugh at them."[37]

The question sent to Isaac Kimḥi stemmed from the talmudic law stipulating that a mourner may not cut his hair or his beard until the end of the thirty-day mourning period.[38] Kimḥi was asked whether this law applied to a Jewish mourner who was close to the royal government (*karov la-malkhut*), possibly

34. Abraham ben Isaac of Narbonne, *She'elot u-Teshuvot*, no. 217, ed. Yosef Kafaḥ (Jerusalem, 1962), 167: "What the French sages do, that they permit the bread of non-Jews with a twig that they throw into the oven"; Hayyim ben Isaac Or Zaru'a, *She'elot u-Teshuvot*, no. 144, ed. Menahem Avitan (Jerusalem, 2002), 134: "In the land of Provence they avoid making the oven kosher because of the accusation of witchcraft."

35. On some of the tensions and challenges raised by differing cultural forms of mourning, see Rochelle Almeida, *The Politics of Mourning: Grief Management in Cross-Cultural Fiction* (Madison, 2004).

36. bMo'ed Katan 15a and 24a.

37. Solomon ben Isaac (Rashi), *Responsa*, ed. Israel Elfenbein (New York, 1943), 343–344; Yitshak (Eric) Zimmer, *Olam ke-minhago noheg: Perakim be-toldot ha-minhagim, hilkhotehem, ve-gilgulehem* (Society and Customs: Studies in the History and Metamorphosis of Jewish Customs) (Jerusalem, 1996), 193–195.

38. bMo'ed Katan 14b.

referring to the court of Robert of Anjou, Count of Provence or to that of the pope, where his friend Gersonides was sometimes to be found.[39]

There was a talmudic precedent for granting an exemption from hair-cutting law for Jewish courtiers.[40] Similarly, a rabbi in thirteenth century Languedoc ruled that the ban against shaving with a razor could be bent "for clerks and communal leaders who come and go in the courtyards of the kings and rulers (*ha-melakhim veha-shiltonim*)."[41] In line with these precedents, the questioner hoped that Kimḥi would permit the mourning Jew to shave before appearing before state officials.

Kimḥi did not follow the path suggested by his questioner. First, he asserted that the problem was inconsequential since the mourner could simply postpone his appearance at court until the thirty-day period was over.[42]

> Even if he does need to attend the court, if it is for such a limited amount of time, it will not cause him shame because, when the knights and the king's ministers suffer a loss, they cover themselves with sacks and wear black and grow their hair. If they come before the king during that period, they are not ashamed because it is known that they are in mourning. Therefore, since they are accustomed to [similar mourning customs], there is no shame.

Kimḥi replaced the language of inter-religious suspicion found in earlier sources with an expectation of mutual understanding. The courtiers would surely recognize that this Jew was in mourning because they would behave in a similar way if they were in mourning. Therefore, there was no reason for the Jew to hide his religious practice.

The custom of wearing black clothes did indeed play an important role in Christian mourning rituals, particularly among late medieval Provençal lay and

39. BnF Héb. 1391, fol. 90r (see Appendix, source 3, pp. 123–124). On Gersonides' links to the papal court, see Bernard Goldstein and David Pingree, "Levi ben Gerson's Prognostication for the Conjunction of 1345," *Transactions of the American Philosophical Society*, new series, 80 (1990): 1–60.

40. bSotah 49b: "For it has been taught: To trim the hair in front (*le-saper komi*) is of the ways of the Amorites; but they permitted Abtilus b. Reuben to trim his hair in front because he had close associations with the Government (*karov la-malkhut*)."

41. Jacob ben Levi (Jacob of Marvège; Joseph Shatzmiller has demonstrated that this placename is a mistake, and Jacob was probably from Viviers), *She'elot u-teshuvot min ha-shamayim*, no. 51, ed. Reuven Margaliot (Jerusalem, 1957), 73. On this work, see Pinchas Roth, "*Responsa* from Heaven: Fragments of a New Manuscript of 'She'elot u-teshuvot min ha-shamayim' from Gerona," *Materia Guidaica* 15–16 (2010–2011): 555–564.

42. BnF Héb. 1391, fol. 90r.

ecclesiastical aristocracy.[43] Growing hair long in mourning, however, does not seem to have been accepted in medieval Christian Europe, at least not for men.[44] Southern French society in general frowned upon excessive display of grief, and specifically curtailed mourning rituals involving tearing hair.[45] Kimḥi's confidence that the other courtiers would accept the Jew's appearance with understanding and empathy seems to have been misinformed. Perhaps he was not used to visiting noble courts and did not know first-hand how formal and inflexible court etiquette actually was.

Kimḥi's optimistic approach to cultural difference may provide the key to an enigmatic *responsum* regarding the donation of lamp oil to a synagogue by a Muslim.[46]

> Regarding the oil donated by an Ishmaelite etc. There are different aspects to such donations. If someone donated an object that is meant (*hora'ato*) for use in the synagogue, it belongs to the synagogue and there is no concern that it is holy (*Hekdesh*)[47] and requires burial (*genizah*) ... But if he donated something that is not normally used in the synagogue – such as money or fruit – then even if he mentioned the synagogue there is a concern that it is *Hekdesh* and that it requires burial because he may have meant to dedicate it to Heaven. Now let us see, what is [this oil] similar to? It seems that it is similar to the candelabrum and the lamp [that are used in the synagogue], and it is as though he said explicitly "I donated it according to the intention

43. Jacques Chiffoleau, *La comptabilité de l'au-delà: Les hommes, la mort et la religion dans la région d'Avignon à la fin du moyen âge (vers 1320–vers 1480)* (Rome, 1980), 141–142; Danièle Alexandre-Bidon, *La mort au moyen âge: XIIIe–XVIe siècles* (Paris, 1998), 166–169; Joëlle Rollo-Koster, "Death of Clergymen: Popes and Cardinals' Death Rituals," in *Death in Medieval Europe: Death Scripted and Death Choreographed*, ed. Joëlle Rollo-Koster (London, 2017), 164–185 (esp. 175–177).

44. Robert Bartlett, "Symbolic Meanings of Hair in the Middle Ages," *Transactions of the Royal Historical Society*, 6th series, 4 (1994): 43–60.

45. Chris Sparks, *Heresy, Inquisition and Life Cycle in Medieval Languedoc* (Woodbridge, 2014), 139–140.

46. BnF Héb. 1391, fols. 88v–89r (see Appendix, source 4, p. 124).

47. In this context, *hekdesh* refers to the property of the Jerusalem Temple, which is considered sacred and may not be used outside of the Temple. Ashkenazic Jewry emphasized the similarity between the Temple and the synagogue, a theme which stands at odds with the approach of the Babylonian Talmud, and by extension Iberian and Provençal communities, which considered synagogues legally inferior to the Temple. Israel M. Ta-Shma, *The Early Ashkenazic Prayer: Literary and Historical Aspects* (Jerusalem, 2003), 199–213 (Hebrew); Jeffrey R. Woolf, *The Fabric of Religious Life in Medieval Ashkenaz (1000–1300)* (Leiden, 2015), 82–104.

of the Jews,"[48] and they can light from it in the synagogue and there is no concern of prohibition.

The query is presented in truncated form, and tantalizingly omits almost all the details of the case. One wonders where this happened, how a Muslim came to find himself in Provence, why he chose to donate oil to a synagogue and why the local community thought that his donation was problematic. To be sure, although no permanent Muslim community is known to have existed in southern France during the High Middle Ages, rabbinic sources from twelfth-century Languedoc refer to Muslims as a regular feature of the local demography.[49] Most likely, these were Muslim merchants passing regularly through the ports of Christian Europe, as was the Muslim donor to the synagogue.[50]

The fact that a Muslim performed an act of piety towards a Jewish religious institution fits nicely into the emerging picture of trans-confessional religiosity in medieval Europe and the Near East. Recent studies have demonstrated that Jews prayed at Christian and Muslim shrines, that Christians visited Muslim holy places and that Muslims did the same at Christian sites.[51] His choice of donating

48. bArakhin 6a: "If a Gentile dedicated a beam [for the synagogue – according to most manuscripts of the Talmud] and the [divine] name is inscribed upon it, they check him. If he said 'I dedicated it to [thus in London, British Library, Add. 25717, fol. 48r; other manuscripts: in] the intention of Israel', he should cut off [the name] and use the rest. If not, it requires genizah, because we are concerned that his heart was for heaven."

49. Israel M. Ta-Shma, *Ritual, Custom and Reality in Franco-Germany, 1000–1350* (Jerusalem, 1996), 241–261 (Hebrew); Jacob Katz, "On Moslems as Intermediaries in Judeo-Christian Commerce," *Tarbiz* 48 (1979): 374–376 (Hebrew). During the early Middle Ages, regions of southern France were ruled by Muslim forces, and some archeological remains reflect this period. Philippe Senac, "Présence musulmane en Languedoc: Réalités et vestiges," *Cahiers de Fanjeaux* 18 (1983): 43–57; Mohammad Ballan, "Fraxinetum: An Islamic Frontier State in Tenth-Century Provence," *Comitatus* 41 (2010): 23–76. Other Muslims lived in the region as slaves of Christians, but it seems unlikely that a slave would make a donation. P.S. van Koningsveld, "Muslim Slaves and Captives in Western Europe During the Late Middle Ages," *Islam and Christian-Muslim Relations* 6 (1995): 5–23.

50. Brian Catlos, *Muslims of Medieval Latin Christendom, c. 1050–1614* (Cambridge, 2014), 229: "In the Middle Ages there were no significant or durable communities of free Muslims in the lands that would become France, Germany, Britain, or northern Italy. Those few who did come of their own volition did not come to settle, but rather to do business, whether commercial or official, and return to their homelands." See also John H. Pryor, *Geography, Technology, and War: Studies in the Maritime History of the Mediterranean, 649–1571* (Cambridge, 1988), 147.

51. Bernard Hamilton, "Our Lady of Saidnaiya: An Orthodox Shrine Revered by Muslims and Knights Templar at the Time of the Crusades," in *The Holy Land, Holy Lands, and Christian History*, ed. R.N. Swanson (Woodbridge, 2000), 207–215; Benjamin Z. Kedar, "Con-

oil to the synagogue may reflect the shared Muslim-Jewish ideal of making donations to religious institutions.[52] Donations of oil for synagogue lamps were a particularly prominent form of pious charity in medieval Egypt.[53] In regions where Jews and Muslims lived under Christian rule, tensions often arose between the two minority communities.[54] In this case, since no larger Muslim community existed in Provence, the Muslim visitor may have been drawn to the only religious minority he found.

Kimḥi's positive response permitting the oil donation was drawn almost verbatim from the Code of Maimonides.[55] However, while Maimonides included the concern that the non-Jewish donor might be offended and claim "I donated something to the synagogue of the Jews, and they sold it for themselves," this concern is missing from Kimḥi's version. In light of his more explicit comment about a mourning Jew in the comital court, it seems possible that here too Kimḥi aimed to transcend a rhetoric of inter-religious suspicion – precisely the type of suspicion that probably motivated the person who posed the question to Kimḥi in the first place.

---

vergences of Oriental Christian Muslim and Frankish Worshippers: The Case of Saydnaya," in *De Sion exhibit lex et verbum domini de Hierusalem: Essays on Medieval Law, Liturgy, and Literature in Honour of Amnon Linder*, ed. Yitzhak Hen (Turnhout, 2001), 59–69; Joseph W. Meri, *The Cult of Saints Among Muslims and Jews in Medieval Syria* (Oxford, 2002); Alexandra Cuffel, "From Practice to Polemic: Shared Saints and Festivals as 'Women's Religion' in the Medieval Mediterranean," *Bulletin of the School of Oriental and African Studies* 68 (2005): 401–419; Ephraim Shoham-Steiner, "'For a prayer in that place would be most welcome': Jews, Holy Shrines and Miracles – A New Approach," *Viator* 37 (2006): 369–395; Ephraim Shoham-Steiner, "Jews and Healing at Medieval Saints' Shrines: Participation, Polemics, and Shared Cultures," *Harvard Theological Review* 103 (2010): 111–129; Ora Limor, "Sharing Sacred Space: Holy Places in Jerusalem Between Christianity, Judaism, and Islam," in *In Laudem Hierosolymitani: Studies in Crusades and Medieval Culture in Honour of Benjamin Z. Kedar*, ed. Iris Shagrir, Ronnie Ellenblum and Jonathan Riley-Smith (Aldershot, 2007), 219–231.

52. Moshe Gil, *Documents of the Jewish Pious Foundations from the Cairo Geniza* (Leiden, 1976); Judah Galinsky, "Jewish Charitable Bequests and the Hekdesh Trust in Thirteenth-Century Spain," *Journal of Interdisciplinary History* 35 (2005): 423–440; Johannes Pahlitzsch, "Christian Pious Foundations as an Element of Continuity between Late Antiquity and Islam," in *Charity and Giving in Monotheistic Religions*, ed. Miriam Frenkel and Yaacov Lev (Berlin, 2009), 125–151; Hmida Toukabri, *Satisfaire le ciel et la terre: Les fondations pieuses dans le judaïsme et dans l'islam au moyen âge* (Paris, 2011); Adam J. Davis, "The Social and Religious Meanings of Charity in Medieval Europe," *History Compass* 12 (2014): 935–950.

53. Moshe Gil, "Supplies of Oil in Medieval Egypt: A Geniza Study," *Journal of Near Eastern Studies* 34 (1975): 63–73.

54. David Nirenberg, *Communities of Violence: Persecution of Minorities in the Middle Ages* (Princeton, 1996), 166–199.

55. *Mishneh Torah*, Laws of Gifts to the Poor 8: 6–8.

One of Kimḥi's best-known contemporaries was Menaḥem ha-Me'iri, who resided in Perpignan from 1249 until his death around 1316. He has probably received more scholarly attention in recent decades than any other medieval rabbi from the region, and the main reason for this inordinate amount of attention is his unique approach to the talmudic laws on Gentiles.[56] According to ha-

56. David Tsevi Hoffmann, *Der Schulchan-Aruch Und Die Rabbinen Über Das Verhältnis Der Juden Zu Andersgläubigen: Zur Berichtigung Des Von Prof. Gildemeister in Dem "isaakiade"–Prozesse Abgegebenen Gerichtlichen Gutachtens* (Berlin, 1885), 3–6; Ḥanokh Albeck, *Shishah sidre Mishnah meforash perush ḥadash* (Six orders of Mishnah with a new commentary) (Jerusalem, 1959), 4: 321–323; see the following works by Jacob Katz, "Religious Tolerance in the Halakhic and Philosophical System of Rabbi Menahem Hame'iri," *Zion* 18 (1953): 15–30 (Hebrew); *Exclusiveness and Tolerance: Studies in Jewish-Gentile Relations in Medieval and Modern Times* (Oxford, 1961), 114–128; "Religious Tolerance in the Halakhic System of Rabbi Menahem Hame'iri – A Reply," *Zion* 46 (1981): 243–246 (Hebrew); see also Efraim Elimelech Urbach, "Rabbi Menahem ha-Meiri's Theory of Tolerance: Its Origin and Limits," in *Studies in the History of Jewish Society in the Middle Ages and in the Modern Period Presented to Professor Jacob Katz on his Seventy-Fifth Birthday*, ed. Immanuel Etkes and Yosef Salmon (Jerusalem, 1980), 34–44 (Hebrew) (reprinted in Efraim Elimelech Urbach, *Studies in Judaica*, ed. Moshe D. Herr and Jonah Fraenkel [Jerusalem, 1998], 366–376); David Novak, *The Image of the Non-Jew in Judaism: An Historical and Constructive Study of the Noahide Laws* (New York, 1983), 351–356; Lawrence Zalcman, "Christians, *Noserim* and Nebuchadnezzar's Daughter," *Jewish Quarterly Review* 81 (1991): 411–426; J. David Bleich, "Divine Unity in Maimonides, the Tosafists and Me'iri," in *Neoplatonism and Jewish Thought*, ed. Lenn Goodman (Albany, 1992), 237–254 (revised version in J. David Bleich, *The Philosophical Quest: Of Philosophy, Ethics, Law and Halakhah* [Jerusalem, 2013], 33–52); the following works by Gerald J. Blidstein, "Maimonides and Me'iri on the Legitimacy of Non-Judaic Religion," in *Scholars and Scholarship: The Interaction Between Judaism and Other Cultures*, ed. Leo Landman (New York, 1990), 27–35; "R. Menahem ha-Me'iri: Aspects of an Intellectual Profile," *Journal of Jewish Thought and Philosophy* 5 (1995): 63–79; "Menahem Meiri's Attitude Toward Gentiles – Apologetics or Worldview?," *Binah: Jewish Intellectual History in the Middle Ages* 3 (1994): 119–133; see also Gary Remer, "Ha-Me'iri's Theory of Religious Toleration," in *Beyond the Persecuting Society: Religious Toleration Before the Enlightenment*, ed. John Christian Laursen and Cary J. Nederman (Philadelphia, 1998), 71–92; the following by Moshe Halbertal, "Menahem ha-Me'iri – Talmudist and Philosopher," *Tarbiz* 63 (1993): 63–118 (Hebrew); "Ones Possessed of Religion: Religious Tolerance in the Teachings of the Me'iri," *Edah Journal* 1 (2000): 1–24; *Between Torah and Wisdom: Rabbi Menachem ha-Meiri and the Maimonidean Halakhists in Provence* (Jerusalem, 2001) (Hebrew); see also David Goldstein, "A Lonely Champion of Tolerance: R. Menachem ha-Meiri's Attitude Towards Non-Jews," *Talk Reason* (2002), http://www.talkreason.org/articles/meiri.cfm; Hannah Kasher, "The Meiri on Christian Allegorical Exegesis on the Consumption of Pork," *Zion* 69 (2004): 357–360 (Hebrew); Philippe Haddad, *Le Méiri: Le rabbin catalan de la tolérance* (Perpignan, 2007); Gedalya Oren, "R. Menahem ha-Meiri's Attitude toward the 'Other,'" *Da'at: A Journal of Jewish Philosophy and Kabbalah* 60 (2007): 29–49 (Hebrew); Gregg Stern, *Philosophy and Rabbinic Culture: Jewish Interpretation and Controversy in Medieval Languedoc* (London, 2009); the following works by David Berger, "Jews, Gentiles, and the

Me᾽iri, the Christians and Muslims of his own time were not idolators. They were civilized members of a proper religion. Hence, he concluded, many of the laws in the Talmud which discriminate between Jews and non-Jews were not applicable to the Gentiles of the Middle Ages. Scholars have argued at length whether ha-Me᾽iri truly meant what he said about Christians being fundamentally different to the Gentiles of the Talmud. They have also disputed the degree of innovation to be found in ha-Me᾽iri's rulings, since many of the leniencies he extrapolated from this principle of civilization had already been issued as practical rulings by earlier authorities without using his terminology.[57] Moshe Halbertal has made a strong case for explaining ha-Me᾽iri's legal approach as an outgrowth of his philosophical sources – specifically, the link between monotheism and civilization that is found in the philosophical writings of Samuel ibn Tibbon and Jacob Anatoli.[58] While ha-Me᾽iri's specific legal rulings about non-Jews were admittedly not novel, he gave them a philosophical rationale and systematic justification that had not previously been expressed.

Ha-Me᾽iri's legal-philosophical approach to inter-religious tolerance was not echoed or emulated by any other rabbinic commentator, medieval or modern. However, a different type of tolerance emerges from the rulings of Isaac Kimḥi. Kimḥi's approach seems to stem, not from any philosophical stance on the legitimacy of other religions, as in the case of ha-Me᾽iri, but from a deep-seated assumption about the commonality of man. Unlike Menaḥem ha-Me᾽iri, Isaac Kimḥi never enunciated a systematic halakhic approach to Gentiles. But in dealing with questions of applied Jewish law, Kimḥi found commonality and kinship – between Jews and Gentiles, and between different factions of Jews – where others did not. Perhaps his particular strain of tolerance is best understood in light of what Cary Nederman has called "tolerant internationalism," an accept-

---

Modern Egalitarian Ethos: Some Tentative Thoughts," in *Formulating Responses in an Egalitarian Age*, ed. Marc Stern (Lanham, 2005), 83–108; *Persecution, Polemic and Dialogue: Essays in Jewish-Christian Relations* (Boston, 2010), 51–74, 158–176; *Cultures in Collision and Conversation: Essays in the Intellectual History of the Jews* (Boston, 2011), 78; see also Yaakov Elman, "Meiri and the Non-Jew: A Comparative Investigation," in *New Perspectives on Jewish-Christian Relations in Honor of David Berger*, ed. Elisheva Carlebach and Jacob J. Schacter (Leiden, 2012), 265–296; Israel Ben Simon, "The Origins of the Meiri's Commentary on the Book of Proverbs and the Concept of Nations Bound by the Ways of Religion," *Jewish Studies Internet Journal* 11 (2013): 199–137 (Hebrew); Ari Berman, "*Ger Toshav* in the Halakhic Literature of the High Middle Ages" (PhD diss., Hebrew University of Jerusalem, 2015), 251–300; Alon Goshen-Gottstein, *Same God, other God: Judaism, Hinduism, and the Problem of Idolatry* (New York, 2016), 107–126.

57. Urbach, "Rabbi Menahem ha-Meiri's Theory of Tolerance."

58. Halbertal, "Ones Possessed of Religion"; Halbertal, *Between Torah and Wisdom*; Ben-Simon, "The Origins."

ance of difference between geographically and ethnically diverse groups by virtue of their different origins.[59] In the words of Nicholas of Cusa:

> Where conformity of mode cannot be had, nations are entitled to their own devotions and ceremonies, provided faith and peace be maintained. Perhaps, as a result of a certain diversity (*ex quadam diversitate*), devotion will even be increased.[60]

When confronted with difference on the communal level, Kimḥi believed that French Jews and Provençal Jews could follow their distinct customs without causing offense to each other, that Jews performing their religious rituals in the presence of Christian nobles would be met with understanding and that a Muslim making pious gifts to Jewish synagogues ought to be embraced by Jews. Yet Kimḥi was also fiercely proud of his own group and its heritage. He upheld the autochthonous Jewish traditions of Provence and Languedoc in the face of self-appointed intellectuals and French Jewish bigots, just as he gently reprimanded Jewish courtiers who preferred to efface their own difference.

Kimḥi's *responsa* reflect the tensions of his time even when he personally took a more tolerant position than most of his contemporaries would have contemplated. The questions of Jewish law that were addressed to him were not neutral musings of theoretical interest. They were drafted by Provençal Jews who turned to him because they believed that he, and the tradition of rabbinic learning that he represented, could provide a satisfying answer to the problems they faced. Encoded into queries about how to wash their hands and how to bake

59. Cary Nederman, "Toleration in Medieval Europe: Theoretical Principles and Historical Lessons," in *Bridging the Medieval-Modern Divide: Medieval Themes in the World of the Reformation*, ed. James Muldoon (Farnham, 2013), 45–64 (at 60); Cary Nederman, *Worlds of Difference: European Discourses of Toleration, c. 1100–c.1550* (University Park, 2000), 85–97.

60. Nicholas of Cusa, *De pace fidei* XIX, ed. Raymond Klibansky and Hildebrand Bascour (Hamburg, 1959), 62; trans. Jasper Hopkins, *Nicholas of Cusa's De pace fidei and Cribratio Alkorani: Translation and Analysis*, 2nd ed. (Minneapolis, 1994), 669 (http://jasper-hopkins.info/DePace12–2000.pdf). Scholarly opinion is divided whether Nicholas of Cusa was truly tolerant, and certainly his attitude towards Jews was not particularly welcoming. Thomas Izbicki, "Nicholas of Cusa and the Jews," in *Conflict and Reconciliation: Perspectives on Nicholas of Cusa*, ed. Inigo Bocken (Leiden, 2004), 119–130; Yossef Schwartz, "Ernst Cassirer on Nicholas of Cusa: Between Conjectural Knowledge and Religious Pluralism," in *The Symbolic Construction of Reality: The Legacy of Ernst Cassirer*, ed. Jeffrey Andrew Barash (Chicago, 2008), 17–39; Jozef Matula, "Nicholas of Cusa's Discourse of Tolerance in Modern Thought," *Intellectual History Review* 26 (2016): 33–41. As Classen comments, "[w]e cannot expect from Nicholas truly tolerant opinions ..." Albrecht Classen, *Toleration and Tolerance in Medieval and Early Modern European Literature* (New York, 2018), 212.

bread was the deeply troubling fear that Provençal Jewish culture lacked the intellectual rigour that was needed to face the challenges of the fourteenth century. The recently arrived Jewish migrants from northern France were only too happy to reinforce that fear, as they too found themselves drawn into the cultural politics of their haven in Provence.

CHAPTER FOUR

Northern French Jews in Provence

Over the course of the thirteenth century, French influence in Languedoc and Provence grew by leaps and bounds. In the political realm, the king of France took full advantage of his victory in the Albigensian Crusade by converting his military success into what would eventually become full political control of Languedoc.[1] To be sure, the transition was not smooth, and local aristocrats and bourgeoisie rebelled against the French regime repeatedly, but these rebellions were quelled in the end. Languedoc struggled to preserve its legal traditions and musical culture, which differed fundamentally from those of northern France.[2] Most significantly, the language (or family of languages) spoken throughout southern France, which modern scholarship refers to as Occitan or Provençal, remained a strong reminder of the region's difference from the French-speaking north.[3]

The distinction between north and south was applied quite explicitly by contemporary Jews to their own culture. As Joseph Shatzmiller has pointed out:[4]

> The division of medieval France into lands of customary law and lands of written law, and the almost parallel division between speaking "oïl" and speaking "oc," roughly echoes the division between *Ẓarfat* and Provence that we find in our Hebrew texts.

1. James Given, *State and Society in Medieval Europe: Gwynedd and Languedoc under Outside Rule* (Ithaca, 1990).

2. Elizabeth Aubrey, "The Dialectic between Occitania and France in the Thirteenth Century," *Early Music History* 16 (1997): 1–53; Christopher K. Gardner, "Practice and Rhetoric: Some Thirteenth-Century Perspectives on the Legal Frontier Between 'France' and Toulouse," in *Frontiers in the Middle Ages: Proceedings of the Third European Congress of Medieval Studies*, ed. Outi Merisalo (Turnhout, 2006), 223–235.

3. As Linda Paterson put it: "For twenty-first century medievalists, medieval Occitan identity is to be found not within political or territorial confines but in its language and culture." Linda Paterson, *Culture and Society in Medieval Occitania* (Farnham, 2011), chapter 1, 4.

4. Joseph Shatzmiller, *Recherches sur la communauté juive de Manosque au moyen âge* (Paris, 1973), 16 (my translation).

The influence of northern rabbinic culture, in the form of the *Tosafot,* began to be felt by the middle of the twelfth century.[5] With the growing encroachment of France as a political entity in addition to internal Jewish developments over the following century, rabbinic interactions between north and south developed negative undertones. Towards the end of the thirteenth century, large numbers of Jews left France and migrated to Provence, where they shared the space with existing Jewish communities.[6] From this point onwards, the France-Provence fault line was more than a symptom of Capetian influence in the south.[7] It became a central aspect of daily Jewish life, and very few people followed Isaac Kimḥi's lead in responding to it with tolerance.

One of the most prolific figures who can be identified as a French Jew in Provence, thanks to Shatzmiller's research, was Rabbi Isaac ben Judah ha-Kohen of Manosque.[8] Manosque was home to a significant population of French Jews, although not all Manosquin Jews were French. Isaac rose to prominence, both within the French migrant community and in Provençal Jewish society, by virtue of his impressive learning and his stormy personality. Both characteristics are readily visible in his *responsa,* which form the basis of this chapter.

Isaac's role as an arbiter within the French émigré community of Provence is recorded formally in a Hebrew document from 1313. The Jewish community of Reillanne (not far from Manosque) drew up ordinances detailing the rules for collecting and disposing of charity. The original text was preserved on a parchment page that was later cut up by binders and tucked into a Hebrew prayerbook.[9] The ordinances were signed by Yekutiel ben Samuel and, possibly, by

5. Avraham (Rami) Reiner, "From France to Provence: The Assimilation of the Tosafists' Innovations in the Provençal Talmudic Tradition," *Journal of Jewish Studies* 65 (2014): 77–87.

6. Unfortunately, the available data does not allow for any clear quantitative conclusions about the number of French Jewish migrants in Provence, or even about their relative proportion of the Provençal Jewish population. Shatzmiller, *Recherches sur la communauté juive de Manosque,* 16–26.

7. William Chester Jordan, *The French Monarchy and the Jews: From Philip Augustus to the Last Capetians* (Philadelphia, 1989), 225–232.

8. Joseph Shatzmiller, "Rabbi Isaac Ha-Cohen of Manosque and His Son Rabbi Peretz: The Rabbinate and Its Professionalization in the Fourteenth Century," in *Jewish History: Essays in Honour of Chimen Abramsky,* ed. Ada Rapoport-Albert and Steven J. Zipperstein (London, 1988), 61–83.

9. Paris, Bibliothèque nationale de France, Hébreu 651 (2). The text was first published by Simon Schwarzfuchs, "A Takkanah of the Year 1313," *Bar Ilan Annual* 4–5 (1967): 209–219 (Hebrew). Its connection to Reillanne was demonstrated by Joseph Shatzmiller, "Ordinances of a Jewish Community in Provence, 1313," *Kiryat Sefer* 50 (1975): 663–667 (Hebrew).

Isaac of Manosque.[10] The French-Ashkenazic handwriting proves that the scribe who copied out the ordinances was himself a Frenchman. The ordinances include the following provision:[11]

> We also agreed that if any doubt should arise regarding a word or an expression in this text, it shall be clarified and resolved by our teacher, Rabbi Isaac ha-Kohen son of Judah ha-Kohen, as long as he does not detract anything from the ordinances.

The fact that Isaac of Manosque was specified as the arbiter for a community that was not his own is ample testimony to his stature within the larger community – at least, among the French Jews of the Provençal hinterland. However, the final clause preventing Isaac from overturning the ordinances may hint at some qualms felt by the Reillanne community about his trustworthiness.

Such qualms would have been well-founded. Over the course of his career Isaac of Manosque was involved in bitter arguments, some of which escalated into the pronouncement of excommunicatory bans (*nidui*). The first instance occurred, perhaps before 1280,[12] when Isaac was a prominent student in the *yeshivah* led by Baruch of Digne, an immigrant from France.[13] The other students in Baruch's academy probably came from a similar French background. Isaac's seniority among the students may have caused tension with the master, which erupted into an incident that Isaac described with ostensible objectivity:[14]

10. The signatures were convincingly identified by Abraham Mordechai Albert, *Sefer Ma'aser Kesafim* (Jerusalem, 1977), 44. The upper edge of the name Isaac is visible, but the following word is almost entirely lost. The ordinances mention another Isaac, one of the communal officials (*berurim*), and he may be the one who signed the document. Yekuti'el ben Samuel is named among the sages of Arles in Abba Mari ben Moses of Lunel, *Minḥat Kena'ot*, chapter 42, in Solomon ben Abraham ibn Adret, *Teshuvot ha-Rashba*, ed. Haim Zalman Dimitrovsky (Jerusalem, 1990), 431 (according to ms. B).

11. Schwarzfuchs, "A Takkanah," 218.

12. If the case was referred to by Isaac of Corbeil (see below, n19), who died in 1280, that would provide a terminus ad quem. For Isaac of Corbeil's year of death, see Simcha Emanuel, *Fragments of the Tablets: Lost Books of the Tosaphists* (Jerusalem, 2006), 198–199 (Hebrew).

13. For a mention of the *schola judeorum* of Digne, see Danièle Iancu-Agou, *Provincia Judaica: dictionnaire de géographie historique des juifs en Provence médiévale* (Paris, 2010), 51.

14. Isaac ben Immanuel de Lattes, *She'elot u-Teshuvot*, ed. Mordechai Tzvi (Max Hermann) Friedländer (Vienna, 1860), 34, on the basis of Vienna, Oesterreichische Nationalbibliothek, Cod. Hebr. 24, fol. 94r. A slightly different version of the story appears in the *responsum* of Mordechai Kimḥi published by Shemu'el Eli'ezer Stern, "Teshuvat Rabenu Mordechai ben Rabbi Yitzhak me-ḥakhme Provincia be-'inyan bizuy talmide ḥakhamim (A

> My question concerns two scholars who are arguing with each other about Halakhah. Each has studied Bible, each has studied Mishnah, each has served rabbinic scholars. The fire of disagreement raged between them, and for some reason one of them[15] cursed the other[16] and humiliated him, calling him a fool, ignoramus, a wicked and obdurate sinner. The other responded in anger: "Even if I am an ignoramus, it is not through my laziness or slack attendance of the study halls, because I did not travel to other lands."[17] As for calling him obdurate (*sarban*),[18] [Isaac] said: "If I am obdurate, you are just as obdurate."

In his carefully crafted description, which he distributed widely among the rabbis of the region, Isaac acknowledged wrongdoing on both sides. He emphasized that the two men were evenly matched in intellectual stature and portrayed his own contribution to the fight, while not negligible, as more restrained than that of his master. The parity that Isaac claimed to exist between them may have been precisely what threw Baruch of Digne into a rage. Baruch declared that Isaac had insulted a rabbinic sage and must therefore be placed under ban.[19] Isaac offered to apologize, but Baruch rebuffed him and travelled to northern France, where he recruited rabbis to issue an additional ban against Isaac.[20] Isaac responded by issuing a public statement:[21]

---

responsum by Rabbi Mordechai ben Isaac, from the sages of Provence, about the denigration of a sage)," *Moriah* 28:1–2 (2006), 12–14. The case was discussed briefly by Heinrich Gross, "Zur Geschichte der Juden in Arles," *Monatsschrift für Geschichte und Wissenschaft des Judenthums* 28 (1879): 418–431, at 423–427; Shatzmiller, "Rabbinate," 73–75.

15. Later revealed to be Baruch of Digne.

16. Isaac of Manosque.

17. "Teshuvat Rabenu Mordechai," ed. Stern, 12. "[t]o Rome and across the sea."

18. A person who refused to appear when summoned to court could be branded obdurate (*sarban*) and placed under ban. See e.g. Maimonides, *Mishneh Torah*, ed. Shabse Frankel (Jerusalem, 1975–2003), Laws of Sanhedrin 25:5.

19. bMo ʿed Katan 17a: "A scholar who issued a ban for his own honour, his ban is valid."

20. One of those rabbis may have been Isaac of Corbeil, whose collection of legal rulings includes the following: "A student who cursed or belittled his master, who then placed him under ban before he offered to make amends, must consider himself under ban. All the students of that master must treat him as banned, even though he offered to make amends after the ban, and it remains in force until he makes amends." "Piske Rabenu Ri me-Corbeil (Rulings by Rabbi Isaac of Corbeil)," in *Sefer Ner le-Shem ʿayah*, ed. Hayim Shelomoh Sha ʾanan (Bene Berak, 1988), 5–32, at 28.

21. Isaac ben Immanuel de Lattes, *She ʾelot u-Teshuvot*, ed. Friedländer, 38.

> I the undersigned declare to all those who see this statement of mine that to this day I remain willing to make amends for all that I have sinned against Rabbi Baruch, in a manner to be determined by two sages from among the sages of Provence. I have said this numerous times, and I still stand by it, even though in my opinion I did not sin against him. I accepted this upon myself on the day that the rabbi from Digne left to travel to France. Since I have always been willing, and since I told him this in public before he left, I now declare that I cannot believe that any rabbi in France could have issued any slander or reprimand against me. If, God forbid, one of them made an error and wrote something unworthy against me – Heaven forfend! – a reprimand or slander or ban (*nidui*), I respond to him: "*Adrabah* (on the contrary)! His reprimand or slander or ban shall redound upon him." So that all those who see my words will find them credible, and in order to save my soul, I have written this to show it to everyone and I have signed my name here.

Baruch of Digne responded by placing Isaac under yet another ban, this time for insulting the rabbis of France, and Isaac retorted with another "*Adrabah*" deflecting the ban back onto Baruch himself. Realizing, however, that this type of sparring would ultimately do him no good, Isaac of Manosque recounted his version of the story and sent it to the sages of Avignon and Carpentras. The Provençal rabbis responded diplomatically by conceding that Baruch of Digne's behaviour was reprehensible, but that his ban was nonetheless valid. However, they bridled against the intervention of French rabbis in what they considered to be their local jurisdiction, complaining that "even if [the French rabbinic] court is the greatest court (*bet ha-va'ad*), they still ought to have applied to the court in our land in order to summon him before them."[22] Bickering among French emigres was of little interest to these Provençal rabbis in comparison with the alarming intervention of a French court in affairs that took place in Provence.

Some twenty-five years after these events, in 1305, Isaac of Manosque sent a series of three questions to the sages of Arles, Aix and Avignon, and to Solomon ben Abraham ibn Adret in Barcelona.[23] The first of his questions related to marriage: according to the Talmud, a widow whose baby was still nursing could not

22. Isaac ben Immanuel de Lattes, *She'elot u-Teshuvot*, ed. Friedländer, 40.

23. Isaac ben Immanuel de Lattes, *She'elot u-Teshuvot*, ed. Friedländer, 42–45; Solomon ben Abraham ibn Adret, *She'elot u-Teshuvot*, ed. Aharon Zaleznik (Jerusalem, 1997–2005), 1: no. 460, no. 723, no. 724 (= 3: no. 105). The identification of 1: nos. 723–724 as *responsa* addressed to Isaac of Manosque is based on the fact that they answer the same questions addressed by the sages of Arles and Avignon, who were explicitly responding to Isaac of Manosque.

remarry until her child had reached the age of twenty-four months, at which stage it could safely be weaned. If, despite this prohibition, the mother did marry, the couple was forced to divorce until the end of the twenty-four-month nursing period. Hiring a wetnurse to replace the mother was not a satisfactory solution because, according to the Talmud, the nurse might quit her job, leaving the baby without a source of nourishment.[24] Jewish laypeople and scholars throughout medieval Europe debated bitterly whether there were any circumstances under which this limitation could be loosened or bypassed.[25] Isaac of Manosque described an arrangement that was designed to circumvent the prohibition: "she gave her son to two wetnurses, who provided guarantees that they would nurse until the agreed time, and they also swore an oath that they would not change the agreed conditions."[26] Isaac may have modeled his lenient suggestion on a French precedent, such as the opinion of Tuviah of Vienne (in the Dauphine, not so far from Manosque) who had issued a permissive ruling under similar circumstances in the mid-thirteenth century.[27] However, Isaac of Manosque admitted that "in this land they are accustomed to forbid it." In fact, the rabbis of Arles, Aix and Avignon all responded that remarriage was forbidden even under these circumstances, confirming that "this land" was Provence.

The second question addressed an institutional conflict between France and Provence:[28]

> You also asked about two people who bickered with each other about something. One of them decided to go to France, to compel the other to be judged there before the sages of that land. Does the law require him to be judged by the French sages? He is willing to appear before the most learned advisors[29] of his land, Provence.

Solomon ibn Adret responded that, since the rabbis of Provence were quite capable of dealing with legal cases, the French court had no advantage over them and the case should be tried locally.[30] The rabbis of Avignon, apparently, thought that this conclusion was so obvious that they did not bother to spell it out.[31]

24. bKetubbot 60b; Elisheva Baumgarten, *Mothers and Children: Jewish Family Life in Medieval Europe* (Princeton, 2004), 123–124.

25. Baumgarten, *Mothers and Children*, 147–152.

26. Ibn Adret, *She'elot u-Teshuvot*, ed. Zaleznik, 1: no. 723, 1: 347–348.

27. Baumgarten, *Mothers and Children*, 150.

28. Ibn Adret, *She'elot u-Teshuvot*, 1: no. 24, ed. Zaleznik, 1: 7 with emendations based on the version in ibn Adret, *She'elot u-Teshuvot* 3: no. 105, 3: 67.

29. Cf. Isaiah 19:11.

30. Ibn Adret, *She'elot u-Teshuvot* 1: no. 724, ed. Zaleznik, 1: 348.

31. Isaac ben Immanuel de Lattes, *She'elot u-Teshuvot*, ed. Friedländer, 44.

The third question was the richest in detail, and it was retold by ibn Adret in the opening to his response:[32]

> To Manosque. You asked: There was a case of a student who had studied before his master most of his life. He went to a different teacher, and told him defamatory words about his first master, alleging some disqualification in him and his descendants. When the [first] master heard of this, he leapt trembling to his feet and called together his entire study circle, twenty-five wise men. Holding a Torah scroll, he declared: "With the consent of God and yourselves, I pronounce a *nidui* (ban) and *herem* and *shamta* (excommunication) against the man who spread slander about me, if he is indeed one of my students, if his mouth indeed spoke this lie." They all answered "Amen! We agree with you, our teacher, and the man who spread this rumour is under ban." When this tale was told to the [second] teacher, he stood on his feet and cancelled the ban, explaining that the rabbis of France had decreed that no scholar could pronounce a ban for his own honour.

Despite the position of the French rabbis, ibn Adret and the Provençal rabbis all responded that the offended teacher's ban was valid and justified.

The fact that these three questions were sent by Isaac of Manosque at the same time and to multiple recipients strongly suggests that they recount successive stages in a single narrative.[33] A possible reconstruction of that narrative emerges: Isaac of Manosque had married the recently widowed mother of an infant.[34] Fully aware of the talmudic prohibition against marrying a nursing widow, Isaac and his new wife took care to arrange two wetnurses to care for the child. Since Isaac was a *kohen* (priest), and priests are barred from marrying divorced women (Lev. 21:7) and even their own divorcées, the couple would not have been able to remarry if they had followed this opinion, and they chose

32. Ibn Adret, *She'elot u-Teshuvot*, ed. Zaleznik, 1: no. 460, 1: 242.

33. To be sure, the three questions could bear no relationship whatsoever to each other and could have arisen independently. Nevertheless, their appearance together in a single correspondence invites the attempt to suggest a single chain of events that would connect them all.

34. The story might equally have occurred in a previous generation of Isaac's family, and resurfaced in Isaac's time in order to besmirch his reputation. For similar attempts in regard to other medieval rabbis, see Bernard Septimus, "Piety and Power in Thirteenth-Century Catalonia," in *Studies in Medieval Jewish History and Literature*, vol. 1, ed. Isadore Twersky (Cambridge, MA, 1979), 197–230; Elchanan Reiner, "*Yihus* and Libel: Maharal, the Bezalel Family, and the *Nadler* Affair," in *Maharal, Overtures: Biography, Doctrine, Influence*, ed. Elchanan Reiner (Jerusalem, 2015), 101–126 (Hebrew).

to ignore it. Some people felt that this arrangement was illegal and one of them reported it to another rabbi of French extraction. When Isaac of Manosque issued his ban against whoever spread the rumour about his questionable marriage, the other French rabbi dismissed the ban. In the ensuing argument, Isaac demanded that the case be tried before a court in Provence, while the opposing rabbi insisted that they both travel back to their motherland to appear before a court of French rabbis.

Two important aspects of Isaac of Manosque's personality emerge from these two stories. The first is that Isaac was prone to verbally violent confrontations with his rabbinic colleagues. His use and abuse of the rabbinic ban and counter-ban (*ʾadrabah*) was less a personal proclivity than a sign of the times. The ban pronounced by Solomon ibn Adret in 1305 against the study of philosophy was essentially shrugged off by most Provençal Jews, who felt that ibn Adret had no business interfering in their internal affairs and fired off an "ʾadrabah" against their opponents.[35] Isaac was particularly fond of it, however. In 1310 he placed a ban upon two men, Jacob ben Joseph and Leonetus son of Bonafos – an act that led to two separate lawsuits against him in Christian courts.[36]

The second commonality to the stories is that they both erupted within the confines of the French émigré community of Provence. For that community, the rabbis who remained in France served (until 1306) as a practical forum for resolving conflicts that arose among those who had left. At the same time, they symbolized the French rabbinic tradition as a whole – a tradition that, in the eyes of the émigré community, easily outshone the local rabbis in Provence. In this respect, however, Isaac of Manosque stood apart from his community. Whether by his own inclination or because he had burnt his bridges among the French, Isaac turned to the Provençal rabbinic class for support in his struggles. While they did not provide the full-throated approbation that he may have hoped for, the animus towards the French rabbinate harboured by the sages of Aix, Avignon and Arles served Isaac's interests.

Isaac of Manosque's ambiguous stance between the French and Provençal rabbinic communities led him to occasionally serve as a bridge between the two groups, but he was not necessarily the most objective of intermediaries. In one case, he was asked to intervene in a divorce case, which ethnic tensions between French and Provençal Jews had rendered too difficult for other rabbis to handle.[37] A man named Elijah had planned to emigrate from Provence (possibly

35. See above, Chapter 1.

36. Shatzmiller, *Recherches*, 43–54; Shatzmiller, "Rabbinate," 71–72.

37. *Teshuvot Ḥakhme Provinẓia (Teshuvot Ḥakhme Provintsya)* (*Responsa* of the Sages of Provence), no. 69, ed. Abraham Sofer (Schreiber) (Jerusalem, 1967), 239–243.

from Avignon) to the Land of Israel. He secured the cooperation of his father's widow, who was to make the trip with him and presumably to finance the enterprise. Elijah's wife Merauda was less enthusiastic about the scheme; she refused to leave Provence, and the couple divorced, leaving Elijah free to travel. But when Elijah's step-mother discovered that he had divorced his wife, she was disgusted: "Now that you have caused a disaster and divorced the wife of your youth, I will not uphold a single one of the commitments that I made to you."[38] Without her financial support, the trip was no longer viable, and since Elijah realized he would in any case remain in Provence, he asked his wife to remarry him. Merauda, however, refused his offer. Rebuffed and enraged, Elijah turned to Isaac of Manosque for help in forcing Merauda back into the marriage.

Isaac of Manosque recounted that he had initially refused to take on the case because other, more senior scholars lived closer to Elijah's home – Abba Mari and Shelemiah Nasi in Arles, and Don Crescas of Bagnols in Orange.[39] When Elijah heard this response, he gathered his friends, "from the leading men of the town," and intimidated the scholars of Arles and Orange. The scholars were quoted as saying that "there are some light-headed Frenchmen who do not obey the rabbis ... and they say: "We are Frenchmen! What do we have with them?"[40] Fearing a confrontation that would erode their authority even further, the scholars of Arles and Orange preferred not to get involved in the case. Once they had recused themselves, Isaac of Manosque felt that his turn had come, and wrote a *responsum* wholeheartedly supporting Elijah's cause.

Isaac ruled that the divorce granted by Elijah to Merauda was invalid, and therefore that the couple was still married. He based this decision on three arguments. First, although the divorce writ did not contain an explicit clause linking it to Elijah's travel plans, everyone involved was fully aware that Merauda's refusal to leave Provence was the reason for the divorce. Therefore, once the sole motivation for divorce fell away, the divorce itself ought to be considered null. To this argument, Isaac added two technical flaws that Elijah claimed were found in the text of the writ. One word was missing from the required text, and the writ had been copied in thirteen lines instead of the usual twelve. For these three reasons, Isaac concluded that Merauda must present her divorce writ to a rabbinic court for inspection. If the court determined that her divorce was invalid, she must return to her husband without further ado. If it found that the divorce was valid or was unable to decide because the divorce writ was lost, she must remarry Eli-

38. *Teshuvot Ḥakhme Provinẓia (Teshuvot Ḥakhme Provintsya)* no. 69, ed. Sofer, 240.

39. On Abba Mari of Lunel, see Chapter 5. The other figures mentioned here are not known from other sources.

40. *Teshuvot Ḥakhme Provinẓia (Teshuvot Ḥakhme Provintsya)*, no. 69, ed. Sofer, 240.

jah in a new wedding ceremony. In any case, then, Merauda would be forced back into her marriage.

Isaac's decision, which he believed would be endorsed by the scholars of Arles and Orange, seems extraordinary when read in the wider context of Jewish divorce law. The very idea of re-examining a divorce writ that had already been granted and ratified was opposed strenuously and categorically by Rabenu Tam (Jacob ben Meir, d. 1171) in the twelfth century.[41] Rabenu Tam's prohibition against retroactively questioning a divorce was not widely adopted, even in his native France, but the practice was certainly frowned upon, since it exposed every divorced woman (and every man who married a divorced woman) to the threat that her divorce might one day be invalidated.

Another problematic practice was granting a conditional divorce, which was both legally fraught and ethically suspect.[42] Yet Isaac went out of his way to claim that Elijah's divorce had been conditional even though no such condition had been expressed at any stage of the divorce proceedings. Isaac's departure from accepted norms of rabbinic discourse on this point is signaled by his proof-texts, which are taken exclusively from the Talmud without any support from medieval commentators.[43] His claim that the writ was disqualified because it was written in thirteen lines is especially baffling since, by his own admission, writing a divorce writ in twelve lines was merely a custom and not a binding rule.[44] Finally, the husband's assertion that a word was missing from the divorce writ was neither convincing, since he did not say which word was missing, nor was it verifiable, since the original divorce writ had almost certainly been destroyed. Standard procedure in Jewish divorce (at least according to the French tradition) was for the divorce writ to be presented to a rabbinic court and then to be destroyed.[45] Yet Isaac claimed that if Merauda had destroyed her writ (which, if she had done so, was in accordance with court procedure), that itself could be used as proof that her divorce was invalid. In short, Isaac of

41. Avraham (Rami) Reiner, "Regulation, Law and Everything in Between: The Laws of Gittin as a Reflection of Society," *Tarbiz* 82 (2014): 139–163 (Hebrew).

42. A. Yehuda Warburg, "The Propriety of a Conditional Divorce," *Tradition* 47 (2014): 31–56.

43. *Teshuvot Ḥakhme Provinẓia (Teshuvot Ḥakhme Provintsya)*, no. 69, ed. Sofer, 240–242.

44. *Teshuvot Ḥakhme Provinẓia (Teshuvot Ḥakhme Provintsya)*, no. 69, ed. Sofer, 242. Sofer (Schreiber), who published the text, sensed this problem and suggested (n36) that Isaac must have concluded that there were other problems with the writ, since the number of lines could not possibly disqualify the divorce.

45. Mordechai Margaliot, *Ha-ḥilukim she-ben anshe mizraḥ u-bene erets yisraʾel* (The Differences Between the People of the East and Those of the Land of Israel) (Jerusalem, 1938), 120–121.

Manosque flouted the norms of normative rabbinic law in order to force a divorced woman back into her marriage.

One clue to Isaac's motivation in deciding this dispute so forcefully in favour of one side and against the other lies in the ethnic identities of those sides. Elijah and his friends are clearly identified in the *responsum* as Frenchmen living in Provence.[46] The name of Elijah's wife, given towards the end of the *responsum*, was Merauda.[47] Medieval Jewish women often bore vernacular names rather than Hebrew ones, and Merauda's name seems to have been the Occitan word for emerald, so she was most probably from a local Provençal family.[48] When Elijah and Merauda's marriage broke down, sides were taken along ethnic lines. Merauda probably turned to a local Jewish court, staffed by Provençal rabbis, to ratify her divorce writ. When Elijah decided to dispute the divorce, he enlisted the help of his friends to prevent the case from being heard by other Provençal rabbis, and instead he steered it into the hands of Isaac of Manosque. Elijah's gambit was entirely successful, as Isaac sided with the French husband against the Provençal wife.

The *responsum* is undated, but some scraps of information provide clues to its historical context. As we will see in Chapter 5, Abba Mari of Lunel moved to Arles only after the 1306 expulsion, and since he is mentioned here among the scholars of Arles, the incident must postdate 1306. In the opening to his *responsum*, Isaac of Manosque complained that "God has stripped us of our honour and removed our crown (Job 19:9) – we cannot learn from the mouths of scribes."[49] Isaac was clearly referring to the recent demise of an important rabbinic figure, and the most reasonable candidate is Solomon ibn Adret, who died in approximately 1310. Placing the story in the early fourteenth century adds a further twist. Medieval Jewish emigration from western Europe to the Holy Land was tied directly to the Crusader Kingdom of Jerusalem, and it is assumed to have decreased dramatically when the European foothold in Acre was destroyed

46. As noted by Shatzmiller, *Recherches*, 13–14.

47. *Teshuvot Ḥakhme Provinẓia (Teshuvot Ḥakhme Provintsya)*, no. 69, ed. Sofer, 243.

48. François-Juste-Marie Raynouard, *Lexique roman ou Dictionnaire de la langue des troubadours comparée avec les autres langues de l'Europe latine* (Paris, 1836–1845), 4: 155a; Simon Seror, *Les noms des juifs de France au moyen âge* (Paris, 1989), 187. The French form would be *émeraude*. On some gendered aspects of medieval Jewish naming patterns, see Lilach Assaf, "The Language of Names: Jewish Onomastics in Late Medieval Germany, Identity and Acculturation," in *Konkurrierende Zugehörigkeit(en) Praktiken der Namengebung im europäischen Vergleich*, ed. Christof Rolker and Gabriela Signori (Konstanz, 2011), 149–160; Lilach Assaf, "Lovely Women and Sweet Men: Gendering the Name and Naming Practices in German-Jewish Communities (Thirteenth to Fourteenth Centuries)," in *Intricate Interfaith Networks in the Middle Ages: Quotidian Jewish-Christian Contacts*, ed. Ephraim Shoham-Steiner (Turnhout, 2016), 231–250.

49. *Teshuvot Ḥakhme Provinẓia (Teshuvot Ḥakhme Provintsya)*, no. 69, ed. Sofer, 239.

in 1291.[50] Nevertheless, some Jews continued to arrive from the West during the course of the fourteenth century, including most notably Astori ha-Parḥi, who was exiled from France in 1306 and moved east after spending several years in northern Spain.[51] Elijah evidently aimed to take part in this smaller stream of Jews moving to Mamluk Palestine, but Merauda may have baulked at living under such a foreign regime, precipitating the breakdown of their marriage.

If Isaac of Manosque referred to Rabbi Solomon ibn Adret as "our honour and our crown," it was an extension of the great respect he showed the sage of Barcelona during his lifetime. The *responsa* of ibn Adret include several replies to Isaac the Frenchman, who was probably Isaac of Manosque.[52] Two of the *responsa* provide glimpses not only of Isaac's interaction with a rabbi whose superiority he acknowledged (a rarity, as we have seen), but also of the practical halakhic questions that the Jews of Manosque presented to their local rabbi.

The body of a dead Jew was being transported for burial in a small boat.[53] Traditionally, a Jewish corpse is not left unattended before burial, so someone – perhaps a family relative – would travel along in the boat. Since priests are not allowed to come into contact with the impurity of death (Lev. 21:1–3), Isaac of Manosque ruled that a priest could not serve as the companion, since his slightest movement could cause the boat – and the corpse – to tilt, which for the priest would be considered contact with a dead body. In this case, ibn Adret did indeed endorse Isaac's ruling – "I think that everything you said in this matter was correct." The question probably arose in Manosque, whose Jewish cemetery was situated near a bridge over the Durance river, making the transportation of corpses for burial by boat a natural choice.[54] Other sources demonstrate that the

50. On Crusader Acre and its Jewish community, see Jonathan Rubin, *Learning in a Crusader City: Intellectual Activity and Intercultural Exchanges in Acre, 1191–1291* (Cambridge, 2018).

51. Joshua Prawer, *The History of the Jews in the Latin Kingdom of Jerusalem* (Oxford, 1988), 293; Joseph Hacker, "Links Between Spanish Jewry and Palestine, 1391–1492," in *Vision and Conflict in the Holy Land*, ed. Richard Cohen (Jerusalem, 1985), 111–139.

52. Ibn Adret, *She'elot u-Teshuvot*, 1: no. 27 (=1: nos. 635–636), 1: no. 28 (=1: no. 559, abbreviated), 4: no. 122 (=1: no. 560, abbreviated). The three *responsa* appear consecutively in Cambridge, University Library, Add. 500, fol. 60v–61r. The reliability of ms. Cambridge 500 with regard to sequences of ibn Adret's *responsa* has been demonstrated by Simcha Emanuel, "'From where the sun rises to where it sets': The *Responsa* by Rashba to the Sages of Acre," *Tarbiz* 83 (2015): 465–489 (Hebrew). For another series of three questions that Isaac sent to ibn Adret, see above, n22.

53. Ibn Adret, *She'elot u-Teshuvot*, 1: no. 28, ed. Zaleznik, 1: 18. For similar discussions from other Jewish centers, see Miriam Fenton, "Moving Bodies: Corpses and Communal Space in Medieval Ashkenaz," *Jewish Studies Quarterly* (forthcoming).

54. Iancu-Agou, *Provincia Judaica*, 78.

Manosque cemetery served the Jewish community of Forcalquier, but the river does not connect the two towns, and corpses were transported from Forcalquier by land.[55] However, other communities (for example, Sisteron or Tallard, Isaac's home town) presumably used the Manosque cemeteries as well, and were better positioned to take advantage of the river.[56]

Another question sent by Isaac to ibn Adret also related to a practical issue.[57] A married woman swore an oath that she would drink a fertility potion, over the opposition of her husband who did not want her to become pregnant. Isaac of Manosque ruled that the husband could nullify his wife's oath, since its performance would directly impact their marital relationship and a husband was empowered to annul oaths made by his wife that could be considered to affect him.[58] Isaac believed that the husband's fear that his wife's health would suffer from imbibing the potion was justified, since every medicine is liable to have negative side-effects. Even if the treatment achieved the desired result, the ensuing pregnancy would mar his wife's beauty, which Isaac and the husband considered to be an asset owned by the husband.

Ibn Adret's response was concise and sharply worded. The husband had no authority to interfere with his wife's oath, since it could not be said to directly impair their relationship. If the concern was that the medicine might negatively affect her health, that type of hypothetical concern could be raised about anything – even bread and fruit could sometimes harm a person's health, but no one would suggest that a husband could prevent his wife from eating regular food. The concern that pregnancy would mar her good looks was likewise inadmissible, since pregnancy and childbirth were the primary objectives of marriage, at least from the wife's perspective.[59] She had agreed to the marriage with the intention of becoming pregnant, and the husband's interference violated the agreement at the foundation of their marriage.

Imbibing a medicinal potion in order to become pregnant was a well-established, if sometimes controversial, procedure in fourteenth-century Provence. Scholars and physicians affiliated with the medical school of Montpellier became increasingly interested in, and opinionated about, the medical treatment of infertility during this period.[60] In 1326, a purported fertility expert was charged with

55. Shatzmiller, *Récherches*, 133–135.

56. For Sisteron, see Iancu-Agou, *Provincia Judaica*, 129–132 (no mention of a local cemetery). For Tallard, see Gérard Weil, "Enquêtes et chantiers: Tallard et Espinasses," *Provence Historique* 32 (1982): 437–446.

57. Ibn Adret, *She'elot u-Teshuvot*, 4: no. 122, ed. Zaleznik, 4: 54.

58. mNedarim 11:1.

59. Ibn Adret cited bYevamot 65b: "A woman needs a crutch for her arm and a hoe for her grave" (i.e., a son who will support her in her old age and bury her after she dies).

60. Monica Green, *Making Women's Medicine Masculine: The Rise of Male Authority in Pre-Modern Gynaecology* (Oxford, 2008), 70–91.

fraud by the criminal court of Manosque because he had allegedly been selling local women fake potions and amulets to cure infertility.[61] A Jewish doctor in Orange at around the same time composed a letter to his brother-in-law with practical advice for the treatment of infertility.[62] The letter included a recipe for a syrup (*isirǫp* in Occitan) composed of various spices and roots steeped in white wine and honey.[63] The doctor emphasized the importance of a happy and intimate marital relationship and of cooperation between husband and wife – elements that may have been lacking in the case that came before Isaac of Manosque.[64] In this case, as in the divorce case of Elijah and Merauda, Isaac sided strongly with the husband to the detriment of the wife. Perhaps, like Merauda, the woman struggling with infertility was ethnically Provençal and hence failed to attract Isaac's sympathy. They were also both women, but there were cases in which Isaac of Manosque ruled in favour of women against their husbands.[65]

Ethnic tensions between Jews in Manosque did not always involve the town's rabbi. Joseph Shatzmiller published a number of court documents from Manosque relating to brawls in the synagogues of the town, none of which men-

61. Joseph Shatzmiller and Rodrigue Lavoie, "Médicine et gynécologie au moyen âge: Un exemple provençal," *Razo: Cahiers du Centre d'études Médiévales de Nice* 4 (1984): 133–143; Joseph Shatzmiller, *Médecine et justice en Provence médièvale: Documents de Manosque, 1262–1348* (Aix-en-Provence, 1989), 176–183; Green, *Making Women's Medicine Masculine*, 86; Caley McCarthy, "Midwives, Medicine and the Reproductive Female Body in Manosque, 1289–1500" (MA thesis, University of Waterloo, 2011), 52–60.

62. Oxford, Bodleian Library, Laud. Or. 113 (cat. no. 2142), fol. 248v–250(ii)v; Ron Barkaï, *A History of Jewish Gynaecological Texts in the Middle Ages* (Leiden, 1998), 76–78 (description), 212–222 (transcription and translation).

63. Bodleian Laud. Or. 113, fol. 250(i)r; Barkaï, *A History of Jewish Gynaecological Texts*, 218.

64. Bodleian Laud. Or. 113, fol. 249r–v; Barkaï, *A History of Jewish Gynaecological Texts*, 216: "First of all, my brother and lord, I would advise you to become accustomed – you and your pure companion – to eating sweet foods as much as possible ... You should also become used, with your pure companion, to various types of joy and to avoid misery and groaning, because without this, the goal cannot be achieved" (my translation). On the roles envisaged for men in late medieval infertility treatment, see Catherine Rider, "Men's Responses to Infertility in Late Medieval England," in *The Palgrave Handbook of Infertility in History: Approaches, Contexts and Perspectives*, ed. Gayle Davis and Tracey Loughran (London, 2017), 273–290.

65. In one case, a wife asked to have her divorce case heard by Isaac of Manosque – a choice that her husband claimed stemmed from the fact that Isaac was the brother-in-law of her cousin. Solomon ben Abraham ibn Adret, *Teshuvot ha-Rashba ha-Hadashot*, no. 202 [vol. 8 of *She'elot u-Teshuvot*, ed. Aharon Zaleznik (Jerusalem, 2005), 142]. For another case, see Pinchas Roth, "The *Responsa* of Gersonides and Their Reception," in *Gersonides' Afterlife: Studies on the Reception of Levi ben Gerson's Philosophical, Halakhic and Scientific Oeuvre in the 14th through 20th Centuries*, ed. Ofer Elior, Gad Freudenthal and David Wirmer (Leiden, 2020), 313–320.

tion Isaac of Manosque.[66] The statements by the Jewish protagonists and witnesses, rendered into Latin by the Manosque criminal court, provide precious glimpses of the social dynamics of Jewish life in the town. At times, fights between Manosquin Jews were explicitly coloured by geographic origins.[67] In other instances, although they are not plainly visible, a legal and cultural analysis reveals the undercurrents of ethnic tension that led to violence.

One such case took place sometime after midnight between Sunday and Monday, 23 September 1324.[68] The Jews of Manosque were gathered in their synagogues. The date, which corresponds to the fifth day of Tishre, and the late hour, make it clear that they were reciting the *seliḥot* or *ashmorot*, penitentiary poems recited before dawn during the Ten Days of Penitence between Rosh ha-Shanah (New Year, 1 Tishre) and the Day of Atonement (10 Tishre).[69] Caracausanus the son of Botinus was leading the prayers. Leonetus, a tax-collector and auctioneer (*incantatorem*), entered the synagogue looking for people to help him bury a Jew from Forcalquier. Noticing that the prayers were being led by a boy, he protested:

> It is neither good nor legal for children to recite the prayer now. Rather, it must be recited by an old person who knows the liturgy well (*Non est bonum nec licitum quod infantes decant modo mesterium, ymo debet eum dicere persona antiqua et que bene sciat mesterium*).[70]

66. Joseph Shatzmiller, "Tumultus et rumor in sinagoga: An Aspect of Social Life of Provençal Jews in the Middle Ages," *AJS Review* 2 (1977): 227–255; Joseph Shatzmiller, "Tumultus et rumor in sinagoga: Suite d'une enquête," *Provence historique* 195–196 (1999): 451–459; 208 (2002): 249–258.

67. Joseph Shatzmiller, "Counterfeit of Coinage in England of the 13th Century and the way it was Remembered in Medieval Provence," in *Moneda y Monedas En La Europa Medieval (siglos XII–XV)* (Pamplona, 2000), 387–397.

68. Shatzmiller, "Tumultus et rumor ... An Aspect," 232–233, 245–247.

69. Shatzmiller, "Tumultus et rumor ... An Aspect," 232, suggested that they were reciting *tikkun ḥatzot*, but during the fourteenth century, that midnight vigil was virtually unknown. Elliott Horowitz, "Coffee, Coffeehouses and the Nocturnal Rituals of Early Modern Jewry," *AJS Review* 14 (1989): 17–46 (esp. 23–24). Israel M. Ta-Shma, *Early Franco-German Ritual and Custom* (Jerusalem, 1992), 309 (Hebrew), suggested that the mourner's kaddish was being recited. Among other problems with Ta-Shma's suggestion, it takes no account of the post-midnight timing – an unusual time for regular prayer services.

70. Shatzmiller, "Tumultus et rumor ... An Aspect," 246. I am very grateful to M. Olivier Gorse of the Archives départementales des Bouches-du-Rhône for his assistance in obtaining photographs of the original document, and to Jonathan Rubin for facilitating that connection and for helping me to understand the document.

Botinus, father of the youngster, responded by cursing anyone who should dare to prevent his son from completing the prayer. Leonetus (who was carrying tools for the burial) rammed Bonitus in the belly with a club and punched him in the jaw, and Bonitus punched him back.

It seems unlikely that Carcasaunus was a minor under the age of thirteen. Although there exist some traces of rabbinic opinions that might justify counting a minor for the prayer quorum or allowing him to recite the *kaddish,* no such allowance can be found for leading the prayers.[71] Botinus was unlikely to have taken such umbrage if his son had violated a commonly-known rule of Jewish prayer. Leonetus emphasized that the prayer-leader must be old and well-versed in the prayer, which suggests that Carcasaunus was not simply an under-age child. His words echo a ruling of the French Tosafists, that although throughout the year the prayers could occasionally be led by a teenager, on the Day of Atonement and at the *ma ʿamadot* they must be led by a man with a full beard.[72] *Ma ʿamadot,* in this context, means the penitentiary prayers recited before the Day of Atonement.[73] However, the proviso of the *Tosafot* requiring an older leader for the Days of Penitence liturgy was not adopted by Catalonian commentators on the Talmud when they quoted this line.[74] This suggests that it was a specifically French custom to bar young men from leading the *ma ʿamadot,* while communities in Catalonia and Provence did not distinguish between the penitential prayers and regular services led throughout the year by boys over the age of thirteen. That Leonetus was French, while Botinus and his son were Provençal – and therefore disinclined to conform to a French custom – is also suggested by their names.[75] In this case, a fistfight in the wee hours between two men was triggered by differing assumptions about the liturgy. The conflagration was probably fed by the tensions that had long been simmering beneath the surface between the two ethnic groups living cheek by jowl within the same synagogue.

71. Israel Ta-Shma, *The Early Ashkenazic Prayer: Literary and Historical Aspects* (Jerusalem, 2003), 237–248 (Hebrew).

72. *Tosafot* Sukkah 42a, s.v. *ha-yodeʿa.*

73. Ariel Zinder, "'There they stand at midnight, time and again': Seliḥot for Repentance Nights by Yitzḥak ibn Giyyat" (PhD diss., Hebrew University, 2014), 48–52 (Hebrew); Ismar Elbogen, *Jewish Liturgy: A Comprehensive History,* trans. Raymond P. Scheindlin (Philadelphia, 1993), 191.

74. Solomon ben Abraham ibn Adret, *Ḥidushe ha-Rashba: masekhet Megilah,* ed. Haim Zalman Dimitrovsky (Jerusalem, 1981), 169; Menaḥem ha-Meʾiri, *Bet ha-Beḥirah ʿal masekhet Megilah,* ed. Moshe Herschler (Jerusalem, 1962), 79.

75. Botin or Botinus exclusively in Provence – Seror, *Les noms des juifs,* 52. Carecausa – Robert I. Burns, *Jews in the Notarial Culture: Latinate Wills in Mediterranean Spain, 1250–1350* (Berkeley, 1996), 118. Leon or Leonetus is found in the south, but most frequently in the north of France (Seror, *Les noms des juifs,* 161–162).

Such deep-seated tension could remain even after the Frenchmen left Provence. One such person was Isaac of Manosque's son Peretz ha-Kohen, who was appointed rabbi of Barcelona and died there in 1369.[76] His legacy in Barcelona was preserved by his prominent students Isaac ben Sheshet Perfet and Mattathiah Trèves (who returned to Paris after his studies).[77] During his lifetime, he was also remembered in Provence – when an argument erupted there regarding the validity of a rabbinic court's decision, one of the local sages wrote to Peretz ha-Kohen asking for his opinion.[78] Peretz concluded that the Provençal court's decision was entirely erroneous and must be overturned. This negative attitude towards a court decision from Provence may not have been simply the result of his legal analysis. On more than one occasion, Peretz ha-Kohen expressed deep disdain for the customs of Provence. In regard to the Provençal custom of marrying boys and girls in early childhood, he said that "the custom of Provence is a foolish custom that was created by arrogant people."[79]

Another sharp comment is preserved in a question sent to Isaac ben Sheshet Perfet by his son-in-law Isaac Bonafos, who had known Rabbi Peretz, by then deceased.[80] The question was whether a wild kosher animal (such as a deer; in Hebrew: *ḥayah*) required inspection of the lungs after slaughtering, in the same way that domesticated animals (*behemah*) were routinely inspected.[81] Bonafos

76. Shatzmiller, "Rabbinate," 61–62; Abraham M. Hershman, *Rabbi Isaac ben Sheshet Perfet and His Times* (New York, 1943), 10 n12; Yom Tov Assis, *The Golden Age of Aragonese Jewry: Community and Society in the Crown of Aragon, 1213–1327* (London, 1997), 140. Peretz wrote commentaries on the Talmud, one or two volumes of which have survived: Moshe Yehudah Blau, *Shitat ha-Kadmonim ʿal masekhet Nazir* (New York, 1972), 293–507; Avigdor Arieli, "On the Commentary on Menaḥot Attributed to Rashba," *Alei Sefer* 16 (1989): 149–150 (Hebrew); Peretz ben Isaac ha-Kohen, *Ḥidushim le-ʾeḥad meha-rishonim ʿal masekhet Menaḥot* (Jerusalem, 2000), 5–14.

77. Leon A. Feldman, "R. Nissim ben Reuben Gerondi: Archival Data from Barcelona," in *Exile and Diaspora: Studies in the History of the Jewish People Presented to Professor Haim Beinart*, ed. Aharon Mirsky, Avraham Grossman and Yosef Kaplan (Jerusalem, 1991), 62 n2; Hershman, *Rabbi Isaac ben Sheshet*, 10; Jeffrey R. Woolf, "French Halakhic Tradition in the Late Middle Ages," *Jewish History* 27 (2013): 1–20, at 8.

78. Jacob ben Moses of Bagnols, "Ezrat Nashim," in *Shitat ha-Kadmonim ʿal masekhet Kidushin*, ed. Moshe Yehudah Blau (New York, 1970), 325–346.

79. See Chapter 6.

80. Isaac ben Sheshet Perfet, *Sheʾelot u-Teshuvot*, ed. David Metzger (Jerusalem, 1993), no. 77.

81. Wild animals were apparently consumed only very rarely by Iberian Jews. No remains of wild animals were found in excavations of a site in Tàrrega that has been identified as reflecting Jewish settlement. Silvia Valenzuela-Lamas, "Shechita and Kashrut: Identifying Jewish Populations through Zooarcheology and Taphonomy: Two Examples from Medieval Catalonia (North-Eastern Spain)," *Quaternary International* 330 (2014): 109–117, at 112.

added that he had heard Peretz comment that "in his place" there was a saying: "A *terefah* (a terminally ill animal, such as an animal with damaged lungs) is not a *ḥayah*."[82] Bonafos understood this to mean that a *ḥayah* could not become a *terefah* and therefore a wild animal did not require post-mortem inspection. Perfet responded that such a conclusion was impossible, and that wild animals required the same inspection as domesticated animals: "I do not think that my late teacher said what he told you as a practical ruling, but in order to poke fun at the people of his place who were lenient in this." "The people of his place," the Provençal Jews among whom he had grown up, followed a policy that Peretz considered not only erroneous but ridiculous, and he troubled himself to concoct a fake maxim to emphasize how nonsensical their policy was. The irony of Peretz's comment was lost on Bonafos but not on Perfet, who remembered his teacher's abiding antipathy towards "the people of his place" in Provence.

82. A pun on a talmudic statement (bḤullin 42a and elsewhere): "A *terefah* will not live." A terminally ill animal is not kosher, even if it was slaughtered in the required manner and did not die from its disease, since it would have died eventually due to its condition and is therefore considered dead (and therefore unfit) from the moment of diagnosis.

CHAPTER FIVE

Zealotry and Law

When Greco-Arabic philosophy first began to make inroads into the Jewish culture of southern France during the first decades of the thirteenth century, it aroused strongly polarized responses. By century's end, the rationalization of Provençal Judaism was largely a fait accompli and the only outstanding question was how thoroughly traditional Jewish texts should be reinterpreted to bring them into line with current thinking. It must have come a surprise to many Jewish intellectuals in Provence and Languedoc when, in 1304, a new campaign against the propagation of rationalist ideas was launched by a rabbinic scholar named Abba Mari ben Moses.[1]

Abba Mari was born in Lunel and was known throughout his life as Sen Astruc de Lunel but his home at the beginning of the fourteenth century was in Montpellier.[2] When Kalonymos ben Kalonymos of Arles described Montpellier

1. Abba Mari's campaign is probably the single best-known and best-documented episode in Provençal Jewish history. A.S. Halkin, "Why Was Levi Ben Hayyim Hounded," *Proceedings of the American Academy for Jewish Research* 34 (1966): 65–76; Joseph Shatzmiller, "Between Abba Mari and Rashba: The Negotiations that Preceded the Herem in Barcelona," *Studies in the History of the Jewish People and the Land of Israel* 3 (1974): 121–137 (Hebrew); Marc Saperstein, "The Conflict over the Rashba's Herem on Philosophical Study: A Political Perspective," *Jewish History* 1 (1986): 27–38 [revised version in Marc Saperstein, *Leadership and Conflict: Tensions in Medieval and Modern Jewish History and Culture* (Oxford, 2014), 94–112]; Ram Ben-Shalom, "Communication and Propaganda between Provence and Spain: The Controversy over Extreme Allegorization," in *Communication in the Jewish Diaspora: The Pre-Modern World*, ed. Sophia Menache (Leiden, 1996), 171–224; Ram Ben-Shalom, "The Ban Placed by the Community of Barcelona on the Study of Philosophy and Allegorical Preaching – A New Study," *Revue des études juives* 159 (2000): 387–404; Gregg Stern, *Philosophy and Rabbinic Culture: Jewish Interpretation and Controversy in Medieval Languedoc* (London, 2009); Tamar Marvin, "The Making of Minhat Qena᾿ot: The Controversy over Ideational Transgression in Fourteenth-Century Jewish Occitania" (PhD diss., Jewish Theological Seminary of America, 2013); Tamar Marvin, "A Heretic from a Good Family? A New Look at Why Levi b. Abraham b. Hayim was Hounded," *AJS Review* 41 (2017): 175–201.

2. Henri Gross, "Notice sur Abba Mari de Lunel," *Revue des études juives* 4 (1882): 192–207; Zadok ha-Kohen, "He῾arot be-divre yeme ḥakhme Yisra᾿el" (Comments on the History of Jewish Sages), *Sinai* 21 (1947): 1–25, at 17–20; Binyamin Bar-Tikvah, *Genres and Topics in Provençal and Catalonian Piyyut* (Be᾿er Sheva, 2009), 61–62 (Hebrew).

at that time, he used a series of puns on Abba Mari's name, as if the entire city were merely an extension of that one scholar: "the Mountain of Myrrh (*mor*) which guides (*moreh*) the rebellious (*meri*) house on the straight path."[3] According to Kalonymos, who bore some familial relationship to him, Abba Mari's personal life was miserable:[4]

> I saw with my own eyes, two or three times, how Time had wrought bitter things against him. The door of his home does not swing on its hinge like other women; his wife at home, who was [once] beautiful and pampered, is wan and tormented by afflictions that vary in number. His descendants give him no consolation to restore his beleaguered soul on the day of wrath and his bitter spirit in a time of strife.

It is tempting to speculate that the relentless letter-writing campaign waged by Abba Mari against proponents of philosophy in 1304–1305 provided him with some outlet for his personal anguish. In any case, it struck a chord with generations of scribes and readers who preserved more than half a dozen copies of *Minḥat Kena'ot* (An Offering of Jealousy), the dossier of documents from the campaign that was compiled by Abba Mari and his disciples.[5]

Throughout his career, and especially following the 1306 Expulsion when he moved to Arles and lived there until at least 1337, Abba Mari fielded questions in Jewish law from rabbinic scholars, courts and Jewish laypeople.[6] His halakhic writings reveal a more positive attitude towards Maimonides than a reader of *Minḥat Kena'ot* might expect. They also evince a distinct affinity for Northern French rabbinic culture that accorded better with Abba Mari's worldview. In emotional terms, they suggest an undercurrent of stringency and impa-

3. Joseph Shatzmiller, "Minor Epistle of Apology of Rabbi Kalonymos ben Kalonymos," *Sefunot* 10 (1966): 7–52, at 39 (Hebrew). According to Shatzmiller, the description was written in 1305 or thereabouts.

4. Shatzmiller, "Minor Epistle," 39.

5. *Minḥat Kena'ot*, in Solomon ben Abraham ibn Adret, *Teshuvot ha-Rashba*, ed. Haim Zalman Dimitrovsky (Jerusalem, 1990). The text was first published as Abba Mari ben Moses, *Minḥat Kena'ot*, ed. Mordecai Leib Bisliches (Pressburg, 1838). Dimitrovsky's critical edition was based on seven manuscripts, whose shelfmarks were not specified in the edition (this information was supposed to appear in an introductory volume which Dimitrovsky never published). The manuscripts were identified by Marvin, "The Making of Minhat Qena'ot," 33–34.

6. The last datable incident in which Abba Mari was involved took place around the year 1337. Pinchas Roth, "'My precious books and instruments': Jewish Divorce Strategies and Self-Fashioning in Medieval Catalonia," *Journal of Medieval History* 43 (2017): 548–561. In that study (pages 556–557), I erroneously wrote that the *responsum* was written by Abba Mari's disciple, but in fact it was written by Abba Mari himself.

tience with human frailty that echoes the zealotry of his public campaign. His rabbinic contemporary, Isaac Kimḥi, seems to have been less than enamoured with him. But the Provençal Jews who solicited his opinion on their legal and religious affairs must have respected his personality, for otherwise they would have sent their questions elsewhere.

The earliest of Abba Mari's legal correspondences concerns medical talismans.[7] It was intimately connected to Abba Mari's campaign against rationalism, since, as he explained in the poetic opening to his first letter on the subject:[8]

> There are many people today who have broken through the fences... some of them are immersed in the discipline of logic, and I have seen those who are buried in physical science ... some stake themselves in the laws of the stars, and some prepare figures at auspicious times when the sun is at a specific elevation in the ascent of Scorpio.

The specific culprit in Abba Mari's eyes was Isaac ben Judah de Lattes, a physician who had prepared a talisman for the treatment of kidney ailments. The talisman was shaped like a lion and had been prepared under specific astrological conditions. Maimonides himself had permitted medical talismans, yet Abba Mari found this position inexplicable.[9] He saw such an object as falling under the biblical and rabbinic prohibitions of idolatry and magic, as well as providing a disincentive for prayer, for "if we permit these talismans, a person will not seek out God, nor doctors."[10]

Abba Mari expressed his concerns in writing to Solomon ben Abraham ibn Adret in Barcelona. Ibn Adret responded that he himself had permitted the lion talisman since he believed that the Talmud permitted all medical charms, and added that his teacher Nahmanides had likewise permitted them.[11] The prohibi-

7. *Minḥat Kena'ot* chapters 19–23, in *Teshuvot ha-Rashba*, ed. Dimitrovsky, 1: 270–333. On this exchange, see Joseph Shatzmiller, "In Search of the 'Book of Figures': Medicine and Astrology in Montpellier at the Turn of the Fourteenth Century," *AJS Review* 7/8 (1982–1983): 383–407; David Horwitz, "Rashba's Attitude Towards Science and Its Limits," *Torah u-Madda Journal* 3 (1991–1992): 52–81; Dov Schwartz, *Studies on Astral Magic in Medieval Jewish Thought*, trans. D. Louvish and B. Stein (Leiden, 2005), 123–138; Stern, *Philosophy and Rabbinic Culture*, 146–150.

8. *Minḥat Kena'ot* chapter 19, in *Teshuvot ha-Rashba*, ed. Dimitrovsky, 1: 272.

9. Ibid., referring to Maimonides, *Guide of the Perplexed* 3:37, trans. Shlomo Pines (Chicago, 1963–1979), 2: 544.

10. *Minḥat Kena'ot* chapter 19, in *Teshuvot ha-Rashba*, ed. Dimitrovsky, 1: 274.

11. *Minḥat Kena'ot* chapter 20, in *Teshuvot ha-Rashba*, ed. Dimitrovsky, 1: 275–280. See also Solomon ben Abraham ibn Adret, *Ḥidushe ha-Rashba: masekhet Shabat*, Shabbat 67a, ed. Ya'ir Broner (Jerusalem, 1986), 300. On ibn Adret's position, see Horwitz, "Rashba's Attitude"; Schwartz, *Studies on Astral Magic*, 79–83.

tions in Jewish law barred any active form of worship to astral forces, but not harnessing their power through talismans. At a number of junctures in his letter, ibn Adret self-effacingly commented that he was simply exploring the issue and invited Abba Mari to critique his position.[12] Abba Mari took full advantage of ibn Adret's invitation. He conceded that healing through *materia medica* (*samim*), incantations, amulets against demons, and objects with occult virtues (*segulot*) was permitted.[13] But he asserted that astrological talismans were strictly forbidden and called upon ibn Adret to adopt his position, in which case "we would give thanks and recite: Blessed is God who uprooted idolatry from our land."[14] Unimpressed, ibn Adret responded acerbically: "For a while, I was determined not to respond to the things you wrote to me about what the Torah forbade. I wrote to you as a scholar and enquirer ... and you picked out of my words whatever seemed good to you and without truly accepting my opinion, and the rest you ignored."[15] Moreover, he explained that he would never have become involved had he realized that the talisman had already aroused controversy in Languedoc.[16]

Undeterred by ibn Adret's unenthusiastic response to his letter about the talisman, Abba Mari decided that it was "a favourable time to speak with the Rabbi" and sent him a series of questions about passages in the Palestinian Talmud.[17] The first related to the complex issue of forbidden foods that were mixed into larger quantities of permitted food, and specifically to a statement in the Palestinian Talmud that a non-kosher fish pickled with a larger quantity of kosher fish could be outnumbered in a ratio of 1:960.[18] Why did the Talmud choose this particular ratio?

Abba Mari then turned to a second talmudic passage that permitted the offering of firstborn animals as sacrifices – after the fact – even when they were born outside the Land of Israel.[19] This passage contradicted a ruling by Maimonides who denied the sacral standing of firstborn animals outside the Land of Israel.[20] Tellingly, Abba Mari did not mention that this selfsame challenge to Maimonides had been raised in the twelfth century by Rabad of Posquières, and in the thirteenth century by Moses Nahmanides of Girona and Menaḥem ha-

12. *Minḥat Kena'ot* chapter 21, in *Teshuvot ha-Rashba*, ed. Dimitrovsky, 1: 284, 308.
13. *Minḥat Kena'ot* chapter 23, in *Teshuvot ha-Rashba*, ed. Dimitrovsky, 1: 329.
14. Ibid., 1: 333.
15. *Minḥat Kena'ot* chapter 25, in *Teshuvot ha-Rashba*, ed. Dimitrovsky, 1: 347–348.
16. *Minḥat Kena'ot* chapter 21, in *Teshuvot ha-Rashba*, ed. Dimitrovsky, 1: 282.
17. *Minḥat Kena'ot* chapter 24, in *Teshuvot ha-Rashba*, ed. Dimitrovsky, 1: 333.
18. Ibid., 1: 334–336; pTerumot 10:7, in Palestinian Talmud (*Talmud Yerushalmi*), ed. Yaacov Sussmann (Jerusalem, 2001), 256.
19. pḤallah 4:11, 330.
20. Maimonides, *Mishneh Torah*, ed. Shabse Frankel (Jerusalem, 1975–2003), Laws of Firstborn Animals 1, 5.

Me'iri of Perpignan.[21] Despite those objections, the Jews in southern France followed Maimonides and made no attempt to observe the law of firstborn animals. By contrast, the communities of France and Germany considered the law applicable.[22]

The Palestinian Talmud was studied during the Middle Ages only by a small minority of rabbinic scholars.[23] Abba Mari was not one of those few, and his access to the passages in his two questions was provided by the Mishnah commentary of Samson of Sens, a Northern French scholar and one of the earliest critics of Maimonides.[24] Abba Mari's choice of French reading material, and his attack on Maimonidean law and Provençal practice, demonstrates that his stance on philosophy – that is, against the widespread adoption of Maimonides' religious approach in Provence – also coloured his approach to Halakhah.[25]

Ibn Adret's response was polite but crushing. In regard to the first question, about forbidden mixtures, he explained that he himself could not resolve the problem, nor could he explain the Mishnah satisfactorily "because of the prob-

21. Rabad, gloss to *Mishneh Torah*, Laws of Firstborn Animals 1, 5; Moses Nahmanides, *Hilkhot Bekhorot*, ed. Me'ir Lev (Jerusalem, 1995), 81–82; Menaḥem ha-Me'iri, *Magen Avot*, ed. Yekuti'el Kohen (Jerusalem, 1989), chapter 15 (142–143).

22. Israel M. Ta-Shma, *Ritual, Custom and Reality in Franco-Germany, 1000–1350* (Jerusalem, 1996), 201–215 (Hebrew); Richard I. Cohen, *Jewish Icons: Art and Society in Modern Europe* (Berkeley, 1998), 56–57; David Henshke, "The Firstborn of a Kosher Animal Outside the Land of Israel: From the Talmud to Maimonides and Back," in *Professor Meir Benayahu Memorial Volume* (Jerusalem, 2019), 1: 241–274 (Hebrew). Several decades after Abba Mari's question, this divergence in custom between France and Provence so disturbed a French Jew living in the city of Forcalquier, in northern Provence, that he felt compelled to challenge the local Provençal sages about it. Unconvinced by their reliance on Maimonides, he turned to Nissim ben Reuben of Girona who provided the selfsame reference to Rabad's gloss. Nissim ben Reuben Gerondi, *She'elot u-Teshuvot*, no. 7, ed. Leon Feldman (Jerusalem, 1984), 52.

23. On southern French scholars who did read the Palestinian Talmud directly, see Pinchas Roth, "On Exegesis of the Jerusalem Talmud in Medieval Southern France," *Sidra: Journal for the Study of Rabbinic Literature* 29 (2015): 117–125 (Hebrew).

24. Samson of Sens, commentary on mTerumot 10:8; commentary on mḤallah 4:11. On Samson as a critic of Maimonides, see Bernard Septimus, *Hispano-Jewish Culture in Transition: The Career and Controversies of Ramah* (Cambridge, MA, 1982), 49–51. Abba Mari was probably not the only Provençal scholar to read Samson's Mishnah commentary since Gersonides (Levi ben Gershom) possessed a copy of the entire commentary. Gérard E. Weil, *La Bibliothèque de Gersonide d'après son catalogue autographe*, ed. Frédéric Chartrain (Leuven, 1991), 44.

25. A further example appears in Abba Mari's letter to Asher ben Yehiel, *Minḥat Kena'ot* chapter 6 (in *Teshuvot ha-Rashba*, ed. Dimitrovsky, 2: 588), which cites a passage "that I found in the Palestinian Talmud," which appeared in Samson's commentary that Abba Mari cited only a few lines beforehand.

lems you raised and others," and that he had written all of this in his Talmud commentary.[26] But first he pointed out, in painful detail, all of the errors that Abba Mari had made in surveying the laws of admixtures in the first question – "everything you wrote seems incorrect to me, and this is not what I received from my late teachers."[27] As for the second question, ibn Adret simply quoted the famous scholars Rabad and Nahmanides, who had posed precisely the same challenge to Maimonides that Abba Mari believed he had discovered.[28]

Abba Mari attempted to use his correspondence with ibn Adret on abstruse points of rabbinic law in order to establish himself as an innovative legal expert and to channel some of Rashba's huge prestige. The rebuttal of each of his suggestions as either inaccurate or unoriginal demonstrates that Abba Mari failed to gain ibn Adret's respect. This did not dampen Abba Mari's admiration for ibn Adret, nor did it deter Provençal Jews from turning to Abba Mari over the subsequent decades for religious guidance. Ingenuity was not the sole trait that members of the community looked for in a rabbinic decisor, and for some it may not even have been the most important one. In the first stage of his career, as reflected in *Minḥat Kena'ot*, Abba Mari demonstrated a dogged commitment to legal and theological rectitude. Further characteristics emerge from his *responsa* over the following decades to individuals and communities that turned to him for guidance out of respect for the values that he embodied.

Towards the end of *Minḥat Kena'ot*, Abba Mari described the expulsion of the Jews from the Kingdom of France:

> The year 5066 (1306 AD) was the year when sin caused [calamity] and a note fell from Heaven, decreed by the Watchers.[29] The king of France decreed that all of the Jews in all the cities of his kingdom must be removed from their homes and shorn of their possessions. They were all placed under guard, young and old, children and women on a single day, Friday the tenth of Av, and they were expelled from the land. The Jews in the city of Montpellier were expelled in the year [506]7 in the month of *Ḥeshvan*. Some of them sought refuge in Perpignan, trusting that the king of Majorca would be valiant and would grant them a remnant stay[30] and a regular allotment of food.[31] Others moved to Provence, trusting that God would grant them

26. *Minḥat Kena'ot* chapter 26, in *Teshuvot ha-Rashba*, ed. Dimitrovsky, 1: 355–356.
27. Ibid., 1: 350–355.
28. Ibid., 1: 356–358.
29. Cf. Daniel 4:14.
30. Cf. Jeremiah 40:11.
31. II Kings 25:30.

> mercy and rest... After I was exiled to Provence to the city of Arles, I embarked on a second exile to the city of Perpignan. I arrived there on the first day of *Shevat*, the fourth month of our exile, and was received by many of the notables there, including Moses ben Samuel ben Asher.[32] He told me that it had been reported to our teacher, Rabbi Solomon Adret, by passersby or by my supporters, that I had been exiled to Provence along with some members of our noble group, and that the king's officials would not allow us into the city of Perpignan.[33]

Minḥat Kena'ot contains no further information about Abba Mari's whereabouts, which led some scholars to conclude that he eventually settled in Perpignan, despite his initial bureaucratic troubles.[34] However, Abba Mari's legal writings leave no doubt that he quickly left Perpignan for the Provençal city of Arles, where he lived for three decades until his death.

Four *responsa* by Abba Mari dating from his Arles period were published in *Teshuvot Ḥakhme Provinẓia (Teshuvot Ḥakhme Provintsya)*, each of which brought him into confrontation with rabbis from the Kimḥi family.[35] The first was written to Mordechai Kimḥi (and was discussed from his perspective in Chapter 2). A Jewish husband who wished to divorce his wife in order to marry another woman had coerced Kimḥi into appearing before the city consul to answer a series of questions in Jewish law pertinent to the case. The husband, Pancho of Viviers, had made an oath to avoid sexual relations with his wife, and then claimed that the court must coerce him to grant his wife a divorce since he could not fulfil his marital obligations towards her. Kimḥi realized that the man's aim was to escape a marriage he had tired of, and that the oath was merely a ruse to force the woman into a divorce she did not want. Even under the threat of punishment by the municipal authorities, Kimḥi refused to validate the divorce, but he did agree to explain himself before the consul. Afterwards, he sent an account of the affair to his rabbinic colleagues, asking whether they thought he had acted correctly. Among the two rabbis who responded was Abba Mari.[36] Abba Mari castigated Kimḥi for showing cowardice in the face of pressure and urged him to nullify the husband's oath. Then, in a dizzying swerve, he suggested

32. Abba Mari's relative; see Stern, *Philosophy and Rabbinic Culture*, 229 n9.

33. *Minḥat Kena'ot* chapter 120, in *Teshuvot ha-Rashba*, ed. Dimitrovsky, 2: 835–836.

34. Shatzmiller, "Minor Epistle," 16. Others remained agnostic about his eventual refuge – Gross, "Notice," 194; Stern, *Philosophy and Rabbinic Culture*, 229 n10.

35. A fifth *responsum* remains unpublished in a manuscript held by the Israel National Library: Roth, "My precious books and instruments," 556–557.

36. *Teshuvot Ḥakhme Provinẓia (Teshuvot Ḥakhme Provintsya)* (*Responsa* of the Sages of Provence), no. 64, ed. Abraham Sofer (Schreiber) (Jerusalem, 1967).

that the husband was justified in his desire to escape the marriage if "he hated his wife, out of anger or disgust, something that can happen for a number of reasons."[37] Finally, in closing, Abba Mari pleaded for "either a ruling or a compromise" that would satisfy both parties.[38] Although he appears to have vacillated in his understanding of the legal dimensions of the case, Abba Mari betrayed scant empathy for his elder colleague Mordechai Kimḥi.

Another case in which a Jewish court asked Abba Mari to express his opinion took place some years later, when Mordechai Kimḥi's son Isaac was the leading rabbi in Provence. The case was described in a letter sent to Isaac Kimḥi and Abba Mari by a court convened in Carpentras.[39] A party of reveling Jewish men entered a brothel in Carpentras, where they proceeded to eat and drink with "a certain woman, a prostitute (*kedeshah*), who was available to every passerby." One of the men sent his servant with a silver *clement* to buy wine for the group, but no wine was available. The servant returned the coin to his master, who promptly handed it to the woman dining with the group "for the purpose of betrothal." Testimony given later by members of the party was divided as to the precise wording used by their friend, but they agreed that the woman said nothing in response. However, immediately after this exchange, the members of the party began to argue. "What have you done?," shouted one of them, while another responded "Why do you care? It was nothing but a joke." The woman told them that she never intended to marry the man and that it was all in jest, and the man confirmed that he had not intended to betroth her. The couple then secluded themselves in a private room where, the judges implied, a sexual encounter ensued. Local authorities got wind of the story somehow, interrogated the witnesses and then wrote to the rabbis inquring whether the man and woman ought to be considered legally married. Was this betrothal, presumably followed swiftly by sexual intercourse, considered valid, or did the circumstances make it clear that it was never meant to be legally binding?

Brothels were legally recognized institutions in medieval Provence.[40] Whether all of the women staffing this particular brothel in Carpentras were Jew-

37. *Teshuvot Ḥakhme Provinẓia (Teshuvot Ḥakhme Provintsya)*, no. 64, ed. Sofer, 221, perhaps echoing his own troubled marriage.

38. *Teshuvot Ḥakhme Provinẓia (Teshuvot Ḥakhme Provintsya)*, no. 64, ed. Sofer, 222.

39. *Teshuvot Ḥakhme Provinẓia (Teshuvot Ḥakhme Provintsya)*, no. 27, ed. Sofer, 108–109. Their tone implies that the judges were an ad hoc group convened in order to grapple with a specific case, rather than professional legists.

40. Leah Lydia Otis, *Prostitution in Medieval Society: The History of an Urban Institution in Languedoc* (Chicago, 1985); Jacques Rossiaud, *Medieval Prostitution*, trans. Lydia G. Cochrane (Oxford, 1995); Joëlle Rollo-Koster, "From Prostitutes to Brides of Christ: The Avignonese *Repenties* in the Late Middle Ages," *Journal of Medieval and Early Modern Studies*

ish is difficult to say, but the woman in question was certainly Jewish (since betrothal of a non-Jewish woman would be invalid in any case).[41] It is possible that the description provided by the Carpentras judges was coloured by their own moral views, that the story actually took place in a tavern and that the mixed company and rowdy behavior were enough for the judges to imagine that sexual misconduct was also part of the mix.[42] As for dating the affair, the only clue is provided by the name of the coin given to the servant and then to the woman. Pope Clement V reigned from 1305 until 1314, spending much of that time in Carpentras and the region.[43] However, the *gros* coins minted during his reign, the silver *clementini,* were still in circulation as late as 1334.[44]

The acting judges in Carpentras investigated the circumstances of the case and then formulated two questions, which they posed to Isaac Kimḥi. First, did the language used for the betrothal comply with the technical requirements of betrothal pronouncements? The second question focused on the circumstances immediately following the betrothal – whether sexual intercourse could be assumed to have taken place, and whether such intercourse qualified either as a component of the betrothal or as an indicator of the betrothal's existence, in line with the talmudic pronouncement that "no man wishes to treat his cohabitation as mere fornication."[45]

Kimḥi responded briefly.[46] Regarding the wording, he declared that neither of the versions reported by the witnesses was legally valid. As to the events fol-

32 (2002): 109–144; Kevin Mummey and Kathryn Reyerson, "Whose City is This? Hucksters, Domestic Servants, Wet-Nurses, Prostitutes, and Slaves in Late Medieval Western Mediterranean Urban Society," *History Compass* 9 (2011): 910–922.

41. On Jewish prostitutes in medieval Spain, see Yom Tov Assis, "Sexual Behaviour in Mediaeval Hispano-Jewish Society," in *Jewish History: Essays in Honour of Chimen Abramsky,* ed. Ada Rapoport-Albert and Steven J. Zipperstein (London, 1988), 44–45.

42. For such suspicions, Ruth Mazo Karras, "Sex and the Singlewoman," in *Singlewomen in the European Past, 1250–1800,* ed. Judith M. Bennett and Amy M. Froide (Philadelphia, 1999), 127–145. The men were described in the question as "*anashim poḥazim,*" carousing men. Several classic rabbinic texts describe groups of (Gentile) men disparagingly as "eating, drinking and carousing (*poḥazim*)." See *Genesis Rabbah* 39 (ed. Julius Theodor and Ḥanokh Albeck [Berlin, 1912–1936], 371); *Pesikta de-Rab Kahana,* sec. 28, trans. William G. Braude and Israel J. Kapstein (Philadelphia, 1975), 433. These texts, like that composed by the Carpentras tribunal, imply a causal link between unrestrained eating and sexually immoral behavior.

43. Sophia Menache, *Clement V* (Cambridge, 1998).

44. Peter Spufford, *Handbook of Medieval Exchange* (London, 1986), 123. The silver clement is also mentioned in the parodical *ḥaramot* ("resolutions") from fourteenth-century Provence published by Israel Davidson, *Parody in Jewish Literature* (New York, 1907), 138.

45. bYevamot 107a, bKetubbot 73a; bGittin 81b.

46. *Teshuvot Ḥakhme Provinẓia (Teshuvot Ḥakhme Provintsya),* no. 27, ed. Sofer, 109–113.

lowing the betrothal, they were irrelevant – if the betrothal were invalid, subsequent events would not change that. The Talmud's statement about a man not wanting his sexual interactions to be "mere fornication" was made "about good women who stand to enter betrothal and marriage through purity and holiness – but this woman, according to the description, is a prostitute and available to all, and she prefers illicit intercourse (*be ʿilat kedeshut*) to sacred intercourse (*be ʿilat kedushah*)."[47] Kimḥi's swift response led to a further exchange with one of the judges, Bonafos de Viviers, who explained that all of the judges concurred with Kimḥi, but that a member of the community named Don Josef de Caslar had publicly challenged their ruling.[48]

Josef de Caslar's challenge to their ruling spurred the Carpentras judges to turn to Abba Mari as well, by sending him the same two-fold question.[49] Abba Mari answered that, due to the language used by the man, the betrothal would have been invalid "even if we knew clearly that the man and the woman intended to be betrothed, all the more so when the man and the woman and one of the witnesses all agreed that everything was a joke."[50] Yet, after declaring that there was no betrothal and therefore no need for divorce, Abba Mari continued:[51]

> I believe that this is in accordance with the letter of the law (*shurat ha-din*). However, in order to be on the safe side (*ravḥa de-milta*), and so that the daughters of Israel should not become loose in these matters, it is better to be strict with her and to require her to receive a divorce, and anyone who is stringent in this shall be blessed.

Abba Mari then turned to the question of the presumed sexual encounter that followed the betrothal and responded briefly that it held no legal significance because "all of her intercourse is illicit."[52]

The lenient approach prevailing through most of his *responsum* repeated almost verbatim the opinion already expressed on the matter by Isaac Kimḥi. The passage in which Abba Mari called for a divorce stands in marked contrast to the rest of his *responsum*, in which – both before and after this passage – he

47. *Teshuvot Ḥakhme Provinẓia (Teshuvot Ḥakhme Provintsya)*, no. 27, ed. Sofer, 111.

48. *Teshuvot Ḥakhme Provinẓia (Teshuvot Ḥakhme Provintsya)*, no. 28, ed. Sofer, 113–114. I discussed this aspect of the story in "Asking Questions: Rabbis and Philosophers in Medieval Provence." *Journal of Jewish Studies* 67 (2016): 1–14, at 11–13.

49. *Teshuvot Ḥakhme Provinẓia (Teshuvot Ḥakhme Provintsya)*, no. 30, ed. Sofer, 120–123.

50. *Teshuvot Ḥakhme Provinẓia (Teshuvot Ḥakhme Provintsya)*, no. 30, ed. Sofer, 121.

51. *Teshuvot Ḥakhme Provinẓia (Teshuvot Ḥakhme Provintsya)*, no. 30, ed. Sofer, 122.

52. *Teshuvot Ḥakhme Provinẓia (Teshuvot Ḥakhme Provintsya)*, no. 30, ed. Sofer, 123.

stated clearly that there had been no betrothal, and therefore no need for divorce. Requiring a divorce, even if not legally necessary, could serve as a reassurance for members of the community (like Josef de Caslar) who feared that married women unattached to their husbands could spread sexual promiscuity and cause other men to unwittingly violate the prohibition of adultery. At the same time, Abba Mari must have been aware that his stringent ruling placed the woman at the mercy of her erstwhile client who could now demand financial incentives in return for granting the divorce. Perhaps because he was torn between these alternatives, Abba Mari wrote a *responsum* that was legally disjointed.

The same pair of rabbis, Isaac Kimḥi and Abba Mari, was called upon to resolve another question relating to marital law:[53]

> A terminally ill (*shekhiv me-ra*) husband intended to save his wife from the need to perform levirate marriage in the case that he died of his illness. He ordered the scribe to write, and the witnesses to sign, a valid divorce. The scribe went and wrote the divorce with this clause: "No person will protest against you in my name from this day onwards. It is not a promise (*ʾasmakhta*) nor is it a template (*tofse shetarot*)." Is this divorce invalid and does she need to perform *ḥaliẓah,* or is it not invalid and she is permitted [to remarry] without *ḥaliẓah*? Also, if there is a concern that the divorce is invalid and yet she remarried without *ḥaliẓah,* what is her status in that (second) marriage?

A number of legal issues were bundled into this question. The law of levirate marriage (*yibum*) requires a childless widow to marry her late husband's brother.[54] Alternatively, the widow and her brother-in-law could perform the *ḥaliẓah* ceremony, after which she was free to marry outside her husband's family.[55] Often, neither of these options was palatable (or even feasible) to the woman since both required the cooperation of her brother-in-law. Therefore, husbands who anticipated dying without issue often tried to grant their wives a divorce before they died. After the husband's death, his wife would be considered a divorcee rather than a widow and would be able to remarry freely. In the case under discussion, the divorce written for the husband was called into question after his death

53. Paris, Bibliothèque nationale de France, Hébreu, 1391, fol. 33r (see Appendix, source 5, pp. 124–126).

54. Deut. 25:5.

55. Deut. 25:7–10.

because it included a clause ('It is not a promise nor is it a template') that properly belonged in financial contracts (including marriage contracts, *ketubot*).[56] Such a clause was not generally included in a divorce writ and might therefore invalidate it, in which case the widow/ex-wife would still be bound to her levir and could not marry anyone else. However, in this case, the woman considered herself divorced and had already remarried and therefore a secondary question arose regarding the validity of her second marriage.

Isaac Kimḥi's *responsum* explained briefly that small inaccuracies in the language of the divorce writ were a problem only because an ex-husband might try to use them in the future to invalidate the divorce.[57] In this case there was no such concern since the husband was no longer alive, and therefore the divorce was valid. The redundant phrase was clearly a scribal error, the husband's intention to divorce his wife remained clear, and the woman was free to remarry. Abba Mari responded with a far more restrictive approach, ruling that the woman could maintain her second marriage, but only after performing *ḥaliẓah* with her brother-in-law.[58]

A disciple of Kimḥi named Abun Marwan de Meyrargues wrote a third response to the question.[59] The first half of Marwan's *responsum* rehearsed Kimḥi's ruling, implying that Marwan was serving as a voicepiece for his mentor.[60] The second half served as a response to Abba Mari, pleading: "If the [judges] are as stringent as the law could require (*kefi ha-ẓorekh*), the pillars of the world will be toppled; if they are lenient, as [required by] the subject (*kefi ha-nose*), the blessing of good will come upon them."[61] This was a startling declaration, a rare pre-modern example of what Zvi Zohar has called "teleological halakhah," in which a rabbinic decisor openly acknowledged that his legal considerations were influenced by a pre-conceived result that he believed to be

56. Klein translated this phrase, found in a real estate contract, less literally: "it is not to be regarded as mere rhetoric or as perfunctory legal form." Elka Klein, *Hebrew Deeds of Catalan Jews, 1117–1316* (Barcelona, 2004), 26. For *ketubot*, see José Luis Lacave, *Medieval Ketubot from Sefarad* (Jerusalem, 2002), 104.

57. BnF Héb. 1391, fols. 33r–34r.

58. BnF Héb. 1391, fols. 34r–35r (see Appendix, source 6, pp. 126–129).

59. BnF Héb. 1391, fols. 35r–37r (see Appendix, source 7, pp. 129–132). For the little that is known about Jews in Meyrargues, see Danièle Iancu-Agou, *Provincia Judaica: Dictionnaire de géographie historique des juifs en Provence medieval* (Leuven, 2010), 96–97. Another responsum by Marwan de Meyrargues is found in *Teshuvot Ḥakhme Provinẓia (Teshuvot Ḥakhme Provintsya)*, part II, no. 11, ed. Sofer, 338–345.

60. "All of my turns are to the right (cf. bYoma 58b) of... R Isaac... [son of] R Mordekhai" (BnF Héb. 1391, fol. 37r).

61. BnF Héb. 1391, fol. 37r.

morally correct.[62] By extension, Marwan implied that Abba Mari's ruling, although it might be formalistically justified, was morally wrong.

The third extant question addressed to Isaac Kimḥi and to Abba Mari was sent from Marseilles.[63] It concerned "the divorce of our daughter Freida," who was pregnant at the time of her divorce. Her father was anxious for her to remarry as soon as possible after she gave birth, but there were mutterings in Marseilles to the effect that she must wait a longer period. Freida's father was hoping to enlist rabbinic support for the lenient position that would allow Freida to take a new husband as soon as possible.

The signatories on the question were Isaac Marwan ben Jacob *ha-Seniri* and Moses *ha-Do ʾeg* ben Nathan. Isaac Marwan may be identified with a Marseilles businessman by the same name, son of Ferrier Marvan, and he was probably Freida's father.[64] Isaac Marwan died in 1329, and therefore the question must predate that year.[65] Moses *ha-Do ʾeg*, unknown from other sources, was apparently a rabbinic scholar enlisted by Isaac Marvan to compose the sophisticated question.[66] Their dual roles in composing the question are reflected in Isaac Kimḥi's response, which opened by explaining that he could not refuse the request of "our colleague, and also our ruler (*nagid*) and lord."[67]

62. Zvi Zohar, "Teleological Decision-Making in Halakhah: Empirical Examples and General Principles," *Jewish Law Association Studies* 22 (2012): 331–362. Schremer has argued that such pragmatic considerations played a major but unspoken role in medieval rabbinic ruling. Adiel Schremer, *Ma ʿase Rav: Halakhic Decision-Making and the Shaping of Jewish Identity* (Ramat Gan, 2019) (Hebrew).

63. *Teshuvot Ḥakhme Provinẓia (Teshuvot Ḥakhme Provintsya)*, ed. Sofer, no. 52, 171–176.

64. Juliette Sibon, *Les juifs de Marseille au XIVe siècle* (Paris, 2011), 402–405. According to Deut. 3:9, Hermon Mountain was called Siryon by the Sidonites and the Amorites called it Senir. If Senir is taken as a synonym of Siryon, and Siryon is interpreted as armour (*shiryon*), then the cognomen *Seniri* may refer to Isaac ha-Seniri's father Ferrier, whose Occitan name meant ironmonger. Emil Levy, *Provenzalisches Supplement-Wörterbuch* (Leipzig, 1894–1924), 3: 471. A similar interpretation was suggested by Salomon Kahn, "Les Juifs de la sénéchaussée de Beaucaire," *Revue des études juives* 65 (1913): 181–195, at 183. More likely, however, the cognomen was a midrashic reference to his own name, Isaac, since Senir is identified with Isaac in *Shir ha-Shirim Rabbah* 4:3 (ed. Tamar Kadari, Schechter Institute of Jewish Studies, https://schechter.ac.il/midrash/shir-hashirim-raba/). For attempts to interpret *Seniri* as a toponym, with regard to the thirteenth century Hebrew poet Isaac ha-Seniri, see Binyamin Bar-Tikvah, *Liturgical Poems of Rabbi Yitzhak Hasniri* (Ramat-Gan, 1996), 29–40 (Hebrew); Judith Kogel, *Joseph Seniri: Commentary on the Former Prophets* (Leiden, 2014), 10–11.

65. Sibon, *Les juifs de Marseille*, 402–405.

66. Do ʾeg may perhaps be a hebraized corruption of the name Benadig [cf. Isaac ben Immanuel de Lattes, *She ʾelot u-Teshuvot*, ed. Mordechai Tzvi (Max Hermann) Friedländer (Vienna, 1860), 98; Gross, *Gallia Judaica* (Paris, 1897), 382].

67. *Teshuvot Ḥakhme Provinẓia (Teshuvot Ḥakhme Provintsya)*, no. 53, ed. Sofer, 176.

Any divorced woman or widow was required by talmudic law to wait a minimum of ninety days from the end of her marriage before marrying anew. This was to ascertain whether she was pregnant, and if so, whether the first husband or the second was the father. However, according to the Talmud, a widow who was already pregnant or had recently given birth was required to wait a much longer period of two years after the birth of the child.[68] This was to ensure that her newborn was able to nurse until the age of twenty-four months, which the Rabbis took as the standard age for weaning. If the mother were permitted to remarry during that period, she might become pregnant and her milk might dry up. Under normal circumstances, the mother's spouse would be the father of both the child and the foetus, and he would make the effort to ensure that his child was receiving nourishment from other sources. However, in a case of remarriage, the new husband might not be willing to spend money on his wife's child, and he would allow it to starve to death.[69]

The faction taking a stringent approach to this case and applying the 24-month rule to Frieda based itself on the opinion of Rabbi Jacob Tam of Ramerupt.[70] Moses *ha-Do'eg* marshalled opposing sources – Isaac Alfasi, Maimonides, Abraham of Montpellier and Samson of Falaise (brother-in-law of Rabenu Tam) – all of whom had arguably ruled that a divorced mother, unlike a widow, could remarry three months after her divorce.[71]

In his response, Isaac Kimḥi laid out three conflicting opinions held by earlier authorities: that a divorced mother must wait twenty-four months even if her child was nursing from a nursemaid, that she must wait only if she was nursing the child herself, and that she could remarry without concern for the child.[72] He explained that Rabenu Tam aligned himself with the first, most stringent, position. The second, intermediate, position he found inconsistent and unconvincing. Finally, the lenient position, which held that there was no limitation on the remarriage of a divorcée, was the one that Kimḥi considered the most compati-

68. bKetubbot 60a–b.

69. See above, Chapter 4.

70. *Teshuvot Ḥakhme Provinẓia (Teshuvot Ḥakhme Provintsya)*, no. 52, ed. Sofer, 172; Jacob ben Meir Tam, *Sefer ha-Yashar*, no. 11, ed. Shim'on Shelomoh Schlesinger (Jerusalem, 1975), 20.

71. *Teshuvot Ḥakhme Provinẓia (Teshuvot Ḥakhme Provintsya)*, no. 52, ed. Sofer, 174–175. His interpretation of Alfasi and Maimonides was disputed by others, as shown below. Abraham of Montpellier's opinion was quoted by Moses from his commentary on Ketubbot, which is no longer extant. However, the same lenient opinion is found in his commentary on Yevamot 42b, ed. Avigdor Arieli, *Perush Rabenu Avraham min ha-har 'al Yevamot* (Jerusalem, 2000), 100.

72. *Teshuvot Ḥakhme Provinẓia (Teshuvot Ḥakhme Provintsya)*, no. 53, ed. Sofer, 176–180.

ble with the talmudic sources. He did not think that Alfasi and Maimonides could be proven to have endorsed any of these positions. Since several authorities followed the stringent position, and in the absence of explicit support by Alfasi and Maimonides for the lenient position, Kimḥi was reluctant to issue a ruling, but he made it clear that his personal opinion was to permit the mother's remarriage.

By contrast, Abba Mari expressed no doubts.[73] He believed – like Rabenu Tam – that the Talmud did not distinguish between nursing widows and divorcees, that Maimonides thought the same, and that Isaac Marwan's daughter must wait the full twenty-four months before remarrying. Abba Mari's stringent ruling curtailing Freida's freedom to remarry immediately stood in clear opposition to Isaac Kimḥi's lenient approach. As in the previous cases, Abba Mari can be understood to have given more weight to social control of female sexuality while Isaac Kimḥi emerges as inclined towards minimizing the limits placed on women by Jewish marital law.

Abba Mari has been described as a member of the "moderate Maimonidean" camp within medieval Provençal Jewry.[74] His philosophical statements clarify that he was never opposed to Maimonides himself.[75] Abba Mari's halakhic writings bear this out, as they contain numerous references to Maimonides' *Mishneh Torah,* which often serves as the basis for his rulings. Nonetheless, respect for Maimonides does not a moderate make, nor was Maimonides the only influence on Abba Mari's worldview. Throughout his career, Abba Mari made extensive use of works from northern France. The commentaries by Rashi and the Tosafists, particularly Samson of Sens, played a crucial role in shaping Abba Mari's rulings and interpretations. Abba Mari may have been attracted to the anti-rationalist proclivities of the French scholars, but their reputation for talmudic prowess was certainly an important reason for him to admire and emulate the Tosafists. The logical disjunctures in Abba Mari's *responsa* are evidence that he was not guided by a lucid legal philosophy but by a commitment to social concerns and to a sense of textual fidelity that can be loosely identified with legal formalism. When Abba Mari asked rhetorically, "Can the truth be cowardly or

73. *Teshuvot Ḥakhme Provinẓia (Teshuvot Ḥakhme Provintsya),* no. 54, ed. Sofer, 180–184.

74. Stern, *Philosophy and Rabbinic Culture,* 115–122; Gregg Stern, "What Divided the Moderate Maimonidean Scholars of Southern France in 1305?," *Be'erot Yitzhak: Studies in Memory of Isadore Twersky,* ed. Jay M. Harris (Cambridge, MA, 2005), 347–376; Moshe Halbertal, *Concealment and Revelation: Esotericism in Jewish Thought and its Philosophical Implications,* trans. Jackie Feldman (Princeton, 2007), 120–134.

75. Menachem Kellner, *Dogma in Medieval Jewish Thought: From Maimonides to Abravanel* (Oxford, 1986), 73–74.

bashful?," he was asserting that law ought not to bend to the crooked timber of humanity.[76]

Working with a very different set of assumptions, Isaac Kimḥi's *responsa* proceeded resolutely towards conclusions that would, as his disciple Marwan de Meyrargues put it, bring down "the blessing of good." In the context of the questions preserved and discussed here, that good was expressed by consistently ruling for women's freedom to marry as they liked, even when voices in the community and within the legal tradition called for curtailing that freedom.

The series of legal queries sent in parallel to Kimḥi and to Abba Mari is testimony to mixed feelings among the Jews of fourteenth-century Provence. Kimḥi's brand of what might be called legal pragmatism was undoubtedly attractive to many. But there were those who found Abba Mari's traditionalist zealotry and his formalistic interpretation of Jewish law equally compelling. In each of the four cases when Abba Mari's ruling appears alongside the Kimḥis, what was at stake was a woman's freedom to choose a marital partner. Some observers believed that allowing such freedom was a laudable goal, while others feared that public morality hung in the balance. For them, the halakhic approach offered by Abba Mari was precisely what they wanted to hear.[77]

The Web of Jewish Identity in Fourteenth-Century Provence

The preceding chapters have shed some light on the intricate web of influences and tensions that shaped Provençal Jewish communal identity during the first half of the fourteenth century. The very fact that this emerges as a period of intellectual and religious creativity is significant, since historians have tended to perceive it as a time punctuated only by the 1306 expulsion and the Black Death of 1347 onwards. As the sources discussed here clarify, rabbinic scholars were active throughout this period, composing their own works, corresponding with each other, and responding to queries from Jewish communities and individuals in Provence and beyond.

The involvement of communities and laypeople in the legal process is likewise a fact that bears emphasis. Sending a question to a rabbi in order to receive a *responsum* is not an expression of passivity, nor is bringing a legal suit before a Jewish court. These are strategic acts, designed to elicit specific results. The legal forum chosen to hear the case could have a crucial bearing on the ruling, and the

76. *Teshuvot Ḥakhme Provinẓia (Teshuvot Ḥakhme Provintsya)*, no. 64, ed. Sofer, 221.

77. The compelling appeal of legal formalism in the public imagination is noted by Brian Leiter, "Legal Formalism and Legal Realism: What is the Issue?," *Legal Theory* 16 (2010): 111–133, at 112.

identity of the rabbinic respondent to whom people chose to send their question would influence the tenor of the *responsum* it elicited. Questions and suits were crafted with care, their legal claims and citations chosen so that they would strike a very particular chord in the minds of others, and not only in regard to their immediate addressees in the court or the study hall. The social impact of a *responsum* or a court decision within the wider communal context was of great importance, for plaintiffs and judges alike. Jewish legal discourse, particularly in late medieval Provence, was played out on an open (although not a level) field.

The lines of halakhic engagement in Provence had long been drawn in light of geo-cultural allegiances, along a north-south axis. The influence of Iberian rabbinic traditions, particularly from al-Andalus, ran very deep in the Midi, while the Tosafists of northern France had profoundly impacted Provençal rabbinics from the twelfth century onwards. Towards the end of the thirteenth century that axis developed a new resonance when Provence began to absorb clusters of Jews migrating or fleeing from northern France. Settling in the Provençal hinterland as a self-identifying ethnic group, the French arrivals held themselves apart from the existing Provençal communities. The almost inevitable tension between the two Jewish groups sharing the same space in Provence was expressed in cultural and legal terms, and at times through physical violence.

Steering a course among rabbinic traditions from Sefarad and France had become overlaid not only with the demographic strain of the French diaspora in Provence, but also with the enduring challenge posed to Provençal Jews by rationalist philosophy. Scientific and philosophical concepts and terminology had suffused Provençal Jewish culture to a degree that people like Abba Mari ben Moses found dangerous.

This dense and unstable web of interlocking forces formed the fabric of Jewish life in fourteenth-century Provence. That fabric included other components as well – the trades pursued by Jews and their economic practices, the food they ate, the stories they told, the songs they sang and the learned tracts that some of them translated and composed. But the role played by the different aspects of Jewish law (civil, marital and ritual law) in shaping Jewish communal life and culture was central and pervasive.

From the middle of the fourteenth century, plague, isolation and religious persecution caused that fabric to fray. The number of surviving *responsa* and Jewish court decisions dwindles almost to nothing, but the few surviving Halakhic books composed during those difficult years bear testimony to the ways in which those recurring tensions and new challenges continued to shape Jewish law and identity.

CHAPTER SIX

Archiving Culture during the Plague Years

The Black Death arrived in Avignon in September 1347, and did not fully relinquish its hold on the city until the end of the fourteenth century.[1] The demographic impact of the Plague in Avignon has been assessed by historians primarily on the basis of a single impression, that of Louis Heyligen, a Flemish intellectual at the papal court, who said that "at least half the people in Avignon died."[2] More precise data from nearby Carpentras points to a drop of more than 50% in the Jewish population between 1343 and 1400, with a slightly smaller proportion among Christians.[3] A number of Jewish communities in Provence also suffered violent attacks during the same period, but there is no evidence that this happened in Avignon.[4]

1. Edouard Baratier, *La démographie Provençale du XIIe au XVIe siècle* (Paris, 1961), 82–85; Jacques Chiffoleau, *La comptabilité de l'au-delà: les hommes, la mort et la religion dans la region d'Avignon à la fin du moyen âge (vers 1320–vers 1480)* (Rome, 1980), 92–101; Joëlle Rollo-Koster, *Avignon and Its Papacy, 1309–1417: Popes, Institutions, and Society* (Lanham, 2015), 205–207; Ann G. Carmichael, "Plague Persistence in Western Europe: A Hypothesis," *The Medieval Globe* 1 (2014): 157–191, at 171–177.

2. Andries Welkenhuysen, "La peste en Avignon (1348) décrite par un témoin oculaire, Louis Sanctus de Beringen," in *Pascua Mediaevalia: Studies voor Prof. Dr. J.M. de Smet*, ed. R. Lievens, E. van Mingroot and W. Verbeke (Leuven, 1983), 452–492, at 467; Rosemary Horrox, ed. and trans., *The Black Death* (Manchester, 1994), 43. On Heyligen (d. 1361), see Elena Abramov-van Rijk, "Who Was Francesco Landini's Antagonist in His Defense of Ockham?," *Philomusica on-line* 14 (2015): 1–24. See also Heather Para, "Plague, Papacy and Power: The Effect of the Black Death on the Avignon Papacy," *Saber and Scroll* 5 (2016): 7–22. On a Hebrew response to an outbreak of the Plague in Avignon in 1382, see Susan L. Einbinder, *No Place of Rest: Jewish Literature, Expulsion, and the Memory of Medieval France* (Philadelphia, 2009), 112–136.

3. Robert-Henri Bautier, "Feux, population et structure sociale au milieu du XVe siècle: L'exemple de Carpentras," *Annales: Économies, Sociétés, Civilisations* 14 (1959): 255–268.

4. Joseph Shatzmiller, "Les Juifs de Provence pendant la peste noire," *Revue des études juives* 133 (1974): 457–480; Roger S. Kohn, *Les Juifs de la France du nord dans la seconde moitié du XIVe siècle* (Leuven, 1988), 8–12; Tzafrir Barzilay, "The Investigation of the Jews of Savoy on Suspicion of Poisoning Wells: A Reappraisal," *Chidushim* 21 (2019): 114–143 (Hebrew).

The first rabbinic scholar to emerge in Provence after the Black Death was Jacob ben Moses of Bagnols.[5] His writings are preserved in a sole manuscript, housed in the British Library and formerly owned by Leon Botarel and Menaḥem de Lonzano.[6] Jacob of Bagnols is known only from his own work, although a later gloss incorporated into the main text of the manuscript refers to him as "the Nasi, Sen Jacob de Bagnols," a reference which implies that he was a figure of some note.[7] By his own description, Jacob established *yeshivot* in Carpentras and in Avignon, and spent time in Tarascon and Salon-de-Provence.[8]

A memory of the Black Death, in its 1361 iteration, is found in Jacob's account of a dying man's divorce. That year, "the year of the plague," Jacob was present in Salon-de-Provence when a young man named Don Moses ben Nathan de Lançon ordered a divorce writ prepared for his wife – the daughter of Don Solomon Bonjudas Caille – before he died of the plague shortly before the Sabbath.[9] However, after Moses died, it emerged that the scribe had mistakenly written the date of the divorce as 1362 rather than 1361. Jacob explained that the scribe had been confused "because his thoughts were severed[10] for he had suffered many losses at that time because of the Plague."[11]

5. Adolph Neubauer, "Documents inédits: Jacob fils de Moïse de Bagnols," *Revue des études juives* 9 (1884): 51–58.

6. London, British Library, Or. 2705 (cat. no. 551). See Jordan S. Penkower, *Masorah and Text Criticism in the Early Modern Mediterranean: Moses ibn Zabara and Menahem de Lonzano* (Jerusalem, 2014), 80. The manuscript was purchased by the British Library from Moses Wilhelm Shapira in 1884.

7. BL Or. 2705, fol. 57v. This line, first recognized as a later gloss by Zev Farber, caused some confusion among earlier historians. Neubauer, "Jacob fils de Moïse," 51; Zev Farber, "The Development of the Three-Day Limit for Salting," *Milin Ḥavivin* 1 (2005), 38–72, at 68 n102.

8. BL Or. 2705, fol. 202v: "I saw in Avignon"; fol. 209v: "when I was in my academy (*bet midrashi*) in the city of Carpentras." Jacob ben Moses of Bagnols, "Ezrat Nashim," in *Shitat ha-Kadmonim ʿal masekhet Kidushin*, ed. Moshe Yehudah Blau (New York, 1970), 283: "when I established a *yeshivah* for the student in the city of Avignon." Tarascon – Jacob ben Moses of Bagnols, "Ḥibur Isur ve-Heter," in *Shitat ha-Kadmonim ʿal masekhet Ḥulin*, ed. Moshe Yehudah Blau (New York, 1989), 94, 96. As noted by Binyamin Zeʾev Benedikt, *Merkaz ha-Torah be-Provans* (The Torah Center in Provence) (Jerusalem, 1985), 185 n9, Jacob's academies were specifically for young students.

9. "Ezrat Nashim," ed. Blau, 290. This testimony to a Jew who originated in Lançon should be placed alongside Danièle Iancu-Agou, *Provincia Judaica: dictionnaire de géographie historique des juifs en Provence médiévale* (Leuven, 2010), 76.

10. Job 17:11.

11. "Ezrat Nashim," ed. Blau, 290.

This chapter explores the explicit and the more subtle ways in which the Black Death left its imprint on Jewish life and halakhic culture in Provence, as refracted through the writings of Jacob ben Moses of Bagnols.

Writing Halakhah in Late Fourteenth-Century Provence

The British Library manuscript contains two full-length works, followed by a series of shorter passages. The first (fols. 1r–110v), entitled *Mayshir* (Straightener), is devoted to the laws of kosher food.[12] The second work (fols. 111r–196v) comprises the laws of marriage, divorce and menstrual purity, and is named *Ezrat Nashim* (Women's Courtyard).[13]

Jacob's primary goal in writing his compositions was pedagogical, since he felt he lacked the capacity to write anything truly innovative. As he explained in his introduction to *Mayshir*:[14]

> Making books without limit and much study is a wearying of the flesh.[15] It is not right for us to expand on the subject of the laws of slaughtering, for the Ge᾿onim have already said, at great length, all that can [be said], and any addition would be inappropriate (*lo yikhshar*).

In *Ezrat Nashim,* however, he shed more light on the intellectual and religious context of his work:[16]

> I judge some of my contemporaries favourably, though they do not issue the words of the King.[17] The vicissitudes that daily threaten and speedily come upon us, the riots and terrors and great wars that – for our errors and sins –

12. BL Or. 2705, fol. 2v. This section was published as "Ḥibur Isur ve-Heter" in *Shitat ha-Kadmonim ʿal masekhet Ḥulin,* ed. Blau, 9–137. The title may have been borrowed from Samuel ha-Nagid, *Ben Mishle* (After Proverbs), ed. Shraga Abramson (Tel Aviv, 1948), 238 (proverb 830): "Straightening (*mayshir*) a devious man (*neloz davar,* cf. Proverbs 14:2) with words of rebuke is like planting a sapling in the earth."

13. Published as "Ezrat Nashim" in *Shitat ha-Kadmonim ʿal masekhet Kidushin,* ed. Blau, 271–364.

14. BL Or. 2705, fol. 2v; "Ḥibur Isur ve-Heter," ed. Blau, 10.

15. Ecclesiastes 12:12.

16. "Ezrat Nashim," ed. Blau, 272; see also Neubauer, "Jacob fils de Moise," 54. He revisited this theme elsewhere – "Ḥibur Isur ve-Heter," ed. Blau, 85.

17. Cf. Esther 1:19.

> befall us lower beings from God, have turned their hearts backward,[18] [preventing them] from eating the fatty meat – the discussions of Abaye and Rava,[19] and persimmon,[20] honey, oil and balm – codified law.
>
> For others, the [desire for] power and argument blinds the eyes of the clear-sighted and twists the words of the righteous.[21]
>
> Some find the Oral Law and its battle to be boring, and it is enough for them [to accept] the ruling (*pesak*) of the rabbis ...
>
> Some of them choose external wisdom, the books of Aristotle and the other philosophers. They forget the Torah of our holy Sages, and they shirk everything but the basic principles [of the law]. When a practical question of forbidden mixtures comes into their hands, they are mystified by it. So too with a woman's betrothal and *ketubah*... They stand and do not reply,[22] and they clap their hands to their mouths.[23] Therefore, I decided to build a small house, and I named it *Ezrat Nashim*.

Jacob identified four groups of his contemporaries whose behaviour had precipitated a decline in the study of Halakhah. For the first group, the general circumstances of the time – presumably, the Plague and the violence it brought in its wake – had turned them away from intellectual endeavours altogether. The three remaining factions continued to devote time and energy to their studies despite those calamities, but they did not direct their resources towards intensive halakhic study. One group is described laconically as preferring "power and argument (*nitsuaḥ*)." The appetite for argumentation was not a positive trait in his eyes.[24] Jacob may have been thinking of rabbinic scholars whose study consisted of casuistry and intellectual fireworks and who intended to impress their audience by flummoxing their opponents in intellectual debate.[25] Such learning, Jacob

18. I Kings 18:37.
19. bSukkah 28a, signifying the intricate legal discussions of the Talmud.
20. Cf. Rashi II Kings 20:13.
21. Exodus 23:8.
22. Job 32:16.
23. Job 29:9.
24. Cf. Falaquera's reference to the middle type of soul "that finds pleasure in thought and argument," as opposed to the highest type of soul "that finds pleasure in wisdom and knowledge of truth." Henry Malter, "Shem Tob ben Joseph Palquera, II. His Treatise of the Dream," *Jewish Quarterly Review* N.S. 1 (1911): 451–500, at 484. Elsewhere, Falaquera identified the intermediate class of people with political leaders. Ludwig Venetianer, *Das Buch der Grade von Schemtob b. Joseph ibn Falaquera* (Berlin, 1894), 43.
25. For similar criticism of rabbinic scholars in the thirteenth century, see Haym Soloveitchik, "Three Themes in the Sefer Hasidim," *AJS Review* 1 (1976): 311–357, at 339–354.

implied, was concerned only with self-aggrandizement, and although it was deeply engaged with Halakhah, it would not produce practical knowledge.

Another group went to the other extreme, dispensing altogether with the intricacies of talmudic study and relying entirely on the rulings of others. Their passivity enraged Jacob, although it is unclear whether the reliance he had in mind was upon texts with halakhic decisions or the authority of a living rabbi.[26]

Finally, Jacob turned to "the philosophers", whom he identified primarily by their association with the Aristotelian corpus. This group preferred to spend its time on "external wisdom," but when it did study Jewish law, it spurned the detailed analysis found in most of rabbinic literature and demanded a conceptualized system of basic principles.[27] Jacob complained that such abstract knowledge could not provide answers to the questions of practical law that arose daily in Jewish life.

The central focus of Jacob's critique was not the infiltration of foreign ideas. Jacob ben Moses was not opposed to philosophy, although he was by no means its strongest advocate. *Yesod ha-Hashgaḥah* (The Foundation of Providence), found in the same manuscript, is a short composition in rhyming prose on the Thirteen Divine Attributes and the celestial spheres, based on the works of Maimonides and other Jewish rationalists.[28] The work reveals that Jacob ben Moses was quite well read in the Jewish philosophy of his time, even citing a term coined by Gersonides (Levi ben Gershom, d. 1344).[29] The poem ends with an explanation that the work was an act of piety and thanksgiving:

> In the year 5117 AM (1357 CE), I saw wonders. Ten days later, I again saw terrible things. Ten days later, for a third time, future events were

26. For reliance on written works of Halakhah in fourteenth-century Castile, see Judah Galinsky, "Ashkenazim in Sefarad: The Rosh and the Tur on the Codification of Jewish Law," *Jewish Law Annual* 16 (2006): 3–23 (esp. 13–19); Judah Galinsky, "On Popular Halakhic Literature and the Jewish Reading Audience in Fourteenth-Century Spain," *Jewish Quarterly Review* 98 (2008): 305–327.

27. For a similar approach in fourteenth-century Iberia, see Ari Ackerman, "Hasdai Crescas on the Philosophic Foundation of Codification," *AJS Review* 37 (2013): 315–331; Yoel Marciano, *Sages of Spain in the Eye of the Storm: Jewish Scholars of Late Medieval Spain* (Jerusalem, 2019), 169–177 (Hebrew).

28. BL Or. 2705, fols. 197r–199v (see Appendix, source 8, pp. 132–133).

29. The term "*geshem bilti shomer temunato* (a body that does not keep its shape)" (BL Or. 2705, fol. 198v) is found in Gersonides' *Wars of the Lord* 5.1.28 (unpublished) and 6.2.7 (trans. Seymour Feldman [Philadelphia, 1984–1999], 3: 442), and in his commentary on Genesis 1:1 and Proverbs 30:1. On this term see Ruth Glasner, "The Early Stages in the Evolution of Gersonides' 'The Wars of the Lord,'" *Jewish Quarterly Review* 87 (1996): 1–46, at 35–39; Ruth Glasner, *Gersonides: A Portrait of a Fourteenth-Century Philosopher-Scientist* (Oxford, 2015), 44–46. I am grateful to Ofer Elior and Eliezer Davidovitch for their help.

> revealed to me ... I vowed to write a short composition, made of stanzas and rhymes, balanced on the scales of my thoughts, with a short commentary to explain the meaning of the stanzas so that the reader can run through them. [The stanzas] point to God's providence over His fearers, saving them from the evil that ought to befall them according to the (astrological) system that He set in place to run the world.[30] Therefore I titled it *Yesod ha-Hashgaḥah*. Blessed is God who performed a miracle for me. May God perform miracles and wonders for us and for His people of Israel, Amen Selah.[31]

"The enemy" referenced here may have been Arnaud de Cervola and his mercenaries, who ravaged Avignon and its surroundings in the spring of 1357.[32] Perhaps Jacob, forewarned by his visions, was able to leave the city with his family and to avoid the pillaging and burning. A belief in the capacity of dreams to convey true information about the future was widely accepted among the medieval Jewish philosophers with whose writings Jacob was familiar.[33]

British Library, Or. ms. 2705 ends with a series of short discussions appended by Jacob ben Moses to his full-length works. Most of them stemmed, according to his testimony, from questions posed to him by people who crossed his path in the *yeshivot* of Avignon and Carpentras. The first passage was introduced with his description (cited at the beginning of this chapter) of teaching his students in Avignon a complex talmudic passage with the medieval commentaries of Rashi and Joseph ibn Megas. While he was thus engaged, "a text was brought to me, written by a philosopher who was said to be in Rome, and I was asked to explain it for it was difficult and very obscure."[34] The philosopher from Rome was Judah Romano, and the passage is found at the end of Romano's commentary on the

30. On the tenacious belief by Provençal Jews that all of life's misfortunes were determined by the stars, see Dov Schwartz, *Studies on Astral Magic in Medieval Jewish Thought*, trans. David Louvish and Batya Stein (Leiden, 2005), 124–165.

31. BL Or. 2705, fol. 199v.

32. Norman Housley, "The Mercenary Companies, the Papacy, and the Crusades, 1356–1378," *Traditio* 38 (1982): 253–280; Kenneth Fowler, *Medieval Mercenaries* (Oxford, 2001), 2; Nicole Archambeau, "Miraculous Healing for the Warrior Soul: Transforming Fear, Violence, and Shame in Fourteenth-Century Provence," *Historical Reflections* 41 (2015): 14–27; Rollo-Koster, *Avignon and its Papacy*, 98–99.

33. Howard Kreisel, *Prophecy: The History of an Idea in Medieval Jewish Philosophy* (Dordrecht, 2001), 326–390; Hagar Kahana-Smilansky, "The Mental Faculties and the Psychology of Sleep and Dreams," in *Science in Medieval Jewish Cultures*, ed. Gad Freudenthal (Cambridge, 2011), 230–254.

34. BL Or. 2705, fol. 200r (see Appendix, source 9, pp. 133–135).

Genesis story.[35] It provides two explanations for the prodigious longevity of the biblical figures recorded in the first chapters of Genesis, a topic that perplexed many medieval Jewish thinkers.[36] The first explanation followed "the natural scientists" (*ba'ale ha-teva*): the high quality of the air when the world was young, coupled with the healthy lifestyles of the early humans "who behaved according to reason and good advice and did not pursue the extravagances which kill the body before its time," provided optimal conditions for a long life. The second explanation, which he attributed to "the men of faith and Torah," claimed that the decreasing longevity of man was paradoxically a sign of increasing proximity to the eschatological Afterlife.

This passage by Romano was adapted from sections in the *Summa theologiae* by Thomas Aquinas.[37] Jacob prepared a lengthy word-by-word explanation of the passage.[38] He then quoted another passage, attributed to Plato, that was similarly presented to him in Avignon.[39] This second passage described how the wise person ought to pray – by appealing to divine justice and wisdom rather

35. Caterina Rigo, "The Be'urim on the Bible of R. Yehudah Romano: The Philosophical Method which Comes Out of Them, Their Sources in the Jewish Philosophy and in the Christian Scholasticism" (PhD diss., Hebrew University of Jerusalem, 1996), part 2 (appendix), 44 (Hebrew). On Romano's biblical commentary see Giuseppe Sermoneta, "The Commentary to the First Weekly Reading in Genesis by Judah Romano, and Its Sources," in *Proceedings of the Fourth World Congress of Jewish Studies* (Jerusalem, 1965), 2: 341–342 (Hebrew); Rigo, "The Be'urim on the Bible of R. Yehudah Romano," part 1, 61–67; Saverio Campanini, "Latin into Hebrew (and Back): Flavius Mithridates and His Latin Translations from Judah Romano," in *Latin into Hebrew: Texts and Studies*, vol. 2: *Texts in Contexts*, ed. Alexander Fidora, Harvey J. Hames and Yossef Schwartz (Leiden, 2013), 161–193. Halbertal was the first to suggest that Romano was the author of the passage presented to Jacob of Bagnols. Moshe Halbertal, *Between Torah and Wisdom: Rabbi Menachem ha-Meiri and the Maimonidean Halakhists in Provence* (Jerusalem, 2000), 150 n55 (Hebrew).

36. Frank Talmage, *Apples of Gold in Settings of Silver: Studies in Medieval Jewish Exegesis and Polemics*, ed. Barry Dov Walfish (Toronto, 1999), 49–62; Daniel Lasker, "The Longevity of the Ancients – Faith and Reason in Medieval Jewish Thought," *Diné Israel* 26–27 (2009–2010): 49–65 (Hebrew). My thanks to Eric Lawee for these references. Immanuel of Rome, who borrowed many ideas from Romano without acknowledgement, enthusiastically adopted and amplified the first explanation. David Goldstein, "Longevity, the Rainbow, and Immanuel of Rome," *Hebrew Union College Annual* 42 (1971): 243–250.

37. Rigo, "The Be'urim on the Bible," 1: 61–67; Thomas Aquinas, *Summa theologiae* 1a, 102, 2 and 4 (*Summa theologiae: Latin Text and English Translation*, Blackfriars Edition [London; New York, 1964–1981], 13: 188–195).

38. BL Or. 2705, fols. 200r–202v.

39. BL Or. 2705, fols. 202v–203v (see Appendix, source 10, pp. 135–137).

than by relying on divine mercy.[40] Furthermore, his prayers to God should concern only those matters controlled by God and not "those belonging to the other types," for which a man must pray to "His creations that are below Him." Ever the pedagogue, Jacob ben Moses spiced his explanations with biblical and rabbinic texts even as he adapted the Platonic text to a Jewish audience – a process begun by the unidentified translator who produced the Hebrew version that Jacob read. For Jacob, the person addressed by the passage was not merely wise, since such a person "could be enlightened and wise and could conceive intense, supernal matters, yet he is not meticulous in avoiding sin before God, may He be blessed" and therefore could not rely upon divine grace.[41] "The creations that are below Him," to whom people were encouraged to turn for matters that did not concern God, were apparently a veiled reference to the gods of the Underworld who deserved the prayers of the pious, according to Plato's original formulation.[42] Yet in Jacob's interpretation this became a reference to the astrological power of the stars, which affect the lives of most humans but not "the wise man who becomes unified in some way with the Higher One protecting."[43] This distinction accorded much better with the religious worldview of medieval Provençal Jews.[44] Nevertheless, in each of his philosophical forays, Jacob emphasized that it was a limited enterprise undertaken only because he was asked to explain a difficult text, implying that otherwise his time would have been better spent teaching the Talmud.[45]

As expressed in the introductions to his halakhic works, the crucial question for Jacob of Bagnols was whether a Jew in fourteenth-century Provence was capable of arriving at the correct solution to a problem of practical law that might arise over the course of his life. His goal was to empower his readers with the

40. I have not located this precise passage in any authentic or pseudepigraphic Platonic writings and I am grateful to Charles Manekin and Ruediger Arnzen for their help in the search. However, it seems to echo Plato, *Laws*, 687e and 717a–c, trans. R.G. Bury (Cambridge, MA, 1926), 1: 205 and 297–299. I am grateful to Fred Unwalla for locating the source in the Laws.

41. BL Or. 2705, fol. 203r.

42. Plato, *Laws*, 717b.

43. BL Or. 2705, fol. 203v. Cf. Ecclesiastes 5:7.

44. On the ability of pious individuals to overcome the astrological powers, according to Provençal Jewish thinkers, see, e.g., Gersonides, *The Wars of the Lord* 4.6, trans. Feldman, 2: 183–184; Gad Freudenthal and Resianne Fontaine, "Gersonides on the Dis-/order of the Sublunar World and on Providence," *Aleph* 12 (2012): 299–328.

45. BL Or. 2705, fol. 202v: "Without question, a single volume would be insufficient to contain an expansion beyond the hints in the explanation that I have given ... and a person who understands will understand it"; fol. 203v: "This is a philosophical inquiry that is not worth expanding upon, and a person who understands will understand it."

information required to reach independent halakhic decisions. He tried to strike a balance between discussion of the talmudic sources, interpretations and opinions of medieval rabbinic authorities, and the traditions and customs of different Jewish communities. The geographically local audience he intended for his book is reflected by the frequent mention of Avignon, or more generally Provence (*Provinẓia*), as opposed to Narbonne and "the other bank of the Rhône" (*ʿever Rodna*).[46] The names of several prominent authorities appear with great frequency throughout Jacob's works – Alfasi, Rashi, Maimonides, Rabad of Posquières – but Jacob used other literary sources without acknowledgement. *Sefer Mayshir* contains numerous verbatim citations from regional works like Meir ben Simeon Meʿili of Narbonne's *Sefer ha-Meʾorot* and Menaḥem ha-Meʾiri of Perpignan's *Bet ha-Beḥirah*.[47]

Nevertheless, the works contain a number of original passages in which Jacob ben Moses described his own decision process. For example, when discussing the physical symptoms of terminal disease in an animal's kidney that would render the entire animal non-kosher, Jacob recounted the following incident:[48]

> We investigated this in one case that occurred in the castrum of Salon (*migdol Shiloh*), with a ewe that was slaughtered and inspected during the intermediate days of the Sukkot festival.[49] It was found to be kosher and was sold in its entirety to the members of our community. When the porger came to remove [the sciatic nerve from] its thigh,[50] he removed the kidney and found a small defect and he saw three drops of pure water that dripped from it. When he saw that defect, which was on the smooth part of the kidney

46. For example, Jacob of Bagnols, "Ḥibur Isur ve-Heter," ed. Blau, 30. In one place ("Ḥibur Isur ve-Heter," 21), Jacob referred to "Narbonne and its environs until the Vidourle river."

47. As noted by Blau in his notes on the text. Examples: "Ḥibur Isur ve-Heter," 27 = *Sefer ha-Meorot* Ḥullin, ed. Blau, 153; "Ḥibur Isur ve-Heter," 38 = ha-Meʾiri, *Bet ha-Beḥirah*, Ḥullin 55a. "Ḥibur Isur ve-Heter," 56 = Aaron ha-Kohen of Narbonne (Lunel), *Sefer Orḥot Hayyim*, II (Berlin, 1902), 335. Ha-Meʾiri is cited explicitly at "Ḥibur Isur ve-Heter," 102 and 106.

48. "Ḥibur Isur ve-Heter," ed. Blau, 38.

49. On the kosher abattoir in Salon, see Monique Wernham, *La communauté juive de Salon-de-Provence d'aprés les actes notaries 1391–1435* (Toronto, 1987), 50–52.

50. In accordance with Genesis 32:33, an expert butcher would remove the forbidden sinews from a slaughtered animal's hindquarters. This expert was called *menaker* in Hebrew and porger in modern British Jewish English ("porger, n." OED Online, March 2020, Oxford University Press, https://www.oed.com/view/Entry/266002, accessed May 17, 2020).

> towards its top, he was concerned and showed the kidney to several of our colleagues there. They were concerned by the defect and they brought it to me. I took my knife and opened the kidney, cutting into two pieces, and found the entire kidney complete, clean of any pus or water. I showed them the words of the law in the Talmud ...

This story underscores Jacob's role as a teacher, not only for his formal students, but for the community as a whole. The porger who raised concerns about the kosher status of the meat acted on the basis of his professional training and experience, but he was not a scholar. Jacob's "colleagues" were probably local rabbinic scholars, but they were not versed in these practical laws.[51] When they turned to Jacob, he began by teaching them the basic sources in the Talmud, as well as dissecting the questionable kidney – a step that neither the porger nor the "colleagues" had thought to take.

In Jacob's telling, the story is one of halakhic heroism – he was able to rehabilitate what had seemed to be non-kosher meat, and thus to save the festival banquets of an entire community. But when placed alongside a similar instance that occurred a century earlier in Narbonne, the story seems quite different:[52]

> There was a case in Narbonne of an animal with a diseased kidney. Part of the kidney looked like dead meat, and the defect reached to the hilum (*ḥariẓ*), but it did not reach the white part that is the hilum itself – that is, the white inside the kidney. All of the sages in the city agreed that it was permitted.

The physical condition of the kidney in thirteenth-century Narbonne was more dire than the kidney in fourteenth-century Salon, yet in the earlier case the entire local rabbinic leadership agreed to permit the meat, while in Jacob's time he was the lone voice for leniency. The erosion in halakhic knowledge during the intervening century led from ignorance to stringency.

More often, though, Jacob's position was more stringent than that of his contemporaries, people he considered unworthy of halakhic decision-making. He

51. Elsewhere ("Ezrat Nashim," ed. Blau, 308, 318) Jacob described legal documents that he drew up in Salon together with the local scholars (*ḥakhamim*) and elders (*zekenim*).

52. Aharon ha-Kohen of Narbonne (Lunel), *Sefer Orḥot Hayyim*, vol. 2 ed. Moses Schlesinger (Berlin, 1902), 420 in the name of his grandfather, David ha-Kohen. Aaron of Narbonne left Narbonne in the exile of 1306 and moved to Majorca, where he lived until at least 1313. Judah Galinsky, "Of Exile and Halakhah: Fourteenth-Century Spanish Halakhic Literature and the Works of the French Exiles Aaron ha-Kohen and Jeruham b. Meshulam," *Jewish History* 22 (2008): 81–96. Aharon's grandfather presumably lived around the middle of the thirteenth century.

recounted in detail an incident that he became involved with.[53] A Tarascon Jew purchased an unborn calf whose mother had been slaughtered. Under those circumstances, the calf did not require slaughtering since it was considered biologically attached to its mother that had been slaughtered. However, different opinions existed regarding the application of other laws. The purchaser asked Jacob whether the calf required porging to remove the sciatic nerve and the forbidden parts of fat, and he replied in the affirmative.

> Then [the purchaser] went to one of the leaders of that community, who had studied Torah under the guidance of scholars, and asked him about the status of this calf. [The leader] immediately permitted it to him without porging any nerves or fat. When I heard this, I stood trembling in shock. I revealed the secret to one of my friends who lived there, and he had a word with that decisor about the error he had made. Then [the leader] studied the rulings of the sages, retracted his decision and sent to [the purchaser saying] that he should porge it. If even great scholars of Torah with sound reasoning can sometimes be mistaken in their rulings – whether due to the distractions of their possessions ... or for any other reason – all the more so can those who are lesser than [such scholars], whose waist is thinner than their little finger.

Jacob's rhetoric was harsh and clear – even the greatest scholars of his generation were less than a pale reflection of earlier times, and their lenient rulings were not the result of courageous leadership but of sheer ignorance.

Jacob's dissatisfaction with the religious and intellectual standards of his contemporaries, lay and leaders alike, emerges clearly throughout his works. In introducing the prohibition against cheese produced by Gentiles, he commented:[54]

> I knew that the men of our time would not see my discussion favourably, for it forbids something that has become a permitted practice in some places. But I will not stray right or left from what our predecessors forbade, and will mention briefly what must be avoided, and let justice pierce the mountain.[55]

53. "Ḥibur Isur ve-Heter," ed. Blau, 94.

54. "Ḥibur Isur ve-Heter," ed. Blau, 114.

55. A rabbinic expression first found in tSanhedrin 1:2, signifying pure justice unadulterated by extraneous considerations.

Child Marriage

Although he could be harshly critical of his contemporaries, there were some local practices that Jacob ben Moses was prepared to defend. His discussion of child marriage in Provence is an important example. According to rabbinic law, a pre-pubescent girl (under twelve years of age) could be given in marriage by her father, and such a marriage was fully binding.[56] If her father was not alive, her mother or brothers could supervise her marriage, in which case the marriage was only provisionally binding and she could repudiate it on reaching majority.[57] The father of a young boy, by contrast, did not have similar authority to marry off his son. While the halakhic mainstream used puberty (or the standard age of thirteen, for men) as the transition point between childhood and adulthood, some rabbinic texts treat a nine-year-old boy as a legal adult for some issues, including marriage – that is, child marriage is invalid, but a nine year old was no longer a child.[58] Strictly speaking, therefore, the marriage of an underage male would not be recognized according to any opinion in the rabbinic tradition. A highly influential statement of the law in this context was that of Maimonides: "It is forbidden to marry a woman to a minor (*katan*), because this is similar to prostitution."[59]

The Christian legal situation bore some similarity to Jewish law on this point. Canon law did not allow betrothal or marriage without consent but, according to Gratian and others, consent could be given from the age of seven.[60] According to Alexander III (pope 1159–1181), a marriage contracted after the age of seven and consummated after puberty would become fully valid, but before that final

56. Eve Krakowski, *Coming of Age in Medieval Egypt: Female Adolescence, Jewish Law, and Ordinary Culture* (Princeton, 2018), 113–141.

57. Aharon Shemesh and Moshe Halbertal, "The Me'un (Refusal): The Complex History of a Halakhic Anomaly," *Tarbiz* 82 (2014): 377–393 (Hebrew).

58. Yitzhak Dov Gilat, *Yad le-Gilat (In Memorium): Collected Essays*, ed. Israel Zvi Gilat and Israel M. Ta-Shma (Jerusalem, 2002), 23–49 (Hebrew); Leib Moscovitz, "The Actions of a Minor are a Nullity? Some Observations on the Legal Capacity of Minors in Rabbinic Law," *Jewish Law Annual* 17 (2007): 63–126.

59. Maimonides, *Mishneh Torah*, ed. Shabse Frankel (Jerusalem, 1975–2002), Laws of Forbidden Intercourse 21:25.

60. James A. Brundage, *Law, Sex, and Christian Society in Medieval Europe* (Chicago, 1987), 238; Jessica Goldberg, "The Legal Persona of the Child in Gratian's Decretum," *Bulletin of Medieval Canon Law* 24 (2000): 10–53. Among later legists, puberty became the defining factor for consent. Willy Onclin, "L'âge requis pour le mariage dans la doctrine canonique médiévale," in *Proceedings of the Second International Congress of Medieval Canon Law* (Vatican City, 1965), 237–247.

stage of consummation the marriage could be cancelled for various reasons.[61] In practice, canon law notwithstanding, marriage of young boys (and girls) existed in European Christian society throughout the Middle Ages, although it was not common.[62] Similarly, despite the legal problems involved, various Jewish communities through history chose to marry off their sons and daughters before the legal age of majority.[63] One of the talmudic sources that could be marshalled to justify that practice is a *baraita* (Tannaitic statement not included in the Mishnah) cited twice in the Babylonian Talmud which praises the man who "marries his children off close to their time (*samukh le-pirkan*)."[64] According to Rashi (d. 1105), this meant six months or a year before the age of majority, while this period was reduced by Jonathan of Lunel, a twelfth-century commentator, who spoke of "half a year or two months."[65] The French Tosafists, however, read it as an unqualified endorsement of child marriage for boys.[66] According to their reading of the network of talmudic statements, an under-age boy's marriage was not legally valid, but it was ethically viable.[67]

61. *Liber Extra* 2.4.8, in *Corpus Iuris Canonici,* ed. Emil Friedberg (Leipzig, 1881), vol. 2, col. 675 (Alexander III to Bishop of Bath); Charles Donahue Jr., *Law, Marriage and Society in the Later Middle Ages* (Cambridge, 2007), 20–21.

62. Juliette M. Turlan, "Recherches sur le mariage dans la pratique coutumière (XIIe–XVIe s.)," *Revue historique de droit français et étranger,* 4e sér., 34 (1957): 477–528; Anne J. Duggan, "The Effect of Alexander III's 'Rules on the Formation of Marriage' in Angevin England," *Anglo-Norman Studies* 33 (2010): 1–22; Corinne Wieben, "Unwilling Grooms in Fourteenth-Century Lucca," *Journal of Family History* 40 (2015): 263–276. Child grooms in Islamic society seem to have been very rare during the Middle Ages, and they are similarly absent from Jewish communities in Islamic lands. Carolyn G. Baugh, *Minor Marriage in Early Islamic Law* (Leiden, 2017), 148; S.D. Goitein, *A Mediterranean Society: The Jewish Communities of the Arab World as Portrayed in the Documents of the Cairo Geniza* (Berkeley, 1967–1993), 3: 76–79.

63. Krakowski, *Coming of Age,* 134–140; Shaul Stampfer, *Families, Rabbis and Education: Traditional Jewish Society in Nineteenth-Century Eastern Europe* (Oxford, 2010), 7–25 ("The Social Implications of Very Early Marriage").

64. bYevamot 62b, bSanhedrin 76b. The phrase "*samukh le-pirkan*" appears in tKippurim 4:2, *Tosefta,* ed. Saul Lieberman (New York, 1955–1988), 249, and was interpreted by the Palestinian Talmud (pYoma 8:3, 45a) as age 9 or 10.

65. Rashi, bSanhedrin 76b, s.v. *samukh le-pirkan shani;* Jonathan of Lunel, in *Sanhedri Gedolah le-masekhet Sanhedrin* (Jerusalem, 1968–2018), 2: 142 (to Sanhedrin 76b). Menaḥem ha-Me'iri reported that his teachers explained that the age intended by the Talmud was close to eighteen. Ha-Me'iri, *Bet ha-Beḥirah 'al masekhet Sanhedrin,* ed. Avraham Sofer (Schreiber) (Jerusalem, 1965), 283.

66. *Tosafot* Yevamot 62b, s.v. *samukh; Tosafot* Sanhedrin 76b, s.v. *samukh;* Asher ben Yehiel, *Tosafot Rosh,* ed. Shraga Vilman (Brooklyn, 1996), Yevamot 62b and Sanhedrin 76b.

67. See also Isaac ben Jacob of Corbeil, *Sefer Mitzvot Katan* (Cremona, 1556), no. 183.

From the early thirteenth century onwards, a number of sources from Languedoc and Provence fleshed out legal justifications for the marriage of child grooms:[68]

> The custom in Arles and throughout Provence is that, when marrying off their minor sons, they separate [the bride and groom] from each other until they grow older. Then [after the children reach majority] they have another wedding ceremony, and they are required to perform another betrothal.

The impetus for this custom and its aggressive promotion among the sages of Provence apparently came from northern France. An unsigned *responsum* from the fourteenth century claimed that it was permissible to marry children to each other and to allow them to live together from the outset:[69]

> And this is the custom in many places in Provence, on the basis of the French rabbis and of the sage Don Profiag of Salon. I showed him what I had written and he rejoiced. The sage Rabbi Judah ben Kalonymos of Lunel betrothed his daughter to a child and did not separate them.[70]

This custom provoked the ire of Catalonian rabbis. Solomon ben Abraham ibn Adret wrote that marrying off minors "is forbidden for several reasons" and recalled berating a family that arranged such a marriage.[71] Peretz ha-Kohen, son

68. *Teshuvot Ḥakhme Provinẓia (Teshuvot Ḥakhme Provintsya)* (*Responsa* of the Sages of Provence), no. 31, ed. Abraham Sofer (Schreiber) (Jerusalem, 1967), 123–124; Oxford, Bodleian Library, Opp. Add. 4°127, fol. 111v. A similar position was attributed to Solomon ben Abraham of Montpellier in Bezalel ben Abraham Ashkenazi, *Shitah Mekubetset (Ketubot)* (Constantinople, 1738), 90a. On Solomon of Montpellier and his disciple Jonah of Gerona, see Bernard Septimus, "Piety and Power in Thirteenth-Century Catalonia," in *Studies in Medieval Jewish History and Literature*, vol. 1, ed. Isadore Twersky (Cambridge, 1979), 197–230.

69. *Teshuvot Ḥakhme Provinẓia (Teshuvot Ḥakhme Provintsya)*, no. 32, ed. Sofer, 125; Bodleian Opp. Add. 4°127, fol. 111v–112r.

70. Judah ben Kalonymos of Lunel wrote a *responsum* in *Teshuvot Ḥakhme Provinẓia (Teshuvot Ḥakhme Provintsya)*, ed. Sofer, no. 17 in the closing years of the thirteenth century. He may have been the brother of Kalonymos ben Kalonymos, as implied by Joseph Shatzmiller, "Minor Epistle of Apology of Rabbi Kalonymos ben Kalonymos," *Sefunot* 10 (1966), 22. Don Profiag [Bodleian Opp. Add. 4°127: Porfi] of Salon might be Don Porfiag Moses, who purchased a copy of the *Guide of the Perplexed* in Salon in 1344, according to Cambridge, University Library, Add. 2668, fol. 101r.

71. Solomon ben Abraham ibn Adret, *She᾿elot u-Teshuvot*, 1: no. 803 and 4: no. 207, ed. Aharon Zaleznik (Jerusalem, 1997–2005), 1: 372 and 4: 107.

of Isaac ha-Kohen of Manosque and rabbi of Barcelona, issued a public statement on the topic:[72]

> This is the letter sent by Rabbi Peretz Kohen about a five-year-old boy who betrothed a girl with her father's knowledge. You should know that the betrothal of a boy is invalid even if he understands the meaning of marriage ... The custom of Provence, where they do this, is a foolish custom that was created by arrogant people ...

Despite opposition to the custom, Jacob ben Moses testified that child marriage was very common:[73]

> The custom has spread to most places in this land of Provence, including Avignon, of marrying a young boy to a wife. They treat him like a grown man in all respects – betrothal (*kiddushin*), the wedding blessings, and the *ketubah* (marriage contract) – and when he grows to be thirteen years and one day, they renew a second marriage which is called *renos*. A number of years ago, when I established an academy for students in Avignon, I attended such second weddings more times than I can count. Some of the sages in that city would say that [the groom] needed to perform the betrothal a second time, and that the seven wedding blessings (*sheva berakhot*) must be recited – besides the blessings recited when he was a child. Other sages would say that the groom must perform the betrothal and give the *kiddushin* [ring] to his wife, but that the seven blessings should not be recited. Yet others said that the seven blessings should be recited, but the groom need not give the *kiddushin*. A huge argument would erupt between them. If this argument had erupted once or twice, I would have kept my peace. But, as my soul lives, it happened there and elsewhere too many times to count.

Jacob himself believed that no public ceremony was required at all. However, since the Talmud ruled that the optional components of a minor's marriage contract were not enforceable, upon reaching the age of thirteen the husband should be encouraged to reconfirm the full sum promised in his original *ketubah*.[74] Jacob

72. Amsterdam, Portugees Israëlitisch Seminarium Ets Haim, ms. EH 47 A 31, fourth foliation, fol. 41r, published in Moshe Yehudah Blau, *Shitat ha-Kadmonim ʿal masekhet Nazir*, ed. Moshe Yehudah Blau (New York, 1972), 11.

73. "Ezrat Nashim," ed. Blau, 283.

74. bKetubot 90a. For a short explanation of the *ketubah* and *tosefet*, see Elka Klein, "The Widow's Portion: Law, Custom, and Marital Property among Medieval Catalan Jews," *Viator* 31 (2000): 147–164, at 149.

then copied out the text of a court deed for just such an occasion, that was often appended to the original *ketubah* when the groom reached majority.[75]

The lack of quantitative data, caused in part by the fact that Jewish marriage contracts make no mention of age, hampers any systematic analysis of age-at-marriage patterns among Provençal Jews. Latin documents from late medieval Provence and Roussillon, which occasionally do provide such information, reflect an average age at marriage for Jewish men and women of around 15 years.[76] The rabbinic sources discussed here make it clear that, from the thirteenth century onwards, a discernable number of weddings took place at a much earlier stage – certainly before the age of twelve and, according to Peretz ha-Kohen, as early as five. These early marriages were often (as Jacob ben Moses wrote, "more times than I can count") followed by a second marriage years later, a pattern that was preserved with some changes by Provençal Jews for centuries. Records from seventeeth and eighteenth-century Avignon and Carpentras reveal that engagements (*kiddushin*, or *cadessar* in the French records) were routinely formed between children in their early teens (aged twelve or thirteen), with marriages taking place many years later.[77]

Historians and demographers have offered many different rationales for child marriage, some more universal than others.[78] It is difficult to determine the

75. "Ezrat Nashim," 285. Other copies of this type of deed are found in *Teshuvot Ḥakhme Provinẓia (Teshuvot Ḥakhme Provintsya)*, no. 32, ed. Sofer, 126 and Bodleian Opp. Add. 4°127, fol. 112r.

76. Juliette Sibon, *Les juifs de Marseille au XIVe siècle* (Paris, 2011), 273–274. The age of marriage among Provençal Jews is discussed briefly by Joseph Shatzmiller, *Shylock Reconsidered: Jews, Moneylending, and Medieval Society* (Berkeley, 1990), 30; Ram Ben-Shalom, "The Disputation of Tortosa, Vicente Ferrer and the Problem of the Conversos According to the Testimony of Isaac Nathan," *Zion* 56 (1991): 21–46, at 37–38 (Hebrew).

77. Jackie A. Kohnstamm and René Moulinas, "Archaïsme et traditions locales: Le mariage chez les juifs d'Avignon et du Comtat au dernier siècle avant l'émancipation," *Revue des études juives* 138 (1979): 89–115 (esp. 93); Simone Mrejen-O'Hana, "Le marriage juif sous l'Ancien Régime: l'exemple de Carpentras (1763–1792)," *Annales de démographie historique* (1993): 161–170; Simone Mrejen-O'Hana, *Le Registre d'Élie Crémieux: Ephémérides de la communauté juive de Carpentras (1736–1769)* (Jerusalem, 2009), Hebrew introduction, 29. On the form "cadessar," see Simone Mrejen-O'Hana, "Hebrew in Carpentras and the Surrounding Area (Part One)," in *Sha'arei Lashon: Studies in Hebrew, Aramaic and Jewish Languages Presented to Moshe Bar-Asher*, ed. Aharon Maman, Steven E. Fassberg and Yohanan Breuer (Jerusalem, 2007), 3: 347–367, at 362–363 (Hebrew).

78. Maryanne Kowaleski, "Singlewomen in Medieval and Early Modern Europe: The Demographic Perspective," in *Singlewomen in the European Past, 1250–1800*, ed. Judith M. Bennett and Amy M. Froide (Philadelphia, 1999), 38–81; Maryanne Kowaleski, "Gendering Demographic Changes in the Middle Ages," in *The Oxford Handbook of Women and Gender in Medieval Europe*, ed. Judith M. Bennett and Ruth Mazo Karras (Oxford, 2013), 181–196.

factors that first motivated Jews in Provence to marry their sons and daughters to each other in childhood. But the staying power of the practice testifies that its roots ran deeper than any specific financial or demographic circumstances. It became a deeply ingrained custom, perpetuated by inertia. By Jacob ben Moses's time, it had become an opportunity for scholars to argue among themselves how it should best be practiced – with blessings or without, as a ceremony or as a declaration in court. Their arguments had become a custom in its own right, but those scholars had come to accept that the Provençal practice was at odds with the version of Jewish law expressed by Maimonides, ibn Adret and other major figures, and that they lacked the power to uproot it. In a time of plague and change, a time-honoured marriage ritual may have provided consolation, a sense of permanency and some hope for the future.

Jacob ben Moses of Bagnols saw himself as one of the last bastions of the Provençal rabbinic tradition – a venerable tradition in which careful study of the Talmud was balanced by a commitment to practical law and enriched by the insights of rational philosophy. By guiding his readers to return to the primary texts and to consider a range of possible interpretations, he offered them intellectual independence. In a world wracked by disaster and awash with Hebrew books providing shortcuts to rabbinic and philosophical knowledge, his works might indeed have played an important role. In reality, though, they did not. Judging by the pristine state of the sole surviving exemplar, marked only by the bibliophile Menaḥem Lonzano's reading notes, Jacob's manuscripts did not find many readers in late medieval Provence. The interests of his audience were shifting away from locally produced legal works and towards pan-regional compilations like Jacob ben Asher's *Arba'ah Turim* (Four Columns), completed in Toledo in 1340.[79] Rather than reinvigorating medieval Provençal rabbinic culture, Jacob ben Moses of Bagnols served as one of its last archivists.

79. Judah Galinsky, "'And This Scholar Achieved more than Everyone for All Studied from His Works': On the Circulation of Jacob b. Asher's Four Turim from the Time of Its Composition until the End of the 15th Century," *Sidra* 19 (2004): 25–45 (Hebrew); Judah Galinsky, "On Popular Halakhic Literature and the Jewish Reading Audience in Fourteenth-Century Spain," *Jewish Quarterly Review* 98 (2008): 305–327.

Conclusion

Provençal Jewry had its heyday as a rabbinic trailblazer during the twelfth century, and as a philosophical and scientific powerhouse it continued into the early fourteenth century. The region's intellectual achievements were significant not only for the scholarly elite that produced them, but for the entirety of Jewish society that crafted its sense of identity out of those same materials. As they used and reused halakhic culture, Jewish laypeople inevitably left their mark upon the tradition even as rabbinic scholars studied, conceptualized and applied the texts that underpinned that same culture. Our close study of halakhic literature from late medieval Provence has taught us a great deal about the process followed by rabbinic scholars as they crafted their *responsa* or legal codes in light of their social and cultural environment. It has also revealed the important role played by Halakhah in shaping communal spaces that were shared by a variety of different Jews.

The Jewish courtroom was one of those shared spaces. Ostensibly a bastion of elite authority imposed upon the Jewish populace, the Jewish legal system in southern France underwent changes during the thirteenth century as litigants discovered how, with a modicum of expertise, it could be nudged into serving their interests. As the general legal culture of southern France was transformed through the adoption of Roman law, Jewish courts mostly ceased to function as arbiters of civil law. However, the cases of personal status, marriage and divorce that remained under their jurisdiction were of immediate concern to the Jewish litigants involved in them and held magnetic fascination for the wider community, so that Jewish courts continued to serve as a meaningful and fraught arena of social conflict.

Outside the courtroom and the study hall, halakhic concepts and affiliations provided the vocabulary to express the deep-seated tension between Provençal and northern French Jews as they were forced to rub shoulders in the villages and towns of Provence. How to bake bread in accordance with Jewish law, how to open the solemn prayer service of the Day of Atonement, how to lead the penitential night vigils leading up to that Day, were some of the laws and rituals that marked battle lines between the frictious groups.

Personality, too, played a role in how such battles were fought. Isaac Kimḥi was one rabbi who advocated a path of compromise and tolerance between Provençal and French Jews, just as he sought (or imagined) common ground and understanding between Jews and Gentiles. By contrast, Isaac of Manosque and Abba Mari of Lunel were drawn repeatedly into strife as they staked out confrontational positions. The entanglements they created, and those they were drawn into by others, provide rich insight into their own views, beliefs and fears and into the complex roles they played in the social fabric of a deeply divided community.

The Black Death reached the ports of Provence in late 1347 and remained there, unrelenting, for decades. Focused on bare survival in the face of plague and violence, many Jews lost interest in the details of their legal and intellectual heritage, while the more robust agendas of other Jewish traditions exerted a growing influence. Marriage remained a core element of their culture, their lifeline to the future. The proper observance of wedding rituals remained an abiding concern and a field for thrashing out underlying cultural anxieties. There remained very few local scholars who could join forces with Jacob ben Moses of Bagnols in upholding those traditions and exploring their legal roots.

Tracing the contours of Jewish life east of the Rhône during the Late Middle Ages reveals the drama and dynamic of a small minority community. Dwarfed, influenced and pressured by larger groups, both Jewish and Christian, Provençal Jews charted and often muddled their path through complicated and difficult times. Law served them as a practical system for the resolution of conflicts, but also for publicly airing those same conflicts. Beyond its practice, though, Jewish law served as a cultural language that could unite and divide.

At the very end of the fifteenth century, scant years before they were expelled from the County of Provence in 1501, Jews in the city of Avignon asked a local scholar named Mordechai Nathan to explain the significance of certain Hebrew words that formed part of the distinctive local Jewish dialect.[1]

> The communities of Provence and Venaissin and Avignon customarily appoint leading citizens[2] to deal with communal affairs – whether to collect money from them or to spend that money on their behalf with the government – and they are called the men of the *Ma ʿamad*. In Avignon they asked me what that title signifies ...

1. London, British Library, Add. 22090, fol. 421v. Published in Pinchas Roth, "Mordechai Nathan and the Jewish Community of Avignon in the Late Fifteenth Century," *Jewish Studies Internet Journal* 17 (2019), 11 (https://jewish-faculty.biu.ac.il/files/jewish-faculty/shared/JSIJ17/roth.pdf).
2. *Tove ha-ʿir*, a Hebrew equivalent of *boni viri*.

> They were accustomed in Avignon to refer to anyone who unlawfully sends a bully or a violent man [to threaten] his fellow as *marbiẓ*, and they refer to that action as *harbaẓah*. The terms *malshin* and *halshanah* are used specifically in regard to the court and the lord.[3] They asked me what the words *harbaẓah* and *marbiẓ* signify.

Nathan was unable to uncover the etymological roots of the words, and instead he offered farfetched explanations based on the Bible, the Talmud and the legal code of Maimonides. His feeble attempts to clarify local traditions serve as eloquent testimony to the process of cultural erasure witnessed in the post-Plague years by Jacob of Bagnols. Yet, though their origins were forgotten, the words that Nathan was asked to define were still used by Avignonese Jews. It is surely no coincidence that these words served in the semantic field of communal life and social tension. As we have seen throughout this book, those were precisely the areas in which Jewish traditions and laws were most actively used by medieval Provençal Jews.

In many ways, the medieval Provençal Jewish community was precocious. The ways in which it assimilated new approaches to science and philosophy into its religious worldview and adapted its judicial system to meet the needs of legally sophisticated consumers set the stage for Jewish communities that faced similar challenges centuries later. The tension between French and Provençal groups that coloured so much of Jewish life in fourteenth-century Provence was a precursor of the conflicts that would arise, on a much grander scale, in the sixteenth century when large numbers of Jewish exiled from Spain reached North Africa and the Ottoman Empire. Like the French Jews in Provence two hundred years earlier, the Sefardim carried a proud legacy of rabbinic expertise that they believed was unmatched by the existing communities in the lands of their refuge.

Eroded by waves of plague and persecution, despair and disintegration, the Jews of Provence entered the sixteenth century with only a tattered memory of its past. Some remained within the Papal territories of Avignon, Carpentras, l'Isle and Cavaillon. Most left for Italy or the Ottoman Empire and were quickly subsumed into the much larger Sefardic mass. As the living community faded from view, its medieval legacy of rabbinic law remained as testimony to the lives of Jews in the land of Provence.

3. Elena Lourie, "Mafiosi and Malsines: Violence, Fear and Faction in the Jewish Aljamas of Valencia in the Fourteenth Century," in Elena Lourie, *Crusade and Colonisation: Muslims, Christians and Jews in Medieval Aragon* (Aldershot, 1990), 69–102.

APPENDIX

Previously Unpublished Manuscript Sources

The texts included in this appendix are discussed and contextualized within the book itself. However, since they have not been previously published, the texts appear here in their entirety in order to provide easier access for readers.

Introduction

1. Paris, BnF, Héb. 1391, fol. 89v. A *responsum* by Isaac Kimḥi regarding the mourning practices required of a Jewish agricultural worker. An unnamed rabbi or other person instructed the worker to spend three days of mourning at home, after which he could return to his work. Kimḥi, however, ruled that the mourner must remain at home and refrain from work for the full seven-day *shivʿah* period of mourning. Kimḥi argued that Talmudic passages permitting employment during the mourning period related only to the mourner's employees, not to the mourner himself.

ומה ששאלת אחי באדם שמת לו מת והתירו לו לאחר שלשה לחזר בבית הגרנות ולחמר אחר בהמתו ולישא משוי על כתפו. דעה אחי כי דעתי נוטה לאיסור אע"פ שהוא מוחכר או מושכר ביד אחרים, דלא התירו בגמ'[1] מוחכר או מושכר בידי אחרי' אלא חמריו ופועליו. אבל הוא עצמו אם היה חמר או פועל ודאי אסור כמו ששנינו[2] מלאכת אחרים בידו אע"פ שקבולת לא יעשה וכו'. ואין לך חמר או כתף גדול מזה, מאחר שפעמים מחמר אחר בהמתו או נושא סבל על כתפו. אע"פ שהוא עושה מלאכה בשדה במקום שאינו נראה, אפי' הכי אסור שהרי אסרו הרבצת שדהו להוא עצמו ולא פלוג בין קרוב מן העיר או רחוק. ועוד שאפי' חמריו או פועליו שהרי אמרו ששכיר יום היכא דהוו שכירי יום אסורין אפי' בעיר אחרת שמא נודע שם שהוא אבל, כמו ששנינו בריש פרק מי שהפך זתיו[3] שכיר יום אפי' בעיר אחרת לא יעשה.

1. bMoʿed Katan 11b.
2. Ibid.
3. Ibid.

ומחמריו ופועליו קאמ׳ ולא מהוא עצמו שעדין לא דבר בהוא עצמו. ביום[4] בין קבולת בין שאינו קבולת לא יעשה. נמצאת למד שחמריו ופועליו בזמן שהן אסורין דהיינו כשהן שכירי יום אסורין אפי׳ במקום שלא נודע שהוא אבל, הוא עצמו לא כל שכן שיהא אסור אפי׳ במקום שלא נודע שהוא אבל.

Chapter 3

2. Paris, BnF, Héb. 1391, fols. 84v–85r. A *responsum* by Isaac Kimḥi regarding a French rabbi in Provence who refused to buy bread from local Jewish bakers. Kimḥi explained the two halakhic concerns that could have led to the French rabbi's behaviour. First, when Provençal Jewish women retained a piece from a batch of dough in order to leaven future loaves, they did so after the priestly portion (*ḥallah*) had been removed from the dough. This created problems, according to some legal opinions, when the starter was added to subsequent batches of dough from which *ḥallah* had not yet been removed. Second, the women did not follow the French Jewish practice of tossing a twig into a communal furnace so that the baking process could be considered to have involved Jewish participation.

ומה שכתבת אחי מענין רב צרפתי אחד שלא רצה לאכול פת של ישראל וצוה לקנות מן הפלטר. וחלת פני שאם אדע טעם בדבר שאשלח לך. דע אחי כי זה כמה שנים יצא דבר זה מקצת חכמי צרפת וכמדומה לי שתמצא [85א] קצת הענין לפי׳ המשניות מרבי׳ שמשון ז״ל בספר[5] זרעים וגם מביא ירושל׳ אחד לתקן זה הענין.[6] ושלח אלי אם תמצא. בעבור כי דרך נשים בארץ הזאת, כשנוטלות השאור מן העיסה כדי להצניעו ולשמרו לדמע בו עיסות אחרות, נוטלין אותו לאחר שהרימו תרומה מן העיסה, וכיון שכן הוא הנה הוא פטור מתרומה. וכשמחמיצין בו עיסה אחרת, אותה עיסה הוי פטור וחיוב מעורבין זה בזה. החיוב הוא העיסה שנילושה אם יש בה שיעור חלה והפטור הוא השאור שמשימין בה שבא מעיסה שהרימו ממנה תרומה קודם שיסלקנו מן העיסה. וכיון שהוא מחמץ את העיסה אינו בטל במיעוטו שהוא דבר חשוב, כדחזינן בכמה דוכתי׳[7] דמחמץ בשאור של תרומה שהעיסה אסורה לזרים. וכיון שאינו בטל אותה עיסה מקולקלת מתרומה שכל מה שמסלקין ממנה הוי מן הפטור על החיוב. ומשום הכי נשמרין שאין אוכלין מפת ישראל אלא אם כן יודעין שהשאור שמחמיצין בו את העיסה סלקוהו מן העיסה הראשונה

4. Read: בידו.

5. Read: בסדר.

6. Samson of Sens, commentary on mḤallah 1: 7, Commentary on Mishnah, Zeraʿim, in Babylonian Talmud (*Talmud Bavli*) (Vilna, 1881–1898), 1: 317; pḤallah 1: 7.

7. mOrlah 2: 8–14.

קודם שהרימו ממנה תרומה, דהא הוי מן החיוב על החיוב והעיסה מתקנת לגבי תרומה כדין וכשורה. ועוד מפני שאין עכשיו נזהרות הנשים להכשיר התנור. ומ"ה הוי להו כל מקום כמקום שאין שם פלטר כיון שלפי דעתם אין נעשית לחם ישראל כהוגן וקונים מפלטר גוי.

3. Paris, BnF, Héb. 1391, fol. 90r. A *responsum* by Isaac Kimḥi regarding the mourning practices required of a Jewish courtier. The courtier requested permission to shave or cut his hair before appearing in court, even though such grooming is forbidden for thirty days after the death of a relative. Kimḥi argued that such permission was unnecessary, since the grooming ban was limited to thirty days and because the other people present at court would accept the Jewish mourner's unkempt visage with understanding. He also clarified the difference between this case, in which he ruled stringently, and the ostensibly similar question of shaving during the intermediate Festival days (*ḥol ha-moʿed*), which he had permitted under certain circumstances.

מה ששאלת אחי באדם שהוא קרוב למלכות אם יוכל להסתפר תוך ל' יום לימי אבלו. דעה אחי כי לבי מגמגם בדבר זה כי יש פנים לאיסור בעבור שאינו דומה לגמרי לבלורית, דהתם[8] לא התירו בלורית אלא מפני שהם תמיד עמהם, ואם יאסר להם לעולם יהיה להם גנאי בדבר שיעמדו לפני המלכים והשרים תמיד בשנוי תספורת שאינם רגילים באותו תספורת כלל בשום זמן. אבל זה שאינו כי אם חדש ימים ויכול להכבד ולשבת בביתו או אע"פ שצריך לו ללכת בחצר במעט זמן כזה לא יהיה לו גנאי' שהרי הפרשים ושרי המלך כשיארע אליהם דבר מתכסים בשקים ולובשים שחורים ומשלחים פרע. ואלו יכנסו לפני המלך בכך אין להם גנאי כיון שיודעים בו שהוא אבל. הילכ' בדבר שהם רגילין בו אין גנאי בדבר. ויש לבעל הדין לחלוק כלומ' כלך לדרך זו למי שיסבור שאין תספורת עקר בתורה ולבלורית יש עקר בתורה. אבל טעם האיסור יותר נראה, וכל שכן למי שיסבור תספורת מן התורה.[9] ומה שהסכמתי בתספורת חולו של מועד פונה אל טעמים אחרים כי תספורת חולו של מועד אינו נאסר מצד עצמו אלא כדי שלא יכנס לרגל וכו'.[10] ומפני קלות

8. bSotah 49b, bBava Kamma 83a.

9. This was the opinion of Abraham ben David of Posquières. See, e.g., David ben Levi of Narbonne, *Sefer ha-Mikhtam*, ed. Yosef Hillel (Jerusalem, 2015–2017), vol. 2, Moʿed Katan, 30.

10. bMoʿed Katan 14a. This sentence refers to a different ruling by Kimḥi, probably permitting shaving during the intermediate Festival days for men who shaved before the Festival began.

האיסור מצאנו שהתירוהו לכמה בני אדם כמו שהם שנויים במשנתנו.[11] ומה שהסכמנו להתיר משום דלא גרע מחבוש בבית האסורין ולנאסר בנדר. ובפ' אלו מגלחין מיבעיא לן[12] אומן שאבדה לו אבדה ערב הרגל מהו כיון דאומן הוא מוכחא מילתא או דילמ' כיון דלא מוכחא מלתא כי הנך לא תיקו. ומסתברא דתיקו לרבנן לקולא.

4. Paris, BnF, Héb. 1391, fols. 88v–89r. A *responsum* by Isaac Kimḥi regarding the use of oil donated to a synagogue by a Muslim. Kimḥi ruled that the oil could be used as intended, despite the possible concern that the donation was designated for the Jerusalem Temple and therefore forbidden for use by less holy institutions.

ולענין השמן שהתנדב ישמעאל וכו'. יש בנדבות הללו פנים שונים, שכל שהתנדב בבית הכנסת דבר שהוראתו להיותו לצורך בית הכנסת הרי הוא לבית הכנסת ולא יהיה בו ספק הקדש להיות טעון גניזה. לפיכך גוי שהתנדב מנורה או נר לבית הכנסת מקבלין אותה ואין משנין אותה לדבר [89א] אחר ואפי' לדבר מצוה עד שישתקע שם בעלים ממנה כדאית' בריש ערכין.[13] אבל אם הוא מתנדב דבר שאין הוראתו להיותו לצורך בית הכנסת אע"פ שיזכור לבית הכנסת כגון מעות או פירות יש בזה חשש הקדש וטעון גניזה שמא לבו להקדיש לשמים. נראה למי דומה איברא השמן הזה נראין הדברים שהוא כמנורה וכנר והרי הוא כמי שפירש לדעת ישראל הפרשתי.[14] ומדליקין ממנו בבית הכנסת ואין בזה חשש איסור.

Chapter 5

5. Paris, BnF, Héb. 1391, fols. 33r–34r. A *responsum* by Isaac Kimḥi regarding a childless woman whose husband granted her a divorce on his deathbed. The divorce writ contained an extraneous clause, which gave rise to the concern that the divorce might be invalid, in which case the woman would be considered a childless widow and would therefore have to perform levirate marriage or the *ḥalizah* ceremony before she could marry another

11. mMoʿed Katan 3: 1.
12. bMoʿed Katan 14a.
13. bArakhin 6b.
14. bArakhin 6a.

man.[15] Kimḥi concluded that the extraneous clause did not invalidate the divorce and that the woman was free to marry as she wished.

מה ידענו ולא תדע, והנה ידענוך אב לחכמה אם לבינה, אח ורע ומודע. מצאנוך יסוד התורה עמוד המדע כבר קדשוך שמים ויצא טבעך בשערים נודע. ניצוץ שמש מעלתך נצחנו בנעימותו עד שנעלם ממנו לחזק הראותו.[16] ראינוך כבר פדת יושב ודורש[17] כמשה ותורתו בחדרי תושיה, נוטע אהלי אפדנו וסבב בית אל כי שם ביתו. ועתה מה לך לשתות מי נהר ולהתבשם בקנמוני ואתה עומד בגנה של ורדים בבית היין יין הרקח יין המשומר בענביו ואיך אשקך מעסיס כמוני. ידעתי הכל חפש מחפש בנר שכלך. חכם כמלאך האלהים ואחד קדוש המדבר לפלמוני.[18] ואיש אשר אלה לו וכל סתום לא עממוהו איך יבקש לקשקש בפעמוני. ואתה פלא יועץ כל רז לא אנס לך יושב בשבת תחכמוני. ומפני שאין מסרבין לגדול ואחזת בכנף מעילי, כמצווה ועושה אני מזמן ועונה הנני כי קראת לי. אמרתי זכותך תסייעני לבאר מצות וחקים אע"פ שהקפוני הסבות בשלשת הרחקים להשיב אמרים אמת והדברים עתיקים. ובהיותך ספר תורה ואנך להפיק רצונך ר' מטונך הנני משיב על דבריך כאשר הראוני מן השמים.

שאלה שכיב מרע שכיון לפטור את אשתו מזיקת יבום אם ימות מחליו וצוה הסופר לכתוב ולעדים לחתום גט כשר. ועמד הסופר וכתב הגט בזה הלשון ואנש לא ימחא בידיכי מן שמי מן יומא דנן ולעלם דלא כאסמכתא ודלא כטפסי דשטרי. יפסל גט זה ותצטרך לחלוץ או לא יפסל ותהיה מותרת בלא חליצה.

תשובה מה שדקדקו ז"ל בלשונות הגט[19] כגון לא לכתו' למחך אלא למהך ולא לאתנסבא ולא ליכתו' ודין אלא ודן ולא ליכתוב איגרת [33ב] אלא אגרת ויתר הדקדוקים כל זה מפני שאלו הלשונות סובלים לשבור כונת הגט ולשווי תנאה בגיטא ולבטל הגט מעקרו ומפני זה החמיר הר"ם ז"ל בהל' גירושין פ"ד כי אם שנה באלו הלשונות יפסל הגט וזה לשונו:[20] הרי שכתב בנוסח זה ולא האריך ו"וין אלו או לא כתב היו"דין היתרות או שכתב היודין שאמרנו שלא יכתבו הרי זה גט פסול וכן כל כיוצא בזה בכל לשון פסול ע"כ. אך הראב"ד

15. A widow without children from her late husband must perform either levirate marriage (*yibum*) or the release ceremony known as *ḥaliẓah* (removing the shoe).

16. Cf. Moses Maimonides, *Guide of the Perplexed*, trans. Shlomo Pines (Chicago, 1963–1979), 1: 59 (ibn Tibbon translation).

17. bYevamot 72b.

18. Daniel 8:13.

19. bGittin 85b.

20. Moses Maimonides, *Mishneh Torah*, ed. Shabse Frankel (Jerusalem, 1975–2003), Laws of Divorce 4: 14.

ז"ל כתב בהשגה[21] א"א כתב גאון כל אלו הדקדוקין בשהבעל עומד ומערער. וכתב בעל העטור ז"ל בזה הלשון:[22] ודייקי ריבוותא דכל הני דקדוקי דרבא היכא דכתב ליה בעל גופיה או כתב לו סופר על פיו ובתר הכי אתא בעל ומערער ואמ' אנא הוא דפסילנא ליה בהני דקדוקי לקלקולה איכונית. אבל אמ' הבעל לסופר ולעדים לכתוב לו גט אפי' סתם וטעו הסופר והעדים באחד מאלו האותיות והבעל אינו מערער הגט כשר ותנשא בו. ואם העדים מצויין יעידו בפני ב"ד שטעות סופר הוא. וכן כתב רבי' האיי דאי יהיב בעל רשותא לסופר למכתב גט שלם וטעה בהני כלהו או במקצתהון, אי איתיה לסופר מתקן ליה ואי לא ומינסבא בהאי גיטא לא מפקינן לה. ודאי אי אתיא לאינסובי ואתי בעל ומערער ואמ' הא דכתי' ודין דינא הוא דאמרי אינמי למחך חוכא ולהכי אסרי לא מנסבינן לה. אבל אי מנסבא לא מפקינן לה, דהא קא אמרי'[23] ומשום שלום מלכות תצא והולד ממזר אי ר' מאיר לטעמי' דאמ' כל המשנה ממטבע שטבעו חכמים בגיטין הולד ממזר. וליתה לר' מאי', וכ"ש לענין טעות סופר. ורבנו נסים השיב כן בקבלה מפי הגאונים היכא שכתב הגט הבעל בעצמו אם נשאת וערער תצא ואם האשה טוענת טעות סופר עליה להביא ראיה. אבל אם אין שם ערעור הבעל ויש בו טעות מתחת ידי הסופר וצוה לכתוב גט, כיון דמדעת שלמה רצה לגרש אינה צריכה גט שני וכל טעות שבא מתחת ידי הסופר אין ערעור הבעל מועיל כלום וכן דעת הגאונים ע"כ.[24] ומעתה כל שכן וכל שכן בנדון שלפנינו שהוא שכיב מרע וצוה לכתוב גט כשר ואחזוקי אינשי ברשיעי לא מחזקינן ואין אדם משטה בשעת מיתה שאין [34א] חוששין במה שהוא טעות סופר, ואע"פ שהלשון ההוא מסופק סובל לדונו לשני פנים דבר והפכו. וכל שכן במה שכתוב דלא כאסמכתא ודלא כטופסי דשטרי שהוא לשון ברור ומוכיח כי בדעת שלמה הוא מגרש, ואע"פ שהלשון ההוא לא תקנו אותו חכמים בגיטין כיון שהוא טעות שנפל מיד סופר, לא איכפת לן ואין חוששין לו כלל. וכל שכן שהלשון מיפה כח הגט. הילכ' הגט כשר והיא מותרת להנשא בלא חליצה. כן נראה לי אמת ונכון.

6. Paris, BnF, Héb. 1391, fols. 34r–35r. A *responsum* by Abba Mari ben Moses of Lunel regarding a childless woman whose husband granted her a divorce on his deathbed. This *responsum* concerns the same case that was discussed by Isaac Kimḥi (above, no. 5), but Abba Mari took it for granted that the divorce was invalid (by rabbinic standards, since he conceded that it was valid according to biblical law) while Kimḥi claimed that the divorce was

21. Abraham ben David of Posquières (Rabad), gloss to Maimonides, *Mishneh Torah*, ed. Frankel, Laws of Divorce 4: 14.

22. Isaac ben Abba Mari of Marseilles, *Sefer ha-Ittur*, ed. Meir Yonah (Warsaw, 1874–1885), 1: 27d.

23. bGittin 80a.

24. End of quote from *Sefer ha-Ittur*.

most probably valid. Therefore, Abba Mari focused only on the question of whether a widow who remarried instead of performing levirate marriage could remain in her second marriage. He concluded that, unless her second husband was a *kohen* (priest), the widow must perform the *ḥaliẓah* ceremony with her levir.

שאלה אם יש בגט חשש פסול ונשאת בלא חליצה מה משפטה בנשואין אלו. תשובה גרסי' ביבמות פ' האשה רבה[25] אמ' רב גדל אמ' רב חייא בר יוסף אמ' רב יבמה קדושין אין בה נשואין יש בה משום דמחלפא באשה שהלך בעלה למדינת הים. ופירשה הרי"ף[26] קדושין אין בה אם נתקדשה לאחר קודם שיחלוץ לה יבמה אינה נאסרת על יבמה, נשואין יש בה אם נשאת נאסרה על יבמה משום דמיחלפא באשה שהלך בעלה למדינת הים. והביא הרב ז"ל עלה דההיא מאי דאיתמר משמיה דמר רב יהודאי גאון ז"ל שומרת יבם שנשאת בלא חליצה תצא מזה ומזה, מבעל בגט ומיבם בחליצה, ואסורה להם עולמית. וחלק בין יש לה בנים לאין לה בנים, כדאי' בהלכות.[27] והביא סברא דרבוותא דפליגי עליה דמר יהודאי, דאמרי דהני מילי לאו דסמכא הן דלייתינון בגמ'. ומייתו ראיה ממאי דאיתמ' בירוש' בפ' הזורק[28] יבמה שנשאת בלא חליצה ר' ירמיה אמ' זה חולץ וזה מקיים ור' יוחנן אמ' תצא ור' אילא אמ' תצא. א"ר זבידא מתני' מסייעא לר' יוחנן[29] הכונס את יבמתו וצרתה נשאת לאחר ונמצאת זו אלונית תצא מזה ומזה ושלשה עשר דבר בה. והא מתני' בשיש לה בנים היא וקתני והולד ממזר מזה ומזה. שמעינ' מינה דאפי' יש לה בנים א"ר יוחנן תצא וכו'. ופסק הרי"ף כר' יוחנן וכת' דאילין מילי דאשכחן למקצת רבוותא מילי דסברא אינון דלא שבקינן תלמוד ערוך ואזלינן בתר סברא ע"כ. ואע"פ שהרב בעל המאור לא פי' כן הא דרב גדל דאמ' יבמה קדושין אין בה וכו'. [334ב] מ"מ לענין פסקא סביר' ליה דהלכת' כר' יוחנן דירושל' דאמ' תצא וזה לשונו[30] עלה דההיא דרב גדל אמ' רב יבמה קדושין אין בה פי' להצריכה גט נאמרה שמועה זו, שהנשואין תופסין בה וצריכה גט וקדושין אין תופסין בה ורב לטעמיה דאמ' אין קדושין תופסין ביבמה, ולית הילכת' כותי' אלא קדושין ונשואין כלן תופסין בה כשמואל. ולשמואל הא לא מיחלפא באשה שהלך בעלה למדינת הים [שזו תופסין בה קידושין ונשואין ואשה שהלך בעלה

25. bYevamot 92b.

26. Isaac Alfasi, *Hilkhot ha-Rif,* Yevamot 29a, in Babylonian Talmud, vol. 8.

27. Alfasi, *Hilkhot ha-Rif,* Yevamot 29b, in Babylonian Talmud, vol. 8.

28. pGittin 8: 7, 49c, in Palestinian Talmud (*Talmud Yerushalmi*), ed. Yaacov Sussmann (Jerusalem, 2001), 1089.

29. tGittin 6: 7, in *Tosefta,* ed. Saul Lieberman (New York, 1955–1988), 4: 271.

30. Zeraḥiah ha-Levi, *Sefer ha-Ma᾽or* on Alfasi, *Hilkhot ha-Rif,* Yevamot 29a, in Babylonian Talmud, vol. 8.

למדינת הים][31] אין קדושין תופסין בה אלא נשואין. וכיון דהלכת' כשמואל, לא היה לו לרב אלפסי לכתוב שמועה זו כל עקר דהא לא גמרינ' מינה ולא מידי. ולאוסרה על היבם ממתני' דהכונס את יבמתו והלכה צרתה ונשאת לאחר נפקא ומהתם גמרינ' ולא מדרב כמו שפירשוה בירושל', דהא לצאת מזה ומזה דברי הכל תצא ע"כ. ורבי' יעקב פירש בתשובה[32] אם נתקדשה לאחר קודם חליצה אינה נאסרת על יבמה ואם יבמה ישראל נופק לה השני גט והותרה לו ואם רצה ליבם מיבם ואם רצה לחלוץ חולץ והראשון אם רצה לקיימה מקיים דלא קנסי לה אלא בנשאת ע"כ. אבל רבי' חננאל והלכות גדולות[33] פירשו אפי' בנתקדשה אסורה לחזור לו עולמית אבל אם נשאת נאסרת על יבמה שמא יאמרו חלץ זה ונשא זה ונמצא זה מחזיר חלוצתו ע"כ. נמצא לכלהו רבוותא אם נשאת בלא חליצה תצא מזה ומזה כר' יוחנן וכן פסק הר"ם ז"ל בהלכו' יבום פ"ב.[34] וכל זה ביבמה שהיא זקוקה ודאית, אבל יבמה שיש ספק בזיקתה אם היא זקוקה אם לאו כגון שגרשה בעלה ויש חשש פסול בגט ונשאת בלא חליצה, נראה מספיקא לא מפקינן לה מתותי גברא אלא אם בעלה ישראל היבם חולץ והבעל יקיים ואם בעלה כהן אי הוי חשש פסול הגט וספיקו ספק דדבריהם דלא מצרכינ' לה חליצה כי היכי דלא ליתסר לבעלה שהוא כהן. ומיהו אי מיית בעלה בחיי היבם לא שרינן לה להנשא לעלמא עד דחליץ לה יבם ותפקע זיקה. וראיה מיהא דגרסי' בפ' החולץ[35] אתמר מת בתוך שלשים יום ועמדה ונתקדשה אמ' רבינא משמיה דרבא אם אשת ישראל היא חולצת ואם אשת כהן היא אינה חולצת ורב שרביא אמ' אחד זו ואחד זו חולצת. ופסק הרי"ף וזה לשונו[36] וקימא [35א] לן כרבינא דכיון דאיכא רבנן דפליגי עלי' דרשב"ג דאמרי דאע"ג דלא שהה ולד מעליא הוא גבי אשת כהן דלא אפשר דאי חליץ לה איתסרא על בעלה עבדינן ליה כרבנן ולא מצרכי' חליצה וגבי אשת ישראל דלית בה פסידא עבדינן כרשב"ג הילכ' חליץ לה ועיילא ליה לגברא ואי בנתקדשה מותבינן לה תותי גברא כל שכן אם נשאת דלא מפקינ' לה מתותי גברא. והך דאמרי' התם לענין שומרת יבם שנשאת בלא חליצה לא שייך בהא מילת' דהתם ודאי בעיא חליצה אבל הכא כיון דמיית בתוך שלשים יום ספיקא הוא ומספקא לא מפקינן אתתא מתותי גברא, אלא אי בעלה ישראל חליץ לה יבמה ויתבא תותי גברא ואי בעלה כהן דאי חליץ לה יבמה איתסרא עליה יתבא בלא

31. These words, found in *Sefer ha-Ma'or,* were omitted in the manuscript due to homeoteleuton.

32. Jacob ben Meir Tam (Rabenu Tam), Ramerupt (France), d. 1171. *Sefer ha-Yashar,* ed. Shim'on Shelomoh Schlesinger (Jerusalem, 1975), 49–51 (sec. 54). Cited by Isaac of Marseilles, *Sefer ha-Ittur,* ed. Yonah, 1: 6a.

33. Cited by Isaac of Marseilles, *Sefer ha-Ittur,* ed. Yonah, 1: 6a.

34. Maimonides, *Mishneh Torah,* ed. Frankel, Laws of Levirate Marriage 2: 18.

35. bYevamot 36b.

36. Alfasi, *Hilkhot ha-Rif,* Yevamot 11a, in Babylonian Talmud, vol. 8.

חליצה ע"כ. וכן נראה הדין לכל ספיקא דאתיליד לענין יבמה שהוא ספק דדבריהם. אבל היכא דהוי ספיקא דאוריתא לא איכפת לן אם היא אשת כהן או אשת ישראל ואחת זו ואחת זו חולצת. וכן נראה מדברי הר"ם פ"ב בהלכות יבום וז"ל[37] כל יבמה שהיא ספק דדבריהם אם יש עליה זיקת יבם או אין עליה כגון יבמה שילדה ולד שלא כלו חדשיו ומת בתוך שלשים יום שדינה שתחלוץ מספק דדבריהם כמו שביארנו, אם הלכה ונתקדשה לאחר קודם חליצה, יחלוץ לה יבמה ותשב עם בעלה. ואם נתקדשה לכהן שהוא אסור בחליצה אין אוסרין על זה אשתו שספק דבריהם הוא גרשה הכהן או מת הרי זו חולצת ואחר כך תנשא לאחרים ע"כ. ומדקא תלי טעמ' מפני שספק דבריהם הוא מכלל דהיכא דהוי ספיקא דאורית' עבדינן כרב שרביא דאמ' אחת זו ואחת זו חולצת כן נראה עקר. ואתה שלום וביתך שלום ושלום לאוהבי תורתך כנפשך וכנפש איש בריתך נאמן אהבתך אבא מרי בר' משה בר' יוסף יש"י עמה"ן[38] [המכונה שנאשטרוג דלוניל].[39]

7. Paris, BnF, Héb. 1391, fols. 35r–37r. A *responsum* by Marwan de Meyrargues regarding a childless woman whose husband granted her a divorce on his deathbed. This *responsum* concerns the same case discussed by Isaac Kimḥi (no. 5) and Abba Mari de Lunel (no. 6) and relates to the sources and arguments cited by the two other scholars. Marwan endorsed Kimḥi's position that the divorce was valid and the woman was free to marry.

שאלה שכיב מרע שכיון לפטור את אשתו מזיקת יבום אם ימות מחליו וצוה הסופר לכתוב ולעדים לחתום גט כשר ועמד הסופר וכתב הגט בזה הלשון ואנש לא ימחא בידיכו מן שמי מיומא דנן ולעלם דלא [35ב] כאסמכתא ודלא כטופסי דשטרי, יפסל גט זה ותצטרך לחלוץ או לא יפסל ותהיה מותרת בלא חליצה. עוד אם יש בזה חשש פסול ונשאת בלא חליצה, מה משפטה בנשואין אלו.

תשובה מלשון השאלה נראה שלא נפל ספק בגט אלא מצד לשון דלא כאסמכתא ודלא כטופסי דשטרי. אבל נראה שהגט נעשה כראוי בשאר הדברים הצריכים לו בעקרי התנאי המותנה בגט שכיב מרע, כתקון חכמים ראשוני ראשונים וכתקון הגאונים האחרונים כרבינו האיי והרב הגדול וגאונים אחרים יסדו דרכי תנאי זה כדי שיהיה הגט כריתות בחבוריהם ובתשובות שאלות להם במשפטיו בלפני התרף במה שנקראו תורף ולאחר התרף במה

37. Maimonides, *Mishneh Torah*, ed. Frankel, Laws of Levirate Marriage 2: 21.
38. Isaiah 57:2.
39. Marginal gloss probably added by Menaḥem de Lonzano.

שנקרא אחר התרף. ואם חלק בו הרב בעל המאור[40] ובעל פה ובכתב שלא בתוך הגט ואע"פ שמדין ההלכה יוצא שיוכל לכתוב בתוכו לאחר התורף בעל מנת או מעכשיו לא בחוץ או אפי' לפני התרף במעכשיו ועל מנת לדעת גאוני מחסיא.[41] מהכל נראה שגט זה מתקן כהלכה וכתקון הגאונות, אבל מה שמוליד החשש הוא לשון דלא כאסמכתא וכו'. ויראה שזה הלשון אע"פ שתקונו הוא בגיטי ממון לשופרא דשטרא ומתקון שטרות הוא וכאן אינו ממטבע שטבעו חכמים בגיטי נשים, אומ' אני שהסופר טעה בו אגב שטפיה לצרף דנן ולעלם עם דלא כאסמכתא וכו' כמצורף בשאר שטרות. וכונת המגרש היתה שיכתב הסופר ויחתמו העדים גט כשר לאשתו כתקון גט שכיב מרע ומעכשו שכיון לזה יחול הגט אחר מותו ותהיה מגורשת בגט כשר שיכתבו ויחתמו לה עד כמה עד שיגיע לידה גט כשר וכאלו הגיע לידה מחיים וחל אחריו למפרע מעכשיו בחייו ולא נחוש באין גט לאחר מיתה שאין מבוא בכאן. ועו' דהא איתמר בתלמודא[42] ומשום שלום מלכות תצא והולד ממזר וכו'. ולא קימ' לן כר' מאי' דאמ' כל המשנה ממטבע שטבעו חכמים בגיטין תצא והולד ממזר, שהרי ברור מה שכתבו הגאונים בטעות סופר בגט בריא. ומכאן אתה דן לגט זה שכוון לגט כשר מעכשיו כדי לפטור אותו מזיקה. ואלה דבריהם בספר העטור[43] ודייקי [36א] ריבוותא דכל הני דקדוקי אותיות דגט היכא דכתב ליה בעל גופיה, אינמי דכתב ליה סופר מפומיה, ובתר הכי אתא בעל ומערער ואמ' אנא דפסילנא ליה בהני דקדוקי וכו'. אבל אמ' הבעל לסופר ולעדים לכתוב לה גט ולחתום אפי' חתמו וטעו הסופר והעדים באחד מאלו אותיות והבעל אינו מערער, הגט כשר ותנשא בו. ואם העדים מצויין יעידו בפני ב"ד שטעות סופר היה. וכן כתב רבינו האיי דאי יהיב בעל רשותא לסופר למכתב גט שלם וטעה בהני כלהו או במקצתן אי איתיה לספרא מתקן ליה ואי לא ומנסבא בהאי גיטא לא מפקינן לה. וודאי אתיא לאינסובי וקאי בעל ומערער ואמ' האי דכתי' ודין דינא הוא דאמרי אינמי למחך חוכא ולהכי איכוונית לא מנסבינן לה. אבל אי מינסבא לא מפקינן לה דהא קא אמרי'[44] ומשום שלום מלכות תצא והולד ממזר וכו' וליתה לדר' מאיר וכ"ש לענין טעות סופר. ורבי' נסים השיב כן בקבלה מפי הגאונים והיכא שכתב בעל גט אם נשאת וערער תצא, ואם האשה טוענת טעות סופר היה עליה להביא ראיה. ואם אין שם ערעור הבעל ויש בו טעות סופר וצוה לכתוב גט סתם, כיון דמדעת שלמה רצה לגרש אינה צריכה גט שני. וכל טעות הבא מתחת ידי סופר אין ערער הבעל מועיל כלום וכן דעת הגאונים ע"כ. מכאן אני רואה דכל דכן הוא בגט זה שדעת המגרש היתה שלמה ואנן סהדי שלשלום איכוון כדי לפטור אותה מזיקה בגט שלם וכשר ואם הסופר טעה מה לה ולו. וכ"ש

40. Zeraḥiah ha-Levi, *Sefer ha-Ma ʾor,* on Alfasi, *Hilkhot ha-Rif,* Gittin 44a, in Babylonian Talmud, vol. 8.

41. Isaac ben Abba Mari of Marseilles, *Sefer ha-Ittur,* ed. Yonah, 1: 40a.

42. bGittin 80a.

43. Isaac ben Abba Mari of Marseilles, *Sefer ha-Ittur,* ed. Yonah, 1: 27d.

44. bGittin 80a.

שבטעות מבוארת שאינו סותר הכריתות אבל מיפהו בקצת כשאר שטרות מתקן בהם. ואע"פ שנשתנה ממטבע שטבעו חכמים, אגב שטפא הוא ואם טעה הסופר הרי אין מי שיערער בו והרי היא כאלו מגורשת ממנו מחיים בגט שלם ואינה צריכה גט שני הואיל והכריתה מפיו נעשה כראוי וצוה שיכתב הגט ויחתם בהכשר. ועו' שטעות זו נפלה במקום שקרוב לומ' בו שהוא לאחר התורף, ואפי' יהיה בו כתוב תנאי גמור שמוציאו מידי כריתות ומשיירו לא יפסל בדיעבד לכשיתקיים התנאי, אפי' לפי תקנת הגאונים שתקנו שלא יכתב תנאי [37א] בגט אפי' לאחר התורף דילמ' אתי לאיחלופי בלפני התורף לכתחלה הוא אבל דיעבד כשר. ואין צריך לומ' זה שאינו תנאי אך יפוי. ואם נפל במקרה הוא, אפי' חליצה אינה צריכה ותנשא. ועו' אפי' תימ' שזה יהיה קצת שנוי ויש בו קצת פקפוק מפני ששנה הסופר המטבע, דעתי דלא גרע האידנא מדינא דנפק לן מהבבלי והירושלמי[45] שאלו פסול ושאלו כשר, פי' היכא דאיכא ושאלו חתמו על הכל בגט ובשאלת שלום וכשר. ואין צרי' לומ' כאן בלשון דלא כאסמכתא אע"פ שאין בו ודלא, דינו כדין ושאלו שהרי יש לו קצת יחס בגט וביפויו ואע"פ שנשתנה מעצם המטבע על הכל חתמו והגט כשר.

ולמה ששאל עוד אם יש מי שיחוש לפסלו לחששא בעלמא ונשאת בלא חליצה מה משפטה בנשואיה. אומר דבר ברור הוא בפ' האשה רבה[46] שיבמה לשוק ודאית לדעת רב אליבא דר' עקיבא דאית ליה אין קדושין תופסין בחייבי לאוין ומפר' האי קרא דלא תהיה אשת המת החוצה לאיש זר לא תהיה בה הויה, הולד ממזר הואיל ואין קדושין תופסין בה כדאי' בסוף פ' האומ'[47] וסוף פ' החולץ.[48] ואם נשאת לזה בלא חליצה או נתקדשה אינה צריכה גט משני ולשמואל מספקא ליה וכו'[49] פי' נסתפק פירושא דהאי קרא וצריכה גט מספק משני אליבא דחכמים דאית להו בפ' הזורק[50] אין ממזר מיבמה וקימ' לן הא דשמואל דהא קימ' לן כחכמים. ולדברי רבי' יעקב בתשובת שאלה[51] הוקבע שאם נתקדשה לזר, אם רצה השני מוציאה בגט והיבם אם ישראל הוא ייבם או יחלוץ ואם כהן חולץ, ואם נשאת לזר אפי' יש לה בנים תצא מזה ומזה משו' דמחלפא באשה שהלך בעלה שאם נשאת תצא מזה פי' משני בגט בעל כרחו שמא יאמרו גירש זה ונשא זה ונמצאת אשת איש יוצאה בלא גט. ותצא מראשון בגט שמא יאמרו מחזיר גרושתו אחר שנשאת הם. הכי נמי ביבמה לשוק חיישינן שמא יאמרו חלץ זה ונשא זה ותצא משני בגט בעל כרחו כדי שלא יהא חוטא נשכר ותצא מהיבם בחליצה כדי שלא יאמרו מחזיר חלוצתו

45. bGittin 87a; pGittin 9: 5, 50b, in Palestinian Talmud, ed. Sussmann, 1093.

46. bYevamot 92b.

47. bKiddushin 68a.

48. bYevamot 49a.

49. bYevamot 92b.

50. bYevamot 92a.

51. Jacob ben Meir Tam, *Sefer ha-Yashar,* ed. Schlesinger, 49–51 (sec. 54).

הוא וקם ליה בלא יבנה כיון שלא בנה שוב לא יבנה. אבל מר יהודאי גאון מחמיר שאפי' [37א] נתקדשה לזר מוציא השני בגט בעל כרחו, ומיקל בנשאת שאם יש בנים שיקיים שלא להוציא לעז על הבנים שלא כדין שהרי אין ממזר מיבמה ואם תצא משני מיחלפא באשה שהלך בעלה וכו' שתצא מזה ומזה והולד ממזר בדין מדין אשת איש אליבא דכולי עלמ'. ומדמי האי להאי ולא דמו, וכבר דחה הרב הגדול בהלכותיו[52] על פי דברי ר"ח דברי מר יהודאי וקבע שאפי' יש לה בנים תצא משני ותחלוץ. ובהאי ענינא שהוא ספק יבמה לשוק, דעתי למי שירצה לחוש שאם נשאת בלא חליצה אפי' אין לה בנים או נתקדשה לזה לא תצא משני ותחלוץ מפני ספקא ואזלינן בה לקולא שלא תצא משני כדברי מר יהודאי ביבמה לשוק ודאית היכא דיש לה בנים. ואם נרצה להחמיר אפי' בספיקה תצא משני כדברי הרב בנשאת אפי' יש לה בנים ולא פלגינן בין ודאה לספקה. וחולצת זו ליבם מספק ולא תתיבם מפני שהיא לו ספק ערוה שהיא ספק גרושת אחיו שהרי גרושת אח ערוה שהרי המגרש אשתו ספק גירושין ומת חולצת ולא מתיבמת שמא יפגע בספק גרושת אח. הרי ברור למי שחושש בחשש פסול גט זה שאם נתקדשה לזר או נשאת או לא נשאת כלל חולצת ולא מתיבמת שהרי אסור מצוה הוא זה כלומ' מדברי סופרים מפני שהיא ספק גרושת אח ואין לומ' בו כל העולה ליבום עולה לחליצה כל שאינו עולה ליבום אינו עולה לחליצה[53] שאין אומ' זה אלא באיסור ערוה גמורה. ועמודי עולם יאביחו אם יחמירו כפי הצורך ואם יקלו כפי היושר עליהם תבא ברכת טוב כלבב השואל וכלבב הנשאל ואם השואל הפלמוני הוא פלאי את שמו לא הוגד לי אנכי הנשאל פני כלפי מעלה וכל פניותי אינן אלא לימין אחד העם הים הקדמוני אחד מבני עליה והם מועטין המלאך הדובר בי הוציא הדין לאמתו החכם הכולל ר' יצחק יצ"ו פרי צדיק הותיק אדננו הגדול המורה ר' מרדכי נ"ע. זה שמי אבון מרואן ב"ר משה דמייראנגש צלב"י.[54]

Chapter 6

8. London, British Library, Or. 2705, fol. 199v. Jacob ben Moses of Bagnols, introduction to *Yesod ha-Hashgaḥah* (Foundation of Providence), a short composition on the Thirteen Divine Attributes.

בשנת מאה ושבעה עשר לאלף הששי ליצירה ראיתי נפלאות, וכעשרת הימים שנית חזיתי נוראות, וכעשרת ימים שלישית נראו לי צפונות לעתיד לעד ולאות. והדבר יש לו רגלים הלא הוא כמוס עמדי חתום באוצרות לבי. והנה בשמים עדי ויהי ייי למשען לי ואלהי לצור מחסי. ואקוד ואשתחוה לייי כי לא נמסרה

52. Alfasi, *Hilkhot ha-Rif*, Yevamot 29b, in Babylonian Talmud, vol. 8.
53. bYevamot 3a, 20a, 36a.
54. Habakkuk 2:4.

נפשי ונפש ביתי ביד אויב, וכי גמל עלי ולא עזב חסדו ואמתו מעם עבדו. ואדור נדר לעשות חבור קטן הכמות בנוי בבתים וחרוזות שקולות במאזני רעיוני עם באור קצר לבאר כונת הבתים למען ירוץ קורא בהם. יורו על פנת ההשגחה אשר ישגיח ייי על יראיו להצילם מהרע הנכון לבא עליהם כפי המערכת אשר סדר להנהיג המציאות. על כן קראתיו יסוד ההשגחה כאשר רמזתי בקודם. ברוך המקום ברוך הוא שעשה לי נס. כן יעשה ייי לנו ולעמו ישראל נסים ונפלאות סלה אמן.

9. London, British Library, Or. 2705, fol. 200r. Jacob ben Moses of Bagnols presenting his interpretation of a passage from the Bible commentary of Judah Romano.

הנה בהיותי באוינון בבית המדרש, שונה לתלמידים ההלכה החמורה מקונמות דכתבות[55] עם באור הר״ש והרב רבנו יוסף הלוי אבן מגש מרחיב מאד בהלכה ההיא על פי הר״ש ז״ל, הובא אלי כתב פילוסוף אחד היה מרומה לפי הנשמע לשאול ביאורו כי חמור הוא וסתום מאד יורה על חכמת ממציאו וזה נסחו. סבת הארכת הימים מהקדמונים לפי בעלי הטבע היתה תכונת האויר המקיף אשר היה אז זך ונקי לסבה ידועה. גם האנשים ההם היו מתנהגים על פי השכל והתבונה והעצה ולא היו רודפים אחר המותרות הממיתות הגופות קודם זמנם. אך לפי בעלי אמונה ותורה סבת ההארכה היתה הריחוק מהסדר התכליי הנתון למרוצת הטבע בגזרת החכמה העליונה להיותה מכונת לחדש מציאות יותר נכבד באדם אחר זה המציאות. ועל כן האנשים באלה הזמנים לקרבם אל התכלית אינם מאריכים ימים כאריכות הקודמים. וזה ההתחדשות אשר היה באדם אינו טבעי אך הוא חנינה מוחלטת מהחונן הראשון. ואעפ״י שהוית פרטי אחד במספר אחר הפסדו אינו נופל תחת השכל בתחלת העיון בהיותנו מציירים סבת התרבות הצורות אשר היא בהתרבות התנועות והעדר רבוים להעדר תנועה, ונבנה זה הציור על היות הפועל הראשון פועל בלא תנועה לא נרחיק זה הענין. והבן זה כי עמוק הוא. וכאשר הובא אלי כתב זה הרמוז, עיינתי בו ובארתיו לפי דעתי אני יעקב בר׳ משה דבנויולש עם היותי בהלכה. וזה באורי: [200ב] **סבת הארכת ימי הקדמונים**, כאדם ושת ואנוש וירד ומהללאל ושם ועבר ומתושלח ונח והכתובים בתורה זולתם אשר האריכו ימים. **לפי בעלי הטבע היה תכונת האויר.** היתה תחלת זכות האויר המקיף בהם **לסבה ידועה**, ר״ל לסבת היות זמנם קרוב להתחלת התנועה הסבובית ועדין לא נתעכר ונתעבה האויר בעליות האדים בהתמדה והחלק מן האויר השפל עדין לא נתעפש בעפושי בעלי ההויה וההפסד מזה המציאות השפל, ולכן היו מאריכים ימים האנשים ההם כי החיים תלויים באויר ובהזדככו יאריכון ובהתעפשו יקצרון. **גם האנשים ההם היו מתנהגים על פי השכל והעצה** ר״ל במזונותיהם, כי במאכלים

55. bKetubbot 59a–b.

הדקים מבא גדול לחדוד השכל ולהוליד דם טוב. **ולא היו רודפים אחר המותרות** ואחר המשגל אשר הם סבת מיתת הגוף בלא עתו. **אך לפי דעת בעלי האמונה האמתית והתורה התמימה סבת הארכת ימיהם היתה הריחוק מהסדר התכליי הנתון למרוצת הטבע** כלומ' שהם היו רחוקים מן האמת בהיותם בני מאה או מאתים שנה כי החכמה היתה מאד חסרה בימים ההם ולא היו יודעים רבונם עד אחר חיותם זמן רב כי לא נתפלספו הקדמונים ההם כל כך שיוכלו להשיג ולבא אל הסדר התכליי הוא ידיעת החכמה באמות במעט זמן כמו האחרונים אשר היישרו בה מספרי קדמוניהם אשר נטעו אילן החכמה עץ החיים והאחרונים לקטו הפרי. ומלת **הנתון** נקשרת עם הריחוק, כלומר הריחוק מהסדר [201א] התכליי הנתון למרוצת הטבע, ר"ל שמרוצת הטבע סבה לריחוק מהסדר התכליי כמלה הנותנת יניחוה הפילוסופים במקום סבה. כי האדם מדיני בטבע להתעסק בענינים המדיניים, ככקין עובד אדמה נקרא שמו כן לפי דעת חכם בהתעסקו בקנין המדומה ואין אדם זוכה לשתי שלחנות בעת אחת כי זה מונע זה וזה מסך מבדיל לזה. והארכת ימיהם הרשומה היתה **בגזרת החכמה העליונה** היא גזרת השם ית' וחכמתו **להיותם מכונת לחדש מציאות יותר נכבד באדם אחר זה המציאות**, ר"ל כי כונת החכמה האלהית היתה בהמצא האדם בעל שכל ונפש המדברת משכלת דבקה בחמר האוכל מעץ הדעת טוב ורע אולי ופן ישלח ידו ולקח גם מעץ החיים אשר הוא המציאות היותר נכבד בו המכונה בעדן אחרי המשכו בחמרי ואכל וחי לעולם[56] בהכרחי השכלי. **ועל כן האנשים באלו הזמנים** כלו' בזמננו זה **לקרבם אל התכלית** ר"ל שהמתבודדים והמתפלספים בזמן הזה הם יותר קרובים מן האמת מן הקדמונים ויותר שלמים בחכמה מהם ובזמן מועט ישיגו אמתת הנמצאות וממציאם כל מה שאיפשר להשכילו, **אינם מאריכים ימים כאריכות הקודמים** כי אין צורך בהארכה להשלים הכונה המכוונת מאתו ית' במציאות האדם. **וזה ההתחדשות אשר היה באדם** ממציאותו השני היותר נכבד מהראשון, אשר הוא השלמות האחרון אשר הוא השאר החלק השכלי ממנו, **אינו טבעי אך הוא חנינה מוחלטת מהחונן הראשון** הקדמון ית' על דרך [201ב] כי יי ייתן חכמה מפיו דעת ותבונה[57] בהמציאו אותו בתחלת היצירה בעל הכנה מזגית לקבל כל מושכל. **ואעפ"י שהוית פרטי אחד במספר אחר הפסדו אינו נופל תחת השכל בתחלת העיון** ר"ל אעפ"י שהִשָּׁאֵר והִמָּצֵא החלק השכלי מהאדם אשר הוא פרטי אחד במספר אחר הפסד הגוף אינו נופל תחת השכל בתחלת העיון, כי יחשב בעיון הגס היות החלק השכלי נפסד בהפסד שאר כחות הנפש. וכפי דעת קצת בקיאי הפילוסופים[58] אשר שער האמת נועל בפניהם, וזה שהם חשבו כי מפני שהנפש הדמיונית נפסדת והיא צריכה אל השכל בהגעת שלמותו עד שאי איפשר הגעתו לה מזולתה והוא שלמות לה, הנה יחוייב שיהיה נפסד השכל הנקנה כי בהפסד בעל השלמות יפסד שלמותו.

56. Genesis 3:22.
57. Proverbs 2:6.
58. Beginning of quotation from Gersonides (Levi ben Gershom).

והם לא ידעו שאם היתה הצורה הדמיונית סבה למציאות הצורה המושכלת היה זה ספק אלא שאין הענין כן. וזה שהצורה הדמיונית קרה שתהיה סבה באופן מה בהשגת הצורה המושכלת לא במציאותה אבל בהפך, וזה כי הצורה המושכלת סבה למציאות הצורה המוחשת אשר היא סבה למציאות הצורה הדמיונית. כבר התבאר זה במה שאחר הטבע, כאשר הורנו הרלב״ג.[59] וזה שאלו הענינים המוחשים אי איפשר שיהיה בהם הסדור המתמיד אשר בו יהיו מושכלים אם לא כשיהיו עלולים מסדור מושכל הוא שכל כמו שאי איפשר היות הסדור והיושר בענינים המלאכותיים אלא מפני הסדור המושכל הנמצא מהם בנפש האומן. ובהיות הענין כן רצוני שאין הצורה הדמיונית סבה במציאות [202א] הצורה המושכלת, הנה לא יחוייב כשתפסד הצורה הדמיונית שתפסד הצורה המושכלת, וזה שאין כל מה שהוא סבה בידיעה מסתלקת הידיעה בהסתלקו. והמשל שכבר יודרך האדם בידיעת דבר מהדברים הלמודיים, והוא מבואר שבהפסד התמונה ההיא לא יחויב שתפסד הידיעה אשר הגיעה לו ממנה, וזה מבואר מאד. ומזה יתבאר שהוא איפשר בשכל הנקנה שיהיה נצחי עם הפסד הנפש הדמיונית. עד כאן הולדת באור הנמשך ללשון **ואעפ״י שהוית פרטי אחד במספר אחד אחר הפסדו אינו נופל תחת השכל בתחלת העיון**. ועד מלת **בהיותנו מציירים** הוא הנושא וממלת **בהיותנו** והלאה הוא הנשוא. ויאמר הפילוסוף **בהיותנו מציירים סבת התרבות הצורות אשר הוא בהתרבות התנועות** ר״ל אשר ענין התרבות הצורות והם המושכלות השניות הנקנות בהקש מהמושכלות הראשונות הוא בהתרבות התנועות כי המושכלות הראשונות נקנות מהחוש עם ההשנות תמיד לאין תכלית. **והעדר רבויים להעדר תנועה** ר״ל להעדר תנועת הזוכר והדמיון אשר רבויים בכח שני אלו הכחות כי הדמיון יקנה לנו ענין המוחש עם העלות החוש ובכח הזוכר ישלם ההשנות ולזה יהיו שני אלו הכחות סבה אל קנותנו כל המושכלות באופן מה. **ונבנה זה הציור על היות הפועל הראשון** הוא השכל הפועל אשר אין די בקנין שום מושכל מזולתו **פועל בלא תנועה** כי הוא משפיע משפעו [202ב] על השכל האנושי ומתאחד ומתדבק בו בלא תנועה, והשנוי והחסרון אינו מצדו כלל כי אם מצד המקבל. **לא נרחיק זה הענין** כלומר הוית והשארות החלק השכלי אחר הפסד הגוף. **והבן זה כי עמוק הוא** כי בלי ספק להרחיב באור ברמזי זה הבאור אשר בארתיו לא יספיק ולא יכילהו ספר אחד כי יביא ההכרח ליכנס בעניני כחות הנפש ובמהות השכל האנושי והנפרד. והמבין יבין.

10. London, British Library, Or. 2705, fol. 202v. Jacob ben Moses of Bagnols presenting his interpretation of a passage from an unidentified source, attributed to Plato.

59. Gersonides, *Commentary on Song of Songs* 7.2, trans. Menachem Kellner (New Haven, 1998), 80.

אמר יעקב בר' משה דבאנויולש ראיתי לבאר עוד לשון אחר פילוסופי נראה אלי באוינוין וזה נסח הלשון. אמר אפלטון אין ראוי למשכיל שישען על התפלה לבורא כי הוא יתפלל מנתינת המשפט אל חכמתו. ומי שיבטח בטוב הנהגתו לברואיו ולא ישען על זה אלא מי שהוא צדיק בדרכיו ראוי להענות. ויהיה מה שיתפלל אליו ממה שיהיה לבורא ולא יהיה לזולתו מן הסוגים. ויהיה התחלת תפלתו האלהים אם יהיה זה איפשר כפי חכמתך. ורוב מה שיעזר המשכיל בבורא בהתחננו להכנע כחו המולדית מכחו העליונה. ואולם מה שזולת יתפלל בו למה שלמטה ממנו בבריאותיו ע"כ.

הפירוש. **אין ראוי למשכיל שישען על התפלה לבורא כי הוא יתפלל מנתינת המשפט אל חכמתו** כלומר שאין ראוי למשכיל שישען על התפלה לבד שיתפלל בה לבורא כשהוא יתפלל לו מהדבר הנתן אל משפט חכמתו ית' [203א] לתת לו כי המשכיל מצד היותו משכיל ישאל מאת הבורא הדבר אשר בחקו ית' לתת לו כפי גזרת חכמתו ית' ולא יבקש מאתו הנמנעות בחקו ית'. ואמר הפילוסוף כנותן עצה למשכיל שגם כי הוא ית' ושואל אליו הדבר הראוי והנתן למשפט חכמתו ית' לתתו לו אין ראוי לו שישען על תפלתו לבד. **ומי שיבטח בטוב הנהגתו לברואיו** כלומר ואין ראוי לו למשכיל גם כן שיהיה מי שיבטח בטוב הנהגתו ית' המנהיג בה ברואיו ויתעצל בדבר המצטרך לו ולא יעזור הוא עצמו לבקש ולתור אי זה דרך ישכון אור[60] דרושו ויניח הכל בידי השם. ויאמר על דרך המשל הנה השם ית' חנון ורחום הוא ומשגיח על ברואיו ומשפיע מטובו לכל ובו בטח לבי ונעזרתי והוא יתן לי צרכי וימלא משאלותי, וזה כי אולי המשכיל אינו כדאי להיות תפלתו נשמעת ולהיות מושגח מאתו ית' לפי שמעשיו בלתי רצויים כי אולי לא ידרוך דרך ישר כי ראובן על דרך משל יוכל להיות משכיל ונבון ומשיג דברים נמרצים ועליונים ולא יהיה נזהר להיות נשמר מחטוא לפני הש' ית' אם לפי מזגו וחמרו או על אי זה צד שיהיה. וזהו אמרו אחר זה **ולא ישען על אי זה אלא מי שהוא צדיק בדרכיו ראוי להענות** ר"ל והאמת כי לא יוכל להשען על זה שתקובל תפלתו אלא מי שהוא צדיק וישר בדרכיו תמים עם אלהיו נשמר מחטוא לו ית' כי זה האיש בלי ספק ראוי להענות. **ויהיה מי שיתפלל אליו ממה שיהיה לבורא ולא יהיה לזולתו מן הסוגים** כלומר ובתנאי זה גם כן שיהיה מה שיתפלל אליו הצדיק או המשכיל [203ב] ההוא ממה שיהיה בחק הבורא ובידו ית' לתתו לו ולא יהיה ביד זולתו מן הסוגים לתת לו שאלתו. ואמרו **מן הסוגים** כגון ככב או מזל כי הכל בחלקים השפלים יגיע מצד הסדור זולת המשכיל המתאחד באופן מה בגבוה שומר.[61] **ויהיה התחלת תפלתו האלהים אם יהיה זה איפשר כפי חכמתך** כלומ' שהתחלת תפלתו תהיה כך: השם ית' אני מבקש ממך דבר פלני זה, אם יהיה איפשר כפי גזרת חכמתך לתתו אלי שלא יהיה מכת הנמנע בחקך ית'. **ורוב מה שיעזר המשכיל בבורא** ר"ל רוב מה שיוכל להיות המשכיל נעזר בו ית'

60. Job 38:19.

61. Ecclesiastes 5:7.

בתפלתו, ואם הוא בלתי צדיק ראוי להענות בדרכים אחרים. **בהתחננו להכנע כחו המולדית לכחו העליונה** כלומר כשיתחנן כלו שיעזרהו בהכנע כחו החמרי לפני כחו השכלי על דרך[62] בא ליטהר מסייעין אותו. ותגבר הנפש המשכלת בדרך תוכל לאור באור אשר ממנה חוצבה. **ואולם מה שזולת ית' בו למה שלמטה ממנו בבריאותיו** ר"ל שמה שיתפלל המשכיל לבורא משאר דרושיו ושאלותיו זולת זה הדרוש הרשום הוא מתפלל בו לדבר מה שנתן מאתו ית' תחת ממשלת מי שהוא למטה ממנו ית' מבריאותיו אשר ברא. וזה עיון פילוסופי אין ראוי להאריך בו והמבין יבין. ויש פרשו בלשון הפלוסוף פירוש אחר לא נראה בעיני.

62. bShabbat 104a.

Bibliography

Manuscripts

Amsterdam, Portugees Israëlitisch Seminarium Ets Haim, ms. EH 47 A 31

Cambridge, University Library, Add. 500

Cambridge, University Library, Add. 2668

El Escorial, Real Biblioteca del Monasterio de San Lorenzo, G.IV.3

London, British Library, Add. 22089 (Margoliouth cat. no. 572)

London, British Library, Add. 22090 (cat. no. 573)

London, British Library, Add. 25717 (cat. no. 402)

London, British Library, Or. 2705 (cat. no. 551)

New York, Jewish Theological Seminary of America, MS R34 (8163)

Oxford, Bodleian Library, Opp. Add. fol. 70 (Neubauer cat. no. 2550)

Oxford, Bodleian Library, Laud. Or. 113 (cat. no. 2142)

Oxford, Bodleian Library, Opp. Add. 4°127 (cat. no. 2343)

Paris, Bibliothèque nationale de France, Hébreu 1391

Paris, Bibliothèque nationale de France, Hébreu 651 (2)

Paris, Alliance Israëlite Universelle, H 135 A

Vienna, Oesterreichische Nationalbibliothek, Cod. Hebr. 24

Printed Sources

Abba Mari ben Moses. *Minḥat Kena'ot*. Ed. Mordecai Leib Bisliches. Pressburg: Anton Edlen v. Schmid, 1838.

Abraham ben David of Posquières. *Teshuvot u-Fesakim*. Ed. Yosef Kafaḥ. Jerusalem: Mossad Harav Kook, 1964.

Abraham ben Isaac of Montpellier. *Perush*. Ed. Moshe Yehudah Blau. 3 vols. New York: Blau, 1962–1975.

—. *Perush Rabenu Avraham min ha-har 'al Yevamot*. Ed. Avigdor Arieli. Jerusalem: [s.n.], 2000.

—. *Tosafot Ri ha-Zaken* (Commentary on Kiddushin). In Babylonian Talmud, vol. 11.

Abraham ben Isaac of Narbonne. *Sefer ha-Eshkol*. Ed. Shalom Albeck and Ḥanokh Albeck. 2 vols. Jerusalem: Mekize Nirdamim, 1935–1938.

—. *She'elot u-Teshuvot*. Ed. Yosef Kafaḥ. Jerusalem: Magen, 1962.

Aharon ha-Kohen of Narbonne (Lunel). *Sefer Orḥot Ḥayim*, vol. 2. Ed. Moses Schlesinger. 2 vols. Berlin: Itzkowski, 1902.

Alfasi, Isaac ben Jacob. *Hilkhot ha-Rif*, Yevamot. In Babylonian Talmud, vol. 8.

Amram bar Sheshna. *Seder Rav ʿAmram Ga'on*. Ed. Daniel Goldschmidt. Jerusalem: Mossad Harav Kook, 1971.

Aristotle. *Parts of Animals*. Trans. A.L. Peck. Loeb Classical Library. Cambridge, MA: Harvard University Press, 1937.

Asher ben Yeḥiel. *Tosafot Rosh*. Ed. Shraga Vilman. 4 vols. Brooklyn: Vilman, 1996.

Ashkenazi, Bezalel ben Abraham. *Shitah Mekubetset (Ketubot)*. Constantinople: Yonah ben Yaʿakov, 1738.

Babylonian Talmud (*Talmud Bavli*). 20 vols. Vilna: Romm, 1881–1898.

Bacharach, Ya'ir Ḥayyim ben Moses Samson. *Ḥavot Ya'ir*. Frankfurt am Main: Vaust, 1699.

Benjamin ben Jonah of Tudela. *The Itinerary of Benjamin of Tudela*. Ed. Marcus Nathan Adler. London: Oxford University Press, 1907.

Corpus iuris canonici. Ed. Emil Friedberg. 2 vols. Leipzig: Bernhard Tauchnitz, 1879–1881.

David ben Levi of Narbonne. *Sefer ha-Mikhtam*. Ed. Yosef Hillel. 2 vols. Jerusalem: Ahavat Shalom, 2015–2017.

—. *Sefer ha-Mikhtam ʿal masekhtot Pesaḥim Sukah u-Moʿed Katan*, Ed. Moshe Yehudah Blau. New York: Blau, 1958.

Galen. *On the Usefulness of the Parts of the Body*. Trans. Margaret Tallmadge May. 2 vols. Ithaca: Cornell University Press, 1968.

Genesis Rabbah (Midrah Bereshit Rabbah). Ed. Julius Theodor and Ḥanokh Albeck. 4 vols. Berlin: Itzkowski, 1912–1936.

Gershom ben Solomon. *The Gate of Heaven (Shaʿar ha-Shamayim)*. Ed. and trans. F.S. Bodenheimer. Studies and Texts Towards the Knowledge of the History of Science in the Middle East 1. Jerusalem: Kiryat Sefer, 1953.

Gersonides (Levi ben Gershom). *Commentary on Song of Songs*. Trans. Menachem Kellner. Yale Judaica Series 28. New Haven: Yale University Press, 1998.

—. *The Wars of the Lord*. Trans. Seymour Feldman. 3 vols. Philadelphia: Jewish Publication Society, 1984–1999.

Ḥayyim ben Isaac Or Zaruʿa. *She'elot u-Teshuvot*. Ed. Menahem Avitan. Jerusalem: Avitan, 2002.

Ibn Adret: *see* Solomon ben Abraham ibn Adret

Isaac ben Abba Mari of Marseilles. *Sefer ha-Ittur*. Ed. Meir Yonah. 3 vols. Warsaw: Unterhendler, 1874–1885.

Isaac ben Immanuel de Lattes. *She'elot u-Teshuvot*. Ed. Mordechai Tzvi (Max Hermann) Friedländer. Vienna: Förster, 1860.

Isaac ben Jacob of Corbeil. "Piske Rabenu Ri me-Corbeil (Rulings by Rabbi Isaac of Corbeil)." Ed. Ḥayim Shelomoh Sha'anan. In *Sefer Ner le-Shem ʿayah*, ed. Ḥayim Shelomoh Sha'anan, 5–32. Bene Berak: Be-Hotsa'at ha-Mishpaḥah, 1988.

—. *Sefer Mitsvot Katan*. Cremona: Vincenzo Conti, 1556.

Isaac ben Sheshet Perfet. *She'elot u-Teshuvot.* Ed. David Metzger. Jerusalem: Mekhon Yerushalayim, 1993.

Israel ben Petaḥiah Isserlein. *Terumat ha-Deshen.* Venice: Bomberg, 1519.

Jacob ben Levi (Jacob of Marvège). *She'elot u-teshuvot min ha-shamayim.* Ed. Reuven Margaliot. Jerusalem: Mossad Harav Kook, 1957.

Jacob ben Meir Tam. *Sefer ha-Yashar.* Ed. Shim'on Shelomoh Schlesinger. Jerusalem: Daf Ḥen, 1974.

Jacob ben Moses of Bagnols. "Ezrat Nashim." In *Shitat ha-Kadmonim 'al masekhet Kidushin,* ed. Moshe Yehudah Blau, 271–364. New York: Blau, 1970.

—. "Ḥibur Isur ve-Heter." In *Shitat ha-Kadmonim 'al masekhet Ḥulin,* ed. Moshe Yehudah Blau, 9–137. New York: Blau, 1989.

Kimḥi, Isaac. "Be-din ha-notel yadav lo yekadesh (On the law that a person who washes his hands should not recite the blessing)." In *Sefer Zikaron Ner Sha'ul,* 28–42. Jerusalem: Mekhon Morashah, 2009.

Kimḥi, Mordechai. "Teshuvat Rabenu Mordekhai ben Rabi Yitzḥak me-ḥakhme Provincia be-'inyan bizuy talmide ha-ḥakhmim (A responsum by Rabbi Mordechai ben Isaac, from the sages of Provence, about the denigration of a sage)." Ed. Shemu'el Eli'ezer Stern. *Moriah* 28:1–2 (2006), 12–14.

Kokhavi, David ben Samuel. *Sefer ha-Batim 'al ha-Rambam.* Ed. Moshe Yehudah Blau. 2 vols. New York: Blau, 1978–1979.

Levi ben Gershom: *see* Gersonides

Luria, Solomon. *Yam shel Shelomoh: 'al masekhet Bava Kama.* Prague: Abraham ben Simeon Heide, 1615–1618.

Maḥzor Carpentras le-shalosh regalim. Ed. Avraham Montil. Amsterdam: Hirz Levi Rofe, 1759.

Maimonides, Moses. *Guide of the Perplexed.* Trans. Shlomo Pines. 2 vols. Chicago: University of Chicago Press, 1963–1979.

—. *Mishneh Torah.* Ed. Shabse Frankel. 10 vols. Jerusalem: Kehilat Bene Yosef, 1975–2003.

Manoaḥ of Narbonne, *Sefer ha-Menuḥah.* Ed. Elazar Hurvitz. Jerusalem: Mossad Harav Kook, 1970.

Meir ben Baruch of Rothenburg. *She'elot u-Teshuvot.* Cremona: Vincenzo Conti, 1557.

Ha-Me'iri, Menaḥem. *Bet ha-Beḥirah 'al masekhet Megilah.* Ed. Moshe Herschler. Jerusalem: Mekhon ha-Talmud ha-Yisra'eli ha-Shalem, 1962.

—. *Bet ha-Beḥirah 'al masekhet Sanhedrin.* Ed. Avraham Sofer (Schreiber). Jerusalem: Schreiber, 1965.

—. *Magen Avot.* Ed. Yekuti'el Kohen. Jerusalem: [s.n.], 1989.

Menaḥem de Lonzano. *Shete Yadot.* Venice: Bragadin, 1618.

Meshulam ben Moses of Béziers. *Sefer ha-Hashlamah.* Ed. Judah Lubetzky. Paris: Moeglin, 1885. Ed. Avraham Ḥafuta. 10 vols. Tel-Aviv: Yeshivat ha-Rambam, 1961–1975.

Nahmanides, Moses. *Hilkhot Bekhorot.* Ed. Me'ir Lev. Jerusalem: Mekhon ha-Rav Hershler, 1995.

Nicholas of Cusa. *De pace fidei.* Ed. Raymond Klibansky and Hildebrand Bascour. *Nicolai de Cusa opera omnia* 7. Hamburg: Meiner, 1959.

—. *Nicholas of Cusa's De pace fidei and Cribratio Alkorani: Translation and Analysis.* 2nd ed. Trans. Jasper Hopkins. Minneapolis: Arthur J. Banning Press, 1994.

Nissim ben Reuben Gerondi. *She'elot u-Teshuvot ha-Ran.* Ed. Leon Feldman. Jerusalem: Mekhon Regensburg, 1984.

Palestinian Talmud (*Talmud Yerushalmi*). Ed. Yaacov Sussmann. Jerusalem: Academy of the Hebrew Language, 2001.

Peretz ben Isaac ha-Kohen. *Ḥidushim le-'eḥad meha-rishonim 'al masekhet Menaḥot.* Ed. Mordekhai Gotesgnadeh. Jerusalem: Mekhon Yagdil Torah, 2000.

—. *Shitat ha-Kadmonim 'al masekhet Nazir.* Ed. Moshe Yehudah Blau. New York: Blau, 1972.

Pesikta de-Rab Kahana. Trans. William G. Braude and Israel J. Kapstein. Philadelphia: Jewish Publication Society of America, 1975.

Plato. *Laws.* Trans. R.G. Bury. 2 vols. Loeb Classical Library. Cambridge, MA: Harvard University Press, 1926.

Samson of Sens. Commentary on Mishnah, Ḥallah. In Babylonian Talmud, vol. 1.

—. Commentary on Mishnah, Terumot. In Babylonian Talmud, vol. 1.

Samuel ben Mordechai of Apt. *Perush.* In: *Mishneh Torah,* Vol. 1b (*Sefer Ahavah*). Ed. Shabse Frankel. Jerusalem: Kehilat Bene Yosef, 1975–2003.

Samuel ha-Nagid. *Ben Mishle* (After Proverbs). Ed. Shraga Abramson. Kol Shire Rabi Shemu'el ha-Nagid 4. Tel Aviv: Maḥbarot le-Sifrut, 1948.

Sanhedri Gedolah le masekhet Sanhedrin. 9 vols. Jerusalem: Harry Fishel Institute, 1968–2018.

Shir ha-Shirim Rabbah. Ed. Tamar Kadari, Schechter Institute of Jewish Studies. https://schechter.ac.il/midrash/shir-hashirim-raba/.

Solomon ben Isaac (Rashi). *Responsa.* Ed. Israel Elfenbein. New York: Schulsinger, 1943.

Solomon ben Abraham ibn Adret. *Ḥidushe ha-Rashba: masekhet Megilah.* Ed. Haim Zalman Dimitrovsky. Jerusalem: Mossad Harav Kook, 1981.

—. *Ḥidushe ha-Rashba: masekhet Shabat.* Ed. Ya'ir Bruner. Jerusalem: Mossad Harav Kook, 1986.

—. *She'elot u-Teshuvot.* Ed. Aharon Zaleznik. 8 vols. Jerusalem: Mekhon Yerushalayim, 1997–2005.

—. *Teshuvot ha-Rashba.* Ed. Haim Zalman Dimitrovsky. 2 vols. Jerusalem: Mossad Harav Kook, 1990.

Stern, Shemu'el Eli'ezer. *Me'orot ha-Rishonim.* Jerusalem: Mekhon Yerushalayim, 2002.

Teshuvot Ḥakhme Provinẓia (Teshuvot Ḥakhme Provintsya) (*Responsa* of the Sages of Provence). Ed. Abraham Sofer (Schreiber). Jerusalem: Akiva Yosef, 1967.

Tosefta. Ed. Saul Lieberman. 4 vols. New York: Jewish Theological Seminary of America, 1955–1988.

Thomas Aquinas. *Summa theologiae: Latin Text and English Translation.* Blackfriars Edition. 61 vols. London: Eyre and Spottiswoode; New York: McGraw-Hill, 1964–1981.

Zeraḥiah ha-Levi (Gerondi, Zeraḥiah ben Isaac, ha-Levi). *Sefer ha-Ma'or* on Alfasi, *Hilkhot ha-Rif,* Yevamot. In Babylonian Talmud, vol. 8.

Secondary Literature

Abramov-van Rijk, Elena. "Who Was Francesco Landini's Antagonist in His Defense of Ockham?" *Philomusica on-line* 14 (2015): 1–24.

Abramson, Shraga. "Agav keriʾah (Reading notes)." *Leshonenu* 42 (1978): 314–316.

Ackerman, Ari. "Ḥasdai Crescas on the Philosophic Foundation of Codification." *AJS Review* 37 (2013): 315–331.

Ackerman-Lieberman, Phillip Isaac. *The Business of Identity: Jews, Muslims, and Economic Life in Medieval Egypt.* Stanford: Stanford University Press, 2014.

Albeck, Ḥanokh. *Shishah sidre Mishnah meforash perush ḥadash* (Six orders of Mishnah with a new commentary). 6 vols. Jerusalem: Bialik Institute, 1959.

Albert, Avraham Mordekhai. *Sefer Maʿaser Kesafim.* Jerusalem: Maor, 1977.

Alexandre-Bidon, Danièle. *La mort au moyen âge: XIIIe–XVIe siècles.* Paris: Hachette, 1998.

Almeida, Rochelle. *The Politics of Mourning: Grief Management in Cross-Cultural Fiction.* Madison: Fairleigh Dickinson University Press, 2004.

Archambeau, Nicole. "Miraculous Healing for the Warrior Soul: Transforming Fear, Violence, and Shame in Fourteenth-Century Provence." *Historical Reflections* 41 (2015): 14–27.

Arieli, Avigdor. "On the Commentary on 'Menaḥot' Attributed to Rashba." *Alei Sefer* 16 (1989): 149–150. Hebrew.

Assaf, Lilach. "Lovely Women and Sweet Men: Gendering the Name and Naming Practices in German-Jewish Communities (Thirteenth to Fourteenth Centuries)." In *Intricate Interfaith Networks in the Middle Ages: Quotidian Jewish-Christian Contacts*, ed. Ephraim Shoham-Steiner, 231–250. Studies in the History of Daily Life 5. Turnhout: Brepols, 2016.

—. "The Language of Names: Jewish Onomastics in Late Medieval Germany, Identity and Acculturation." In *Konkurrierende Zugehörigkeit(en) Praktiken der Namengebung im europäischen Vergleich*, ed. Christof Rolker and Gabriela Signori, 149–160. Konstanz: UVK, 2011.

Assaf, Simcha. "Teshuvot ha-Geʾonim mitokh genazav shel R. Moshe Botarel ("Geonic *responsa*" from the archives of Moses Botarel)." In *Sefer ha-Yovel: kovets torani madaʿi mugash le-Dr. Binyamin Menashe Lewin*, ed. J.L. ha-Kohen Fishman, 1–20. Jerusalem: Mossad Harav Kook, 1940. Reprinted in Simcha Assaf, *Tekufat ha-Geʾonim ve-Sifrutah*, 323–340. Jerusalem: Mossad Harav Kook, 1967.

Assis, Yom Tov. *The Golden Age of Aragonese Jewry: Community and Society in the Crown of Aragon, 1213–1327.* London: Littman Library of Jewish Civilization, 1997.

—. "Sexual Behaviour in Mediaeval Hispano-Jewish Society." In *Jewish History: Essays in Honour of Chimen Abramsky*, ed. Ada Rapoport-Albert and Steven J. Zipperstein, 25–59. London: Halban, 1988.

Aubrey, Elizabeth. "The Dialectic between Occitania and France in the Thirteenth Century." *Early Music History* 16 (1997): 1–53.

Balasse, Céline. *1306: L'expulsion des juifs du royaume de France.* Bruxelles: De Boeck Université, 2008.

Ballan, Mohammad. "Fraxinetum: An Islamic Frontier State in Tenth-Century Provence." *Comitatus* 41 (2010): 23–76.

Bar-Asher, Avishai. "Kabbalah and Minhag: Geonic *Responsa* and the Kabbalist Polemic on Minhagim in the Zohar and Related Texts." *Tarbiz* 84 (2015): 195–263. Hebrew.

Baratier, Édouard. *La démographie Provençale du XIIIe au XVIe siècle*. Démographie et sociétés 5. Paris: S.E.V.P.E.N, 1961.

Barkaï, Ron. *A History of Jewish Gynaecological Texts in the Middle Ages*. Leiden: Brill, 1998.

Baron, Salo. *A Social and Religious History of the Jews*. 18 vols. New York: Columbia University Press, 1952–1993.

Bar-Tikvah, Binyamin. *Genres and Topics in Provençal and Catalonian Piyyut*. Be᾿er Sheva: Ben Gurion University, 2009. Hebrew.

—. *Liturgical Poems of Rabbi Yitzhak Hasniri*. Ramat-Gan: Bar Ilan University Press, 1996. Hebrew.

Bartlett, Robert. "Symbolic Meanings of Hair in the Middle Ages." *Transactions of the Royal Historical Society*, 6th series, 4 (1994): 43–60.

Barzilay, Tzafrir. "The Investigation of the Jews of Savoy on Suspicion of Poisoning Wells: A Reappraisal." *Chidushim* 21 (2019): 114–143. Hebrew.

Baugh, Carolyn G. *Minor Marriage in Early Islamic Law*. Leiden: Brill, 2017.

Baumgarten, Elisheva. *Mothers and Children: Jewish Family Life in Medieval Europe*. Princeton: Princeton University Press, 2004.

—. *Practicing Piety in Medieval Ashkenaz: Men, Women, and Everyday Religious Observance*. Philadelphia: University of Pennsylvania Press, 2014.

Bautier, Robert-Henri. "Feux, population et structure sociale au milieu du XVe siècle: L'exemple de Carpentras." *Annales: Économies, Sociétés, Civilisations* 14 (1959): 255–268.

Benedikt, Binyamin Ze᾿ev. *Merkaz ha-Torah be-Provans* (The Torah Center in Provence). Jerusalem: Mossad Harav Kook, 1985.

Benovitz, Moshe. *Kol Nidre: Studies in the Development of Rabbinic Votive Institutions*. Atlanta: Scholars Press, 1998.

Ben-Shalom, Ram. "The Ban Placed by the Community of Barcelona on the Study of Philosophy and Allegorical Preaching – A New Study." *Revue des études juives* 159 (2000): 387–404.

—. "Communication and Propaganda between Provence and Spain: The Controversy over Extreme Allegorization." In *Communication in the Jewish Diaspora: The Pre-Modern World*, ed. Sophia Menache, 171–225. Brill's Series in Jewish Studies 16. Leiden: Brill, 1996.

—. "The Disputation of Tortosa, Vicente Ferrer and the Problem of the Conversos According to the Testimony of Isaac Nathan." *Zion* 56 (1991): 21–46. Hebrew.

—. *The Jews of Provence and Languedoc: Renaissance in the Shadow of the Church*. Ra῾ananah: Open University of Israel, 2017. Hebrew.

Ben-Simon, Israel. "The Origins of the Meiri's Commentary on the Book of Proverbs and the Concept of Nations Bound by the Ways of Religion." *Jewish Studies Internet Journal* 11 (2012): 119–137. https://jewish-faculty.biu.ac.il/files/jewish-faculty/shared/ben-simon.pdf. Hebrew.

Ben–Yehudah, Eliezer. *A Complete Dictionary of Ancient and Modern Hebrew*. 8 vols. New York: International News, 1959. Hebrew.

Berger, David. *Cultures in Collision and Conversation: Essays in the Intellectual History of the Jews*. Boston: Academic Studies Press, 2011.

—. "Jews, Gentiles, and the Modern Egalitarian Ethos: Some Tentative Thoughts." In *Formulating Responses in an Egalitarian Age*, ed. Marc Stern, 83–108. Lanham: Rowman and Littlefield, 2005.

—. *Persecution, Polemic and Dialogue: Essays in Jewish-Christian Relations*. Boston: Academic Studies Press, 2010.

Berkovitz, Jay R. *Protocols of Justice: The Pinkas of the Metz Rabbinic Court, 1771–1789*. Studies in Jewish History and Culture 44. Leiden: Brill, 2014.

Berman, Ari. "*Ger Toshav* in the Halakhic Literature of the High Middle Ages." PhD diss., Hebrew University of Jerusalem, 2015.

Berman, Harold J. *Law and Revolution: The Formation of the Western Legal Tradition*. Cambridge, MA: Harvard University Press, 1983.

Berman, Lawrence V. "A Manuscript Entitled Shoshan Limudim and the Group of Meʿaynim in Provence." *Kiryat Sefer* 53 (1978): 368–372. Hebrew.

Berns, Andrew. "The Importance of Agriculture in Medieval Jewish Life: The Case of Crete." *Jewish History* 33 (2020): 275–298.

Blasco Orellana, Meritxell, José Ramón Magdalena Nom de Déu and Juliette Sibon. "Le *pinqas* (carnet personnel) de Mordacays Joseph (1374–1375), corailleur juif de Marseille." *Revue des études juives* 175 (2016): 251–307.

Bleich, J. David. "Divine Unity in Maimonides, the Tosafists and Meʾiri." In *Neoplatonism and Jewish Thought*, ed. Lenn Goodman, 237–254. Albany: State University of New York Press, 1992. Revised version in *The Philosophical Quest: Of Philosophy, Ethics, Law and Halakhah*, 33–52. Jerusalem: Maggid Books, 2013.

Blidstein, Gerald J. "Maimonides and Meʾiri on the Legitimacy of Non-Judaic Religion." In *Scholars and Scholarship: The Interaction Between Judaism and Other Cultures*, ed. Leo Landman, 27–35. New York: Yeshiva University Press, 1990.

—. "Menahem Meiri's Attitude Toward Gentiles – Apologetics or Worldview?" *Binah: Jewish Intellectual History in the Middle Ages* 3 (1994): 119–133.

—. "R. Menahem ha-Meʾiri: Aspects of an Intellectual Profile." *Journal of Jewish Thought and Philosophy* 5 (1995): 63–79.

Bonfil, Robert. *Rabbis and Jewish Communities in Renaissance Italy*, trans. Jonathan Chipman. Oxford: Oxford University Press for the Littman Library of Jewish Civilization, 1990.

Bonnassie, Pierre. "L'Occitanie, un état manqué?" *L'histoire* 14 (1979): 31–40.

Bos, Gerrit. *Novel Medical and General Hebrew Terminology from the 13th Century*. Vols. 1–3. Oxford: Oxford University Press, 2011–2016.

Bourdieu, Pierre. *The Logic of Practice*. Trans. Richard Nice. Stanford: Stanford University Press, 1990.

Breuer, Mordechai. "The Ashkenazi Semikha." *Zion* 33 (1968): 15–46. Hebrew.

—. *Oholei Torah (The Tents of Torah): The Yeshiva, Its Structure and History*. Jerusalem: Merkaz Shazar, 2003. Hebrew.

Brody, Robert. *The Geonim of Babylonia and the Shaping of Medieval Jewish Culture*. New Haven: Yale University Press, 1998.

Brundage, James A. *Law, Sex, and Christian Society in Medieval Europe*. Chicago: University of Chicago Press, 1987.

—. *The Medieval Origins of the Legal Profession: Canonists, Civilians, and Courts*. Chicago: University of Chicago Press, 2008.

Burns, Robert I. *Jews in Notarial Culture: Latinate Wills in Mediterranean Spain, 1250–1350*. Berkeley: University of California Press, 1996.

Calmann, Marianne. *The Carrière of Carpentras*. Oxford: Oxford University Press for the Littman Library of Jewish Civilization, 1984.

Campanini, Saverio. "Latin into Hebrew (and Back): Flavius Mithridates and His Latin Translations from Judah Romano." In *Latin into Hebrew: Texts and Studies*, vol. 2: *Texts in Contexts*, ed. Alexander Fidora, Harvey J. Hames and Yossef Schwartz, 161–193. Studies in Jewish History and Culture 40. Leiden: Brill, 2013.

Carlin, Marie-Louise. *La pénétration du droit romain dans les actes de la pratique Provençale (XIe–XIIIe siècle)*. Bibliothèque d'histoire du droit et droit romain 11. Paris: R. Pichon et R. Durand-Auzias, 1967.

Carmichael, Ann G. "Plague Persistence in Western Europe: A Hypothesis." *The Medieval Globe* 1 (2014): 157–191.

Catlos, Brian. *Muslims of Medieval Latin Christendom, c. 1050–1614*. Cambridge: Cambridge University Press, 2014.

Chajes, J.H. "He Said She Said: Hearing the Voices of Pneumatic Early Modern Jewish Women." *Nashim* 10 (2005): 99–125.

Chartrain, Frédéric. "Die Siedlung der Juden in der Dauphiné während des Mittelalters." In *Geschichte der Judenim Mittelalter von der Nordsee bis zu den Südalpen*, ed. Jörg R. Müller, 1: 143–168. Forschungen zur Geschichte der Juden. Abteilung A, Abhandlungen 14. 3 vols. Hannover: Hahnsche, 2002.

Chiffoleau, Jacques. *La comptabilité de l'au-delà: Les hommes, la mort et la religion dans la région d'Avignon à la fin du moyen âge (vers 1320–vers 1480)*. Rome: École Française de Rome, 1980.

Chitwood, Zachary. *Byzantine Legal Culture and the Roman Legal Tradition, 867–1056*. Cambridge: Cambridge University Press, 2017.

Classen, Albrecht. *Toleration and Tolerance in Medieval and Early Modern European Literature*. New York: Routledge, 2018.

Cohen, Mordechai Z. "The Qimhi Family." In *Hebrew Bible/ Old Testament: The History of its Interpretation*, ed. Magne Sæbø, I:2, 388–415. 3 vols. Göttingen: Vandenhoeck and Ruprecht, 1996–2015.

Cohen, Richard I. *Jewish Icons: Art and Society in Modern Europe*. Berkeley: University of California Press, 1998.

Cooper, Levi Yitzhak. "Liability According to the Laws of Heaven." LLM thesis, Bar Ilan University, 2001. Hebrew.

Cooperman, Bernard Dov. "Organizing Knowledge for the Jewish Market: An Editor/Printer in Sixteenth-Century Rome." In *Perspectives on the Hebraic Book: The Myron M. Weinstein Memorial Lectures at the Library of Congress*, ed. Peggy K. Pearlstein, 79–129. Washington, DC: Library of Congress, 2012.

—. "Political Discourse in a Kabbalistic Register: Isaac de Lattes' Plea for Stronger Communal Government." In *Be'erot Yitzhak: Studies in Memory of Isadore Twersky*, ed. Jay M. Harris, 47–68. Cambridge, MA: Harvard University Press, 2005.

Cuffel, Alexandra. "From Practice to Polemic: Shared Saints and Festivals as 'Women's Religion' in the Medieval Mediterranean." *Bulletin of the School of Oriental and African Studies* 68 (2005): 401–419.

David, Abraham. "L'expulsion des juifs français à la lumière des sources hébraïques." In *Philippe le Bel et les juifs du royaume de France (1306)*, ed. Danièle Iancu-Agou, 243–252. Nouvelle Gallia Judaica 7. Paris: Cerf, 2012.

—. "Sarid mi-khronikah Ivrit (Fragments from a Hebrew Chronicle)." *Alei Sefer* 6–7 (1979): 198–200.

Davidson, Israel. *Parody in Jewish Literature*. New York: Columbia University Press, 1907.

Davis, Adam J. "The Social and Religious Meanings of Charity in Medieval Europe." *History Compass* 12 (2014): 935–950.

Deshen, Shlomo. "The Enigma of Kol Nidre: An Anthropological and Historical Investigation." In *Studies in the History of Jewish Society in the Middle Ages and in the Modern Period*, ed. Immanuel Etkes and Yosef Salmon, 136–153. Jerusalem: Magnes Press, 1980. Hebrew.

—. "The Kol Nidre Enigma: An Anthropological View of the Day of Atonement Liturgy." *Ethnology* 18 (1979): 121–133.

Dinari, Yedidyah Alter. *The Rabbis of Germany and Austria at the Close of the Middle Ages*. Jerusalem: Bialik Institute, 1984. Hebrew.

Donahue, Charles Jr. *Law, Marriage and Society in the Later Middle Ages*. Cambridge: Cambridge University Press, 2007.

Dossat, Yves. "Les juifs à Toulouse: Un demi-siècle d'histoire communautaire." *Cahiers de Fanjeaux* 12 (1977): 117–139.

Drendel, John. "Jews, Villagers and the Count in Haute Provence: Marginality and Mediation." *Provence historique* 49 (1999): 217–231.

Dubno, Solomon. *Reshimah mi-sefarim rabim va-ḥashuvim* (List of many important books). Amsterdam: Yohanan Levi Rofe, 1814.

Duggan, Anne J. "The Effect of Alexander III's 'Rules on the Formation of Marriage' in Angevin England." *Anglo-Norman Studies* 33 (2010): 1–22.

Dunkelgrün, Theodor. "Dating the Even Bohan of Qalonymos ben Qalonymos of Arles: A Microhistory of Scholarship." *European Journal of Jewish Studies* 7 (2013): 39–72.

Efros, Israel. *Philosophical Terms in the Moreh Nebukhim*. Columbia University Oriental Studies 22. New York: Columbia University Press, 1924.

Eidelberg, Shlomo. *Jewish Life in Austria in the XVth Century*. Philadelphia: The Dropsie College for Hebrew and Cognate Learning, 1962.

Einbinder, Susan L. *No Place of Rest: Jewish Literature, Expulsion, and the Memory of Medieval France*. Philadelphia: University of Pennsylvania Press, 2009.

Elbogen, Ismar. *Jewish Liturgy: A Comprehensive History*. Trans. Raymond P. Scheindlin. Philadelphia: Jewish Publication Society, 1993.

Elman, Yaakov. "Meiri and the Non-Jew: A Comparative Investigation." In *New Perspectives on Jewish-Christian Relations in Honor of David Berger*, ed. Elisheva Carlebach and Jacob J. Schacter, 265–296. Leiden: Brill, 2012.

Elon, Menachem. *Jewish Law: History, Sources, Principles*. Trans. Bernard Auerbach and Melvin J. Sykes. Philadelphia: Jewish Publication Society, 1994.

Emanuel, Simcha. "Additional *Responsa* by Rabbi Shlomo ben Aderet." In *Professor Meir Benayahu Memorial Volume*, ed. Moshe Bar-Asher, Yehuda Liebes, Moshe Assis and Yosef Kaplan, 1: 329–339. 2 vols. Jerusalem: Yad ha-Rav Nissim, 2019. Hebrew.

—. *Fragments of the Tablets: Lost Books of the Tosaphists*. Jerusalem: Magnes Press, 2006. Hebrew.

—. "'From where the sun rises to where it sets': The *Responsa* by Rashba to the Sages of Acre." *Tarbiz* 83 (2015): 465–489. Hebrew.

—. "Halakhic Questions of Thirteenth-Century Acre Scholars as a Historical Source." *Crusades* 17 (2019): 115–130.

—. "The Struggle for Provençal Halakhic Independence in the Thirteenth Century." *Hispania Judaica Bulletin* 9 (2013): 5–14.

Emery, Richard W. *The Jews of Perpignan in the Thirteenth Century: An Economic Study Based on Notarial Records* New York: Columbia University Press, 1959.

Epstein, Isidore. *The Responsa of Rabbi Solomon ben Adreth of Barcelona as a Source of the History of Spain*. London: Paul, Trench, Trubner, 1925.

Farber, Zev. "The Development of the Three-Day Limit for Salting." *Milin Ḥavivin* 1 (2005): 38–72.

Farmer, Sharon. *Surviving Poverty in Medieval Paris: Gender, Ideology, and the Daily Lives of the Poor*. Ithaca: Cornell University Press, 2005.

Feldman, Leon A. "R. Nissim ben Reuben Gerondi: Archival Data from Barcelona." In *Exile and Diaspora: Studies in the History of the Jewish People Presented to Professor Haim Beinart*, ed. Aharon Mirsky, Avraham Grossman and Yosef Kaplan, 56–97. Jerusalem: Ben Zvi Institute, 1991.

Fenster, Thelma and Daniel Lord Smail. "Introduction." In *Fama: The Politics of Talk and Reputation in Medieval Europe*, ed. Thelma Fenster and Daniel Lord Smail, 1–12. Ithaca: Cornell University Press, 2003.

Fenton, Miriam. "Moving Bodies: Corpses and Communal Space in Medieval Ashkenaz." *Jewish Studies Quarterly* (forthcoming).

Fishman, Talya. "Introduction." In *Regional Identities and Cultures of Medieval Jews*, ed. Javier Castaño, Talya Fishman and Ephraim Kanarfogel, 1–18. London: Littman Library of Jewish Civilization, 2018.

Fowler, Kenneth. *Medieval Mercenaries*. Oxford: Blackwell, 2001.

Fram, Edward. *A Window on Their World: The Court Diary of Rabbi Hayyim Gundersheim, Frankfurt am Main, 1773–1794*. Cincinnati: Hebrew Union College Press, 2012.

Fränkel, David. "Biographie des R. Isaac di Lattes." *Alim: A Periodical for Bibliography and History of the Jews* 3 (1937): 27–33. Hebrew.

Frankl, Pinkus Fritz. "Die Familie Kimchi in ihrer Ausbreitung nach Ländern und zeiten." *Monatsschrift für Geschichte und Wissenschaft des Judenthums* 33 (1884): 552–561.

Freidenreich, David M. "Contextualizing Bread: An Analysis of Talmudic Discourse in Light of Christian and Islamic Counterparts." *Journal of the American Academy of Religion* 80 (2012): 411–433.

Freudenthal, Gad. "Abraham Ibn Ezra and Judah Ibn Tibbon as Cultural Intermediaries: Early Stages in the Introduction of Non-Rabbinic Learning into Provence in the Mid-Twelfth Century." In *Exchange and Transmission across Cultural Boundaries: Philosophy, Mysticism and Science in the Mediterranean World*, ed. Haggai Ben-Shammai, Shaul Shaked and Sarah Stroumsa, 52–81. Jerusalem: Israel Academy of Sciences and Humanities, 2013.

—. "Arabic and Latin Cultures as Resources for the Hebrew Translation Movement: Comparative Considerations Both Quantitative and Qualitative." In *Science in Medieval Jewish Cultures*, ed. Gad Freudenthal, 74–105. Cambridge: Cambridge University Press, 2011.

—. "Arabic into Hebrew: The Emergence of the Translation Movement in Twelfth-Century Provence and Jewish-Christian Polemic." In *Beyond Religious Borders: Interaction and Intellectual Exchange in the Medieval Islamic World*, ed. David M. Freidenreich and Miriam Goldstein, 124–143. Philadelphia: University of Pennsylvania Press, 2012.

—. "The Brighter Side of Medieval Christian-Jewish Polemical Encounters: Transfer of Medical Knowledge in the Midi (Twelfth-Fourteenth Centuries)." *Medieval Encounters* 24 (2018): 29–61.

— and Resianne Fontaine. "Gersonides on the Dis-/order of the Sublunar World and on Providence." *Aleph* 12 (2012): 299–328.

— and Resianne Fontaine. "Philosophy and Medicine in Jewish Provence, *anno* 1199: Samuel ibn Tibbon and Doeg the Edomite Translating Galen's *Tegni*." *Arabic Sciences and Philosophy* 26 (2016): 1–26.

Furst, Rachel. "Marriage Before the Bench: Divorce Law and Litigation Strategies in Thirteenth-Century Ashkenaz." *Jewish History* 31 (2017): 7–30.

Galinsky, Judah. "'And This Scholar Achieved more than Everyone for All Studied from His Works': On the Circulation of Jacob b. Asher's Four Turim from the Time of Its Composition until the End of the 15th Century." *Sidra* 19 (2004): 25–45. Hebrew.

—. "Ashkenazim in Sefarad: The Rosh and the Tur on the Codification of Jewish Law." *Jewish Law Annual* 16 (2006): 3–23.

—. "Jewish Charitable Bequests and the Hekdesh Trust in Thirteenth-Century Spain." *Journal of Interdisciplinary History* 35 (2005): 423–440.

—. "The Legacy of R. Judah ben Ha-Rosh, Rabbi of Toledo: A Chapter in the Exploration of the *Responsa* Literature of Christian Spain." *Pe'amim* 128 (2011): 175–210. Hebrew.

—. Of Exile and Halakhah: Fourteenth-Century Spanish Halakhic Literature and the Works of the French Exiles Aaron ha-Kohen and Jeruham b. Meshulam." *Jewish History* 22 (2008): 81–96.

—. "On Popular Halakhic Literature and the Jewish Reading Audience in Fourteenth-Century Spain." *Jewish Quarterly Review* 98 (2008): 305–327.

García y García, Antonio. "The Faculties of Law." In *A History of the University in Europe*, vol. 1: *Universities in the Middle Ages*, ed. Hilde de Ridder-Symoens,and Walter Rüegg, 388–408. Cambridge: Cambridge University Press, 1992.

Gardner, Christopher K. "Practice and Rhetoric: Some Thirteenth-Century Perspectives on the Legal Frontier Between 'France' and Toulouse." In *Frontiers in the Middle Ages: Proceedings of the Third European Congress of Medieval Studies*, ed. Outi Merisalo, 223–235. Turnhout: Brepols, 2006.

Gil, Moshe. *Documents of the Jewish Pious Foundations from the Cairo Geniza*. Leiden: Brill, 1976.

—. "Supplies of Oil in Medieval Egypt: A Geniza Study." *Journal of Near Eastern Studies* 34 (1975): 63–73.

Gilat, Yitzhak Dov. *Yad le-Gilat (In Memorium): Collected Essays*, Ed. Israel Zvi Gilat and Israel M. Ta-Shma. Jerusalem: Bialik Institute, 2002. Hebrew.

Given, James. *State and Society in Medieval Europe: Gwynedd and Languedoc under Outside Rule*. Ithaca: Cornell University Press, 1990.

Glasner, Ruth. "The Early Stages in the Evolution of Gersonides' 'The Wars of the Lord.'" *Jewish Quarterly Review* 87 (1996): 1–46.

—. *Gersonides: A Portrait of a Fourteenth-Century Philosopher-Scientist*. Oxford: Oxford University Press, 2015.

—. "Levi ben Gershom and the Study of Ibn Rushd in the Fourteenth Century." *Jewish Quarterly Review* 86 (1995): 51–90.

Goitein, S.D. *A Mediterranean Society: The Jewish Communities of the Arab World as Portrayed in the Documents of the Cairo Geniza*. 6 vols. Berkeley: University of California Press, 1967–1993.

Goldberg, Jessica. "The Legal Persona of the Child in Gratian's Decretum." *Bulletin of Medieval Canon Law* 24 (2000): 10–53.

Goldhaber, Yehiel. "Amirat Kol Nidre ve-hotsa'at sefer Torah be-lel Yom ha-Kipurim (Recitation of Kol Nidre and the Torah Service on the Eve of Yom Kippur)." *Kovets Bet Aharon ve-Yisrael* 17:1 (2001): 91–105.

Goldstein, Bernard and David Pingree. "Levi ben Gerson's Prognostication for the Conjunction of 1345." *Transactions of the American Philosophical Society*, new series, 80 (1990): 1–60.

Goldstein, David. "A Lonely Champion of Tolerance: R. Menachem ha-Meiri's Attitude Towards Non-Jews." *Talk Reason* (2002), http://www.talkreason.org/articles/meiri.cfm.

—. "Longevity, the Rainbow, and Immanuel of Rome." *Hebrew Union College Annual* 42 (1971): 243–250.

Goshen-Gottstein, Alon. *Same God, other God: Judaism, Hinduism, and the Problem of Idolatry*. New York: Palgrave Macmillan, 2016.

Gouron, André. "Diffusion des consulats méridionaux et expansion du droit romain aux XIIe et XIIIe siècles." *Bibliothèque de l'école des chartes* 121 (1963): 26–76. Reprinted in *La science du droit dans le Midi de la France au moyen âge*, chapter I. London: Variorum, 1984.

—. "Les étapes de la penetration du droit romain au XIIe siècle dans l'ancienne Septimanie." *Annales du Midi* 69 (1957): 103–120.

—. "Les juristes de l'école de Montpellier." *Ius Romanum Medii Aevi* IV, 3a (1970): 3–35.

—. "Note sur les origines de l'université d'Avignon." In *Études offertes à Jean Macqueron*, 361–366. Aix-en-Provence: Faculté de droit et des sciences économiques d'Aix-en-Provence, 1970. Reprinted in *La science du droit dans le Midi de la France au moyen âge*, chapter II.

—. "Le role social des juristes dans les villes méridionales au *moyen âge*." *Annales de la Faculté des Lettres et Sciences Humaines de Nice* 9–10 (1969): 55–67. Reprinted in *La science du droit dans le Midi de la France au moyen âge*, chapter III.

—. "The Training of Southern French Lawyers during the Thirteenth and Fourteenth Centuries." *Studia Gratiana* XV (1972): 217–228. Reprinted in *La science du droit dans le Midi de la France au moyen âge*, chapter IV.

Green, Monica. *Making Women's Medicine Masculine: The Rise of Male Authority in Pre-Modern Gynaecology*. Oxford: Oxford University Press, 2008.

Gross, Heinrich. "Zur Geschichte der Juden in Arles." *Monatsschrift für Geschichte und Wissenschaft des Judenthums* 28 (1879): 418–431.

Gross, Henri. "Notice sur Abba Mari de Lunel." *Revue des études juives* 4 (1882): 192–207.

—. *Gallia Judaica*. Paris: Cerf, 1897.

Hacker, Joseph. "Links Between Spanish Jewry and Palestine, 1391–1492." In *Vision and Conflict in the Holy Land*, ed. Richard Cohen, 111–139. Jerusalem: Ben Zvi Institute, 1985.

Haddad, Philippe. *Le Méiri: Le rabbin catalan de la tolérance*. Perpignan: Mare nostrum, 2007.

Ha-Kohen, Zadok. "He῾arot be-divre yeme ḥakhme Yisra᾽el (Comments on the History of Jewish Sages)." *Sinai* 21 (1947): 1–25.

Halbertal, Moshe. *Between Torah and Wisdom: Rabbi Menachem ha-Meiri and the Maimonidean Halakhists in Provence*. Jerusalem: Magnes Press, 2001. Hebrew.

—. *Concealment and Revelation: Esotericism in Jewish Thought and its Philosophical Implications*. Trans. Jackie Feldman. Princeton: Princeton University Press, 2007.

—. "Menahem ha-Me᾽iri – Talmudist and Philosopher." *Tarbiz* 63 (1993): 63–118. Hebrew.

—. "Ones Possessed of Religion: Religious Tolerance in the Teachings of the Me᾽iri." *Edah Journal* 1 (2000): 1–24.

Halkin, Abraham S. "Why Was Levi Ben Hayyim Hounded." *Proceedings of the American Academy for Jewish Research* 34 (1966): 65–76.

—. "Yedaiah Bedershi's Apology." In *Jewish Medieval and Renaissance Studies*, ed. Alexander Altman, 165–184. Cambridge, MA: Harvard University Press, 1967.

Hamilton, Bernard. "Our Lady of Saidnaiya: An Orthodox Shrine Revered by Muslims and Knights Templar at the Time of the Crusades." In *The Holy Land, Holy Lands, and Christian History*, ed. R.N. Swanson, 207–215. Studies in Church History 36. Woodbridge: Boydell Press, 2000.

Hanuka, Gabriel. "The Philosophy and Halakhic Theory of R. David d'Estelle." PhD diss., Bar Ilan University, 2013. Hebrew.

Harvey, Warren Zev. "Levi ben Abraham of Villefranche's Controversial Encyclopedia." In *The Medieval Hebrew Encyclopedias of Science and Philosophy*, ed. Steven Harvey, 171–188. Dordrecht: Springer, 2000.

Hendry, Jennifer. "Existing in the Hyphen: On Relational Legal Culture." In *Culture in the Domains of Law*, ed. René Provost, 179–190. Cambridge: Cambridge University Press, 2017.

Henshke, David. "The Firstborn of a Kosher Animal Outside the Land of Israel: From the Talmud to Maimonides and Back." In *Professor Meir Benayahu Memorial Volume*, ed. Moshe Bar-Asher, Yehuda Liebes, Moshe Assis and Yosef Kaplan, 1: 241–274. 2 vols. Jerusalem: Yad ha-Rav Nissim, 2019. Hebrew.

Hershman, Abraham M. *Rabbi Isaac ben Sheshet Perfet and His Times.* New York: Jewish Theological Seminary of America, 1943.

Hoffmann, David (Tsevi). *Der Schulchan-Aruch Und Die Rabbinen Über Das Verhältnis Der Juden Zu Andersgläubigen: Zur Berichtigung Des Von Prof. Gildemeister in Dem "isaakiade"-Prozesse Abgegebenen Gerichtlichen Gutachtens.* Berlin: Jüdischen Presse, 1885.

Horowitz, Elliott. "Coffee, Coffeehouses and the Nocturnal Rituals of Early Modern Jewry." *AJS Review* 14 (1989): 17–46.

Horrox, Rosemary, ed. and trans. *The Black Death.* Manchester: Manchester University Press, 1994.

Horwitz, David. "Rashba's Attitude Towards Science and Its Limits." *Torah u-Madda Journal* 3 (1991–1992): 52–81.

Housley, Norman. "The Mercenary Companies, the Papacy, and the Crusades, 1356–1378." *Traditio* 38 (1982): 253–280.

Hyams, Paul R. "Was There Really Such a Thing as Feud in the High Middle Ages?" In *Vengeance in the Middle Ages: Emotion, Religion and Feud,* ed. Susanna A. Throop and Paul R. Hyams, 151–176. Farnham: Ashgate, 2010.

Iancu, Danièle. *Les Juifs en Provence (1475–1501): de l'insertion a l'expulsion.* Marseille: Institut historique de Provence, 1981.

Iancu-Agou, Danièle. "Provence: Jewish Settlement, Mobility and Culture." In *The Jews of Europe in the Middle Ages (Tenth to Fifteenth Centuries),* ed. Christoph Cluse, 175–189. Turnhout: Brepols, 2004.

—. *Provincia Judaica: dictionnaire de géographie historique des juifs en Provence médiévale.* Collection de la Revue des études juives 48. Leuven: Peeters, 2010.

—. "Un siècle d'investigation sur les juifs du Midi médiéval dans les revues savantes juives d'expression française." In *Les revues scientifiques d'études juives,* ed. Simone Claude Mimouni and Judith Olszowy-Schlanger, 83–92. Collection de la Revue des études juives 38. Leuven: Peeters, 2006.

Imbach, Ruedi and Catherine König-Pralong. *Le défi laïque: Existe-t-il une philosophie de laïcs au moyen âge?* Paris: Librairie philosophique J. Vrin, 2013.

Izbicki, Thomas. "Nicholas of Cusa and the Jews." In *Conflict and Reconciliation: Perspectives on Nicholas of Cusa,* ed. Inigo Bocken, 119–130. Leiden: Brill, 2004.

Johnson, Tom. *Law in Common: Legal Cultures in Late-Medieval England.* Oxford: Oxford University Press, 2020.

Jordan, William Chester. "Administering Expulsion in 1306." *Jewish Studies Quarterly* 15 (2008): 241–250.

—. *The French Monarchy and the Jews: From Philip Augustus to the Last Capetians.* Philadelphia: University of Pennsylvania Press, 1989.

—. "Home Again: The Jews in the Kingdom of France, 1315–1322." In *The Stranger in Medieval Society,* ed. F.R.P. Akehurst and Stephanie Cain Van D'Elden, 27–45. Medieval Cultures 12. Minneapolis: University of Minnesota Press, 1997.

—. "The Jews and the Transition to Papal Rule in the Comtat-Venaissin." *Michael* 12 (1991): 213–232.

Kahana-Smilansky, Hagar. "The Mental Faculties and the Psychology of Sleep and Dreams."

In *Science in Medieval Jewish Cultures,* ed. Gad Freudenthal, 230–254. Cambridge: Cambridge University Press, 2011.

Kahn, Salomon. "Les Juifs de la sénéchaussée de Beaucaire." *Revue des études juives* 65 (1913): 181–195.

Kanarfogel, Ephraim. *Jewish Education and Society in the High Middle Ages.* Detroit: Wayne State University Press, 1992.

—. "Rabbinic Attitudes Toward Nonobservance in the Medieval Period." In *Jewish Tradition and the Nontraditional Jew,* ed. Jacob J. Schacter, 3–35. Northvale, NJ: Jason Aronson, 1992.

—. "Schools and Education." In *The Cambridge History of Judaism,* vol. VI: *The Middle Ages: The Christian World,* ed. Robert Chazan, 393–415. Cambridge: Cambridge University Press, 2018.

Kasher, Hannah. "The Meiri on Christian Allegorical Exegesis on the Consumption of Pork." *Zion* 69 (2004): 357–360. Hebrew.

Katz, Jacob. *Exclusiveness and Tolerance: Studies in Jewish-Gentile Relations in Medieval and Modern Times.* Oxford: Oxford University Press, 1961.

—. "Jewish Civilization as Reflected in the Yeshivot – Jewish Centers of Higher Learning." *Cahiers d'histoire mondiale* 10 (1966–1967): 674–704.

—. "On Moslems as Intermediaries in Judeo-Christian Commerce." *Tarbiz* 48 (1979): 374–376. Hebrew.

—. *Out of the Ghetto: The Social Background of Jewish Emancipation, 1770–1870.* New York: Schocken Books, 1978.

—. "Religious Tolerance in the Halakhic and Philosophical System of Rabbi Menahem Hame᾽iri." *Zion* 18 (1953): 15–30. Hebrew.

—. "Religious Tolerance in the Halakhic System of Rabbi Menahem Hame᾽iri – A Reply." *Zion* 46 (1981): 243–246. Hebrew.

—. *Tradition and Crisis: Jewish Society at the End of the Middle Ages.* Trans. Bernard Dov Cooperman. New York: New York University Press, 1993.

Kedar, Benjamin Z. "Convergences of Oriental Christian Muslim and Frankish Worshippers: The Case of Saydnaya." In *De Sion exhibit lex et verbum domini de Hierusalem: Essays on Medieval Law, Liturgy, and Literature in Honour of Amnon Linder,* ed. Yitzhak Hen, 59–69. Cultural Encounters in Late Antiquity and the Middle Ages 1. Turnhout: Brepols, 2001.

Kellner, Menachem. *Dogma in Medieval Jewish Thought: From Maimonides to Abravanel.* Oxford: Oxford University Press for the Littman Library of Jewish Civilization, 1986.

Kelman, Tirza. "The Use of Ashkenazic Decisors in the Beit Yosef Yore Dea 183–200 as a Case Study." MA thesis, Ben-Gurion University, 2012. Hebrew.

Kfir, Uriah. *A Matter of Geography: A New Perspective on Medieval Hebrew Poetry.* Études sur le judaïsme médiéval 74. Leiden: Brill, 2018.

Kirschenbaum, Aaron. *Equity in Jewish Law: Beyond Equity: Halakhic Aspirationism in Jewish Civil Law.* Library of Jewish Law and Ethics 18. New York: Yeshiva University Press, 1991.

Klein, Elka. *Hebrew Deeds of Catalan Jews, 1117–1316.* Publicacions de la Societat d'Estudis Hebraics 1. Barcelona: Societat Catalana d'Estudis Hebraics, 2004.

—. *Jews, Christian Society, and Royal Power in Medieval Barcelona.* Ann Arbor: University of Michigan Press, 2006.

—. "The Widow's Portion: Law, Custom, and Marital Property among Medieval Catalan Jews." *Viator* 31 (2000): 147–164.

Klibansky, Raymond, Erwin Panofsky and Fritz Saxl. *Saturn and Melancholy: Studies in the History of Natural Philosophy, Religion and Art.* London: Nelson, 1964.

Kogel Judith. *Joseph Seniri: Commentary on the Former Prophets.* Leiden: Brill, 2014.

Kohn, Roger S. *Les Juifs de la France du nord dans la seconde moitié du XIVe siècle.* Collection de la Revue des études juives 5. Leuven: Peeters, 1988.

Kohnstamm, Jackie A. and René Moulinas. "Archaïsme et traditions locales: Le mariage chez les juifs d'Avignon et du Comtat au dernier siècle avant l'émancipation." *Revue des études juives* 138 (1979): 89–115.

Koningsveld, P.S. van. "Muslim Slaves and Captives in Western Europe During the Late Middle Ages." *Islam and Christian-Muslim Relations* 6 (1995): 5–23.

Kowaleski, Maryanne. "Gendering Demographic Changes in the Middle Ages." In *The Oxford Handbook of Women and Gender in Medieval Europe,* ed. Judith M. Bennett and Ruth Mazo Karras, 181–196. Oxford: Oxford University Press, 2013.

—. "Singlewomen in Medieval and Early Modern Europe: The Demographic Perspective." In *Singlewomen in the European Past, 1250–1800,* ed. Judith M. Bennett and Amy M. Froide, 38–81. Philadelphia: University of Pennsylvania Press, 1999.

Krakowski, Eve. *Coming of Age in Medieval Egypt: Female Adolescence, Jewish Law, and Ordinary Culture.* Princeton: Princeton University Press, 2018.

Kreisel, Howard. *Judaism as Philosophy: Studies in Maimonides and the Medieval Jewish Philosophers of Provence.* Boston: Academic Studies Press, 2015.

—. *Prophecy: The History of an Idea in Medieval Jewish Philosophy.* Amsterdam Studies in Jewish Thought 8. Dordrecht: Kluwer Academic Publishers, 2001.

Kuehn, Thomas. *Law, Family, and Women: Toward a Legal Anthropology of Renaissance Italy.* Chicago: University of Chicago Press, 1991.

Lacave, José Luis. *Medieval Ketubot from Sefarad.* Trans. Eliahu Green. Hispania Judaica 11. Jerusalem: Magnes Press, 2002.

Lasker, Daniel. "The Longevity of the Ancients – Faith and Reason in Medieval Jewish Thought." *Diné Israel* 26–27 (2009–2010): 49–65. Hebrew.

Lauer, Rena N. *Colonial Justice and the Jews of Venetian Crete.* Philadelphia: University of Pennsylvania Press, 2019.

—. "Jewish Law and Litigation in the Secular Courts of the Late Medieval Mediterranean." *Critical Analysis of Law* 3 (2016): 114–132.

Le Goff, Jacques. *Intellectuals in the Middle Ages.* Trans. Teresa Lavender Fagan. Cambridge, MA: Blackwell, 1993.

Leiter, Brian. "Legal Formalism and Legal Realism: What is the Issue?" *Legal Theory* 16 (2010): 111–133.

Lesné-Ferret, Maïté. "The Notariate in the Consular Towns of Septimanian Languedoc (Late Twelfth-Thirteenth Centuries)." In *Urban and Rural Communities in Medieval France: Provence and Languedoc, 1000–1500,* ed. Kathryn Reyerson and John Drendel, 3–21. Medieval Mediterranean 18. Leiden: Brill, 1998.

Lévi, Israël. "Un recueil de consultations inédites de rabbins de la France méridionale." *Revue des études juives* 38 (1899): 103–122; 39 (1899): 76–84, 226–241; 43 (1901): 237–258; 44 (1902): 73–86.

Levy, Emil. *Provenzalisches Supplement-Wörterbuch.* 8 vols. Leipzig: Reisland, 1894–1924.

Limor, Ora. "Sharing Sacred Space: Holy Places in Jerusalem Between Christianity, Judaism, and Islam." In *In Laudem Hierosolymitani: Studies in Crusades and Medieval Culture in Honour of Benjamin Z. Kedar*, ed. Iris Shagrir, Ronnie Ellenblum and Jonathan Riley-Smith, 219–231. Crusades: Subsidia 1. Aldershot: Ashgate, 2007.

Loeb, Isidore. "Les Juifs de Malaucène." *Revue des études juives* 6 (1882): 270–272.

—. "Le procès de Samuel ibn Tibbon." *Revue des études juives* 15 (1887): 70–79.

Lourie, Elena. *Crusade and Colonisation: Muslims, Christians and Jews in Medieval Aragon.* Collected Studies 317. Aldershot: Variorum, 1990.

Malkiel, David. *Reconstructing Ashkenaz: The Human Face of Franco-German Jewry, 1000–1250.* Stanford: Stanford University Press, 2009.

Malter, Henry. "Shem Tob ben Joseph Palquera, II. His 'Treatise of the Dream.'" *Jewish Quarterly Review* new series 1 (1911): 451–500.

Manekin, Charles. *The Logic of Gersonides.* The New Synthese Historical Library 40. Dordrecht: Kluwer Academic Publishers, 1992.

Marciano, Yoel. *Sages of Spain in the Eye of the Storm: Jewish Scholars of Late Medieval Spain.* Jerusalem: Bialik Institute, 2019. Hebrew.

Margaliot, Mordechai. *Ha-ḥilukim she-ben anshe mizraḥ u-bene erets yisra᾽el* (The Differences Between the People of the East and Those of the Land of Israel). Jerusalem: Reuben Mass, 1938.

Marvin, Tamar Ron. "A Heretic from a Good Family? A New Look at Why Levi b. Abraham b. Hayim was Hounded." *AJS Review* 41 (2017): 175–201.

—. "The Making of Minhat Qena᾽ot: The Controversy over Ideational Transgression in Fourteenth-Century Jewish Occitania." PhD diss., Jewish Theological Seminary of America, 2013.

Matula, Jozef. "Nicholas of Cusa's Discourse of Tolerance in Modern Thought." *Intellectual History Review* 26 (2016): 33–41.

Mazo Karras, Ruth. "Sex and the Singlewoman." In *Singlewomen in the European Past, 1250–1800*, ed. Judith M. Bennett and Amy M. Froide, 127–145. Philadelphia: University of Pennsylvania Press, 1999.

McCarthy, Caley. "Midwives, Medicine and the Reproductive Female Body in Manosque, 1289–1500." MA thesis, University of Waterloo, 2011.

McCleery, Iona. "Both 'Illness and temptation of the enemy': Melancholy, the Medieval Patient and the Writings of King Duarte of Portugal (r. 1433–1438)." *Journal of Medieval Iberian Studies* 1 (2009): 163–178.

Mell, Julie. *The Myth of the Medieval Jewish Moneylender.* 2 vols. New York: Palgrave Macmillan, 2017–2018.

Menache, Sophia. *Clement V.* Cambridge: Cambridge University Press, 1998.

Menkes, Fred. "Une communauté juive en Provence au XIVe siècle: Étude d'un groupe sociale." *Le Moyen Age* 77 (1971): 277–303, 417–450.

Meri, Joseph W. *The Cult of Saints Among Muslims and Jews in Medieval Syria*. Oxford: Oxford University Press, 2002.

Michaud, Francine. *Un signe des temps: Accroisement des crises familiales autour du patrimoine à Marseille à la fin du XIIIe siècle*. Studies and Texts 117. Toronto: Pontifical Institute of Mediaeval Studies, 1994.

Mooney, Catherine M., ed. *Gendered Voices: Medieval Saints and Their Interpreters*. Philadelphia: University of Pennsylvania Press, 1999.

Moscovitz, Leib. "The Actions of a Minor are a Nullity? Some Observations on the Legal Capacity of Minors in Rabbinic Law." *Jewish Law Annual* 17 (2007): 63–120.

Moulinas, René. *Les juifs du pape: Avignon et le Comtat Venaissin*. Présences du judaïsme 6. Paris: Albin Michel, 1992.

Mrejen-O'Hana, Simone. "Hebrew in Carpentras and the Surrounding Area (Part One)." In *Sha'arei Lashon: Studies in Hebrew, Aramaic and Jewish Languages Presented to Moshe Bar-Asher*, ed. Aharon Maman, Steven E. Fassberg and Yohanan Breuer, 3: 344–367. 3 vols. Jerusalem: Bialik Institute, 2007. Hebrew.

—. "Le marriage juif sous l'Ancien Régime: L'exemple de Carpentras (1763–1792)." *Annales de démographie historique* (1993): 161–170.

—. *Le Registre d'Élie Crémieux: Ephémérides de la communauté juive de Carpentras (1736–1769)*. Jerusalem: Bialik Institute, 2009. Hebrew.

Mummey, Kevin and Kathryn Reyerson. "Whose City is This? Hucksters, Domestic Servants, Wet-Nurses, Prostitutes, and Slaves in Late Medieval Western Mediterranean Urban Society." *History Compass* 9 (2011): 910–922.

Mutius, Hans-Georg von. *Rechtsentscheide Isaak Kimchis aus Südfrankreich*. Judentum und Umwelt 35, 45. 2 vols. Frankfurt am Main: Peter Lang, 1992–1993.

—. *Rechtsentscheide Mordechai Kimchis aus Südfrankreich*. Judentum und Umwelt 31. Frankfurt am Main: Peter Lang, 1991.

Nahon, Gérard. "Le figuier du Seigneur: Relations hébraïques méridionales des exiles de 1306." In *Philippe le Bel et les juifs du royaume de France (1306)*, ed. Danièle Iancu-Agou, 211–241. Nouvelle Gallia Judaica 7. Paris: Cerf, 2012.

—. *Inscriptions hébraïques et juives de France médiévale*. Collection franco-judaïca 12. Paris: Les Belles Lettres, 1986.

Nederman, Cary. "Toleration in Medieval Europe: Theoretical Principles and Historical Lessons." In *Bridging the Medieval-Modern Divide: Medieval Themes in the World of the Reformation*, ed. James Muldoon, 45–64. Farnham: Ashgate, 2013.

—. *Worlds of Difference: European Discourses of Toleration, c. 1100–c.1550*. University Park: Pennsylvania State University Press, 2000.

Neubauer, Adolph. "Documents inédits: Jacob fils de Moïse de Bagnols." *Revue des études juives* 8 (1884): 51–58.

—. "Yedaya de Béziers." *Revue des études juives* 20 (1890): 244–248.

Nirenberg, David. *Communities of Violence: Persecution of Minorities in the Middle Ages*. Princeton: Princeton University Press, 1996.

Novak, David. *The Image of the Non-Jew in Judaism: An Historical and Constructive Study of the Noahide Laws*. Toronto Studies in Theology 14. New York: Edwin Mellen Press, 1983.

Oxford English Dictionary Online. Oxford University Press. https://www.oed.com

Olszowy-Schlanger, Judith. "Binding Accounts: A Ledger of a Jewish Pawn Broker from 14th Century Southern France (Ms. Krakow, BJ Przyb/163/92)." In *Books within Books: New Discoveries in Old Book Bindings*, ed. Andreas Lehnardt and Judith Olszowy-Schlanger, 97–147. European Genizah Texts and Studies 2. Leiden: Brill, 2014.

Onclin, Willy. "L'âge requis pour le mariage dans la doctrine canonique médiévale." In *Proceedings of the Second International Congress of Medieval Canon Law*, ed. Stephan Kuttner and John J. Ryan, 237–247. Vatican City: S. Congregatio de seminariis et studiorum universitatibus, 1965.

Oren, Gedalya. "R. Menahem ha-Meiri's Attitude toward the 'Other.'" *Da'at: A Journal of Jewish Philosophy and Kabbalah* 60 (2007): 29–49. Hebrew.

Otis, Leah Lydia. *Prostitution in Medieval Society: The History of an Urban Institution in Languedoc*. Chicago: University of Chicago, 1985.

Paden, William D. *Two Medieval Occitan Toll Registers from Tarascon*. Medieval Academy Books 115. Toronto: University of Toronto Press, 2016.

Pahlitzsch, Johannes. "Christian Pious Foundations as an Element of Continuity between Late Antiquity and Islam." In *Charity and Giving in Monotheistic Religions*, ed. Miriam Frenkel and Yaacov Lev, 125–151. Berlin: De Gruyter, 2009.

Para, Heather. "Plague, Papacy and Power: The Effect of the Black Death on the Avignon Papacy." *Saber and Scroll* 5 (2016): 7–22.

Paterson, Linda M. *Culture and Society in Medieval Occitania*. Variorum Collected Studies Series, CS 970. Farnham: Ashgate 2011.

—. *The World of the Troubadours: Medieval Occitan Society, c. 1100–c. 1300*. Cambridge: Cambridge University Press, 1993.

Pécout, Thierry. *L'invention de la Provence: Raymond Bérenger V (1209–1245)*. Paris: Perrin, 2004.

Penkower, Jordan S. *Masorah and Text Criticism in the Early Modern Mediterranean: Moses ibn Zabara and Menahem de Lonzano*. Jerusalem: Magnes Press, 2014.

Perles, Joseph. *R. Salomo b. Abraham b. Adereth: Sein Leben und seine Schriften*. Breslau: Schletter, 1863.

PESHAT: Philosophic and Scientific Hebrew Terminology. University of Hamburg. (https://peshat.gwiss.uni-hamburg.de/)

Pick, Shlomo H. "Jewish Aristocracy in Southern France." *Revue des études juives* 161 (2002): 97–121.

—. "Medieval Provençal Jewish Self-Government." *Trumah* 15 (2005): 105–138.

Pormann, Peter E. "Melancholy in the Medieval World: The Christian, Jewish, and Muslim Tradition." In *Rufus of Ephesus: On Melancholy*, ed. Peter E. Pormann, 179–196. Tübingen: Mohr Siebeck, 2008.

Poznanski, Samuel. "Sur un fragment d'une collection de consultations rabbiniques du XIVe siècle." *Revue des études juives* 40 (1900): 91–94.

Prawer, Joshua. *The History of the Jews in the Latin Kingdom of Jerusalem*. Oxford: Clarendon Press, 1988.

Preuss, Julius. *Biblical and Talmudic Medicine*. Trans. Fred Rosner. Northvale: Jason Aronson, 1993.

Pryor, John H. *Business Contracts of Medieval Provence: Selected Notulae from the Cartulary of Giraud Amalric of Marseilles, 1248*. Studies and Texts 54. Toronto: Pontifical Institute of Mediaeval Studies, 1981.

—. *Geography, Technology, and War: Studies in the Maritime History of the Mediterranean, 649–1571*. Cambridge: Cambridge University Press, 1988.

Radding, Charles M. and Antonio Ciaralli. *The Corpus Iuris Civilis in the Middle Ages: Manuscripts and Transmission from the Sixth Century to the Juristic Revival*. Brill's Studies in Intellectual History 147. Leiden: Brill, 2006.

Ray, Jonathan. *After Expulsion: 1492 and the Making of Sephardic Jewry*. New York: New York University Press, 2013.

—. *The Sephardic Frontier: The Reconquista and the Jewish Community in Medieval Iberia*. Ithaca: Cornell University Press, 2006.

Raynouard, François-Juste-Marie. *Lexique roman ou Dictionnaire de la langue des troubadours comparée avec les autres langues de l'Europe latine*. 6 vols. Paris: Silvestre, 1836–1844.

Reiner, Avraham (Rami). "From France to Provence: The Assimilation of the Tosafists' Innovations in the Provençal Talmudic Tradition." *Journal of Jewish Studies* 65 (2014): 77–87.

—. "Regulation, Law and Everything in Between: The Laws of Gittin as a Reflection of Society." *Tarbiz* 82 (2013): 139–163. Hebrew.

Reiner, Elchanan. "Maʿase she-ira be-k.k. Vermaiza ba-raʿash ha-gadol bi-shenat 396 (A story that happened in the community of Worms at the time of the great earthquake in 1626)." *Haaretz*, 4 October 2006.

—. "*Yihus* and Libel: Maharal, the Bezalel Family, and the *Nadler* Affair." In *Maharal, Overtures: Biography, Doctrine, Influence*, ed. Elchanan Reiner, 101–126. Jerusalem: Zalman Shazar Center, 2015. Hebrew.

Reyerson, Kathryn L. and Debra A. Salata, eds. *Medieval Notaries and Their Acts: The 1327–1328 Register of Jean Holanie*. Kalamazoo: Medieval Institute Publications, 2004.

Remer, Gary. "Ha-Meʾiri's Theory of Religious Toleration." In *Beyond the Persecuting Society: Religious Toleration Before the Enlightenment*, ed. John Christian Laursen and Cary J. Nederman, 71–92. Philadelphia: University of Pennsylvania Press, 1998.

Richler, Benjamin. *Guide to Hebrew Manuscript Collections*. Jerusalem: Israel Academy of Sciences and Humanities, 2014.

—. "Hebrew Manuscripts that were Separated." *Assufot* 1 (1987): 105–158. Hebrew.

Rider, Catherine. "Men's Responses to Infertility in Late Medieval England." In *The Palgrave Handbook of Infertility in History: Approaches, Contexts and Perspectives*, ed. Gayle Davis and Tracey Loughran, 273–290. London: Palgrave Macmillan, 2017.

Rigo, Caterina. "The Beʾurim on the Bible of R. Yehudah Romano: The Philosophical Method which Comes Out of Them, Their Sources in the Jewish Philosophy and in the Christian Scholasticism." PhD diss., Hebrew University of Jerusalem, 1996. Hebrew.

Roach, Andrew. "Occitania Past and Present: Southern Consciousness in Medieval and Modern French Politics." *History Workshop Journal* 43 (1997): 1–22.

Robinson, James T. "Al-Farabi, Avicenna, and Averroes in Hebrew: Remarks on the Indirect Transmission of Arabic-Islamic Philosophy in Medieval Judaism." In *The Judeo-Christian-Islamic Heritage: Philosophical and Theological Perspectives*, ed. Richard C. Taylor and Irfan

A. Omar, 59–87. Marquette Studies in Philosophy 75. Milwaukee: Marquette University Press, 2012.

—. "Secondary Forms of Philosophy: On the Teaching and Transmission of Philosophy in Non-Philosophical Literary Genres." In *Vehicles of Transmission, Translation, and Transformation in Medieval Textual Culture*, ed. Robert Wisnovsky, Faith Wallis, Jamie C. Fumo and Carlos Fraenkel, 235–248. Turnhout: Brepols, 2011.

Rogoziński, Jan. "Ordinary and Major Judges." *Studia Gratiana* 15 (1972): 589–611.

—. *Power, Caste, and Law: Social Conflict in Fourteenth-Century Montpellier.* Medieval Academy Books 91. Cambridge, MA: Medieval Academy of America, 1982.

Rollo-Koster, Joëlle. *Avignon and Its Papacy, 1309–1417: Popes, Institutions, and Society.* Lanham: Rowman and Littlefield, 2015.

—. "Death of Clergymen: Popes and Cardinals' Death Rituals." In *Death in Medieval Europe: Death Scripted and Death Choreographed*, ed. Joëlle Rollo-Koster, 164–185. London: Routledge, 2017.

—. "From Prostitutes to Brides of Christ: The Avignonese *Repenties* in the Late Middle Ages." *Journal of Medieval and Early Modern Studies* 32 (2002): 109–144.

Rosen-Zvi, Ishay. *The Mishnaic Sotah Ritual: Temple, Gender and Midrash.* Trans. Orr Scharf. Supplements to the Journal for the Study of Judaism 160. Leiden: Brill, 2012.

Rosman, Moshe. *How Jewish is Jewish History?* Oxford: Littman Library of Jewish Civilization, 2007

Rossiaud, Jacques. *Medieval Prostitution.* Trans. Lydia G. Cochrane. Oxford: Blackwell, 1995.

Roth, Pinchas. "A Responsum by Rabbi Isaac ben Mordechai Kimhi about a Needle in an Animal's Liver." *Yeshurun* 29 (2013): 28–32. Hebrew.

—. "Asking Questions: Rabbis and Philosophers in Medieval Provence." *Journal of Jewish Studies* 67 (2016): 1–14.

—. "Halakhah and Criticism in Southern France: R. David ben Saul on the Laws of Wine Made by Gentiles." *Tarbiz* 83 (2015): 439–463. Hebrew.

—. "Kosher Wine in Medieval Provence and Languedoc – Production and Commerce." *Revue des études juives* 178 (2019): 59–78.

—. "Later Provençal Sages – Jewish Law (Halakhah) and Rabbis in Southern France, 1215–1348." PhD diss., Hebrew University, 2012. Hebrew.

—. "Legal Strategy and Legal Culture in Medieval Jewish Courts of Southern France." *AJS Review* 38 (2014): 375–393.

—. "Manuscript Fragments of Early Tosafot in Perpignan." *European Journal of Jewish Studies* 14 (2020): 117–136.

—. "Mordechai Nathan and the Jewish Community of Avignon in the Late Fifteenth Century." *Jewish Studies Internet Journal* 17 (2019): 1–17. https://jewish-faculty.biu.ac.il/files/jewish-faculty/shared/JSIJ17/roth.pdf. Hebrew.

—. "Mourning Murderers in Medieval Jewish Law." In *Medieval and Early Modern Murder: Legal, Literary and Historical Contexts*, ed. Larissa Tracy, 77–95. Woodbridge: Boydell Press, 2018.

—. "'My precious books and instruments': Jewish Divorce Strategies and Self-fashioning in Medieval Catalonia." *Journal of Medieval History* 43 (2017): 548–561.

—. "The Nasi, the Judge and the Hostages: Loans and Oaths in Thirteenth-Century Narbonne." *Diné Israel* 33 (2019): 99–136.

—. "On Exegesis of the Jerusalem Talmud in Medieval Southern France." *Sidra: Journal for the Study of Rabbinic Literature* 29 (2015): 117–125. Hebrew.

—. "Rabbinic Politics, Royal Conquest and Provençal Jewish Identity." In *Regional Identities and Cultures of Medieval Jews*, ed. Talya Fishman, Ephraim Kanarfogel and Javier Castaño (London: Littman Library of Jewish Civilization, 2018), 173–191.

—. "Regional Boundaries and Medieval Halakhah: Rabbinic *Responsa* from Catalonia to Southern France in the Thirteenth and Fourteenth Centuries." *Jewish Quarterly Review* 105 (2015): 72–98.

—. "*Responsa* from Heaven: Fragments of a New Manuscript of 'She᾿elot u-teshuvot min ha-shamayim' from Gerona." *Materia Guidaica* 15–16 (2010–2011): 555–564.

—. "The *Responsa* of Gersonides and Their Reception." In *Gersonides' Afterlife: Studies on the Reception of Levi ben Gerson's Philosophical, Halakhic and Scientific Oeuvre in the 14th through 20th Centuries*, ed. Ofer Elior, Gad Freudenthal and David Wirmer, 311–340. Leiden: Brill, 2020.

Rubin, Jonathan. *Learning in a Crusader City: Intellectual Activity and Intercultural Exchanges in Acre, 1191–1291*. Cambridge Studies in Medieval Life and Thought, 4th Series, 110. Cambridge: Cambridge University Press, 2018.

Ruderman, David B. *Early Modern Jewry: A New Cultural History*. Princeton: Princeton University Press, 2010.

Saige, Gustave. *Les Juifs du Languedoc antérieurement au XIVe siècle*. Paris: Picard, 1881.

Saperstein, Marc. "The Conflict over the Rashba's Herem on Philosophical Study: A Political Perspective." *Jewish History* 1 (1986): 27–38. Revised version in *Leadership and Conflict: Tensions in Medieval and Modern Jewish History and Culture*, 94–112. Oxford: Littman Library of Jewish Civilization, 2014.

—. *Decoding the Rabbis: A Thirteenth-Century Commentary on the Aggadah*. Harvard Judaic Monographs 3. Cambridge, MA: Harvard University Press, 1980.

—. *Jewish Preaching 1200–1800: An Anthology*. Yale Judaica Series 26. New Haven: Yale University Press, 1989.

Schremer, Adiel. *Ma῾ase Rav: Halakhic Decision-Making and the Shaping of Jewish Identity*. Ramat Gan: Bar Ilan University Press, 2019. Hebrew.

Schwartz, Dov. *Central Problems of Medieval Jewish Philosophy*. Brill Reference Library of Judaism 26. Leiden: Brill, 2005.

—. *Studies on Astral Magic in Medieval Jewish Thought*. Trans. David Louvish and Batya Stein. Brill Reference Library of Judaism 20. Leiden: Brill, 2005.

Schwartz, Yossef. "Ernst Cassirer on Nicholas of Cusa: Between Conjectural Knowledge and Religious Pluralism." In *The Symbolic Construction of Reality: The Legacy of Ernst Cassirer*, ed. Jeffrey Andrew Barash, 17–39. Chicago: University of Chicago Press, 2008.

Schwarzfuchs, Simon. "A Takkanah of the Year 1313." *Bar Ilan Annual* 4–5 (1967): 209–219. Hebrew.

—. "Rabbi Isaac Joshua ben Immanuel of Lattes and the Jews of the Apostolic States." *Italia Judaica* 6 (1998): 66–79.

Sela, Shlomo. "Queries on Astrology Sent from Southern France to Maimonides: Critical Edition of the Hebrew Text, Translation and Commentary." *Aleph* 4 (2004): 89–190.

Sénac, Philippe. "Présence musulmane en Languedoc: Réalités et vestiges." *Cahiers de Fanjeaux* 18, *Islam et Chrétiens du Midi, XIIIe et XIVe siècles.* (1983): 43–57.

Septimus, Bernard. *Hispano-Jewish Culture in Transition: The Career and Controversies of Ramah.* Harvard Judaic Monographs 4. Cambridge, MA: Harvard University Press, 1982.

—. "Piety and Power in Thirteenth-Century Catalonia." In *Studies in Medieval Jewish History and Literature*, vol. 1. ed. Isadore Twersky, 197–230. Cambridge, MA: Harvard University Press, 1979.

Sermoneta, Giuseppe. "The Commentary to the First Weekly Reading in Genesis by Judah Romano, and Its Sources." In *Proceedings of the Fourth World Congress of Jewish Studies*, 2: 341–342. 2 vols. Jerusalem: World Union of Jewish Studies, 1965. Hebrew.

Seror, Simon. *Les noms des juifs de France au moyen âge.* Paris: Centre National de la recherche scientifique, 1989.

Shafat, Shoval. "The Interface of Divine and Human Punishment in Rabbinic Thought." PhD diss., Ben Gurion University of the Negev, 2011. Hebrew.

Shailat, Itzḥak. *The Letters and Essays of Moses Maimonides.* 2 vols. Ma ʿaleh Adumim: Shailat, 1995. Hebrew.

Shatzmiller, Joseph. "Between Abba Mari and Rashba: The Negotiations that Preceded the Herem in Barcelona (1303–1305)." *Studies in the History of the Jewish People and the Land of Israel* 3 (1974): 121–137. Hebrew.

—. "Community and Super-Community in Provence in the Middle Ages." In *Judenvertei-bungen in Mittelalter und früher Neuzeit*, ed. Friedhelm Burgard, Alfred Haverkamp and Gerd Mentgen, 441–448. Hannover: Verlag Hahnsche Buchhandlung, 1999.

—. "Counterfeit of Coinage in England of the 13th Century and the Way it was Remembered in Medieval Provence." In *Moneda y Monedas En La Europa Medieval (siglos XII–XV)*, 387–397. Pamplona: Gobierno de Navarra, 2000.

—. "In Search of the 'Book of Figures': Medicine and Astrology in Montpellier at the Turn of the Fourteenth Century." *AJS Review* 7/8 (1982–1983): 383–407.

—. Les Juifs de Provence pendant la peste noire." *Revue des études juives* 133 (1974): 457–480.

—. *Justice et injustice au début du XIVe siècle: l'enquête sur l'archevêque d'Aix et sa renunciation en 1318.* Sources et documents d'histoire du moyen âge 2. Rome: École française de Rome, 1999.

—. *Médecine et justice en Provence médiévale: Documents de Manosque, 1262–1348.* Aix-en-Provence: Université de Provence, 1989.

—. "Minor Epistle of Apology of Rabbi Kalonymos ben Kalonymos." *Sefunot* 10 (1966): 7–52. Hebrew.

—. "Ordinances of a Jewish Community in Provence, 1313." *Kiryat Sefer* 50 (1975): 663–667. Hebrew.

—. "Rabbi Isaac Ha-Cohen of Manosque and His Son Rabbi Peretz: The Rabbinate and Its Professionalization in the Fourteenth Century." In *Jewish History: Essays in Honour of Chimen Abramsky*, ed. Ada Rapoport-Albert and Steven J. Zipperstein, 61–83. London: Halban, 1988.

—. *Recherches sur la communauté juive de Manosque au moyen âge: 1241–1329*. Paris: Mouton, 1973.
—. *Shylock Reconsidered: Jews, Moneylending, and Medieval Society*. Berkeley: University of California Press, 1990.
—. "Les tossafistes et la première controverse maimonidienne." In *Rashi et la culture juive en France du nord au moyen âge*, ed. Gilbert Dahan, Gérard Nahon and Elie Nicolas, 57–82. Collection de la Revue des études juives 16. Paris: Peeters, 1997.
—. "Tumultus et rumor in sinagoga: An Aspect of Social Life of Provençal Jews in the Middle Ages." *AJS Review* 2 (1977): 227–255.
—. "Tumultus et rumor in sinagoga: Suite d'une enquête." *Provence historique* 195–196 (1999): 451–459, 208 (2002): 249–258.
—. "Terminologie politique en hébreu médiéval: Jalons pour un glossaire." *Revue des études juives* 142 (1983): 133–140.
— and Rodrigue Lavoie. "Médicine et gynécologie au moyen âge: Un exemple provençal." *Razo: Cahiers du Centre d'études Médiévales de Nice* 4 (1984): 133–143.
Shemesh, Aharon and Moshe Halbertal. "The Me'un (Refusal): The Complex History of a Halakhic Anomaly." *Tarbiz* 82 (2014): 377–393. Hebrew.
Shoham-Steiner, Ephraim. "'For a prayer in that place would be most welcome': Jews, Holy Shrines and Miracles – A New Approach." *Viator* 37 (2006): 369–395.
—. "Jews and Healing at Medieval Saints' Shrines: Participation, Polemics, and Shared Cultures." *Harvard Theological Review* 103 (2010): 111–129.
—. *On the Margins of a Minority: Leprosy, Madness, and Disability among the Jews of Medieval Europe*. Trans. Haim Watzman. Detroit: Wayne State University Press, 2014.
Sibon, Juliette. *Les juifs de Marseille au XIVe siècle*. Nouvelle Gallia Judaica 6. Paris: Cerf, 2011.
Sirat, Colette. *A History of Jewish Philosophy in the Middle Ages*. Cambridge: Cambridge University Press, 1985.
—. "Entering the Field of Philosophy: Provence, Mid-Fourteenth Century." In *Jewish Education from Antiquity to the Middle Ages: Studies in Honour of Philip S. Alexander*, ed. George J. Brooke and Renate Smithius, 398–411. Ancient Judaism and Early Christianity 100. Leiden: Brill, 2017.
—. "Paléographie hébraïque médiévale." *Annuaire de l'École Pratique des Hautes Études* (1971/1972): 399–409.
—. "Studia of Philosophy as Scribal Centers in Fifteenth-Century Iberia." In *The Late Medieval Hebrew Book in the Western Mediterranean: Hebrew Manuscripts and Incunabula in Context*, ed. Javier del Barco, 46–69. Études sur le judaïsme médiéval 65. Leiden: Brill, 2015.
— and Marc Geoffroy. "The Modena Manuscript and the Teaching of Philosophy in Fourteenth and Fifteenth Century Spain." In *Study and Knowledge in Jewish Thought*, ed. Howard Kreisel, 185–202. Be'er-Sheva: Ben Gurion University Press, 2006.
Smail, Daniel Lord. *The Consumption of Justice: Emotions, Publicity, and Legal Culture in Marseille, 1264–1423*. Ithaca: Cornell University Press, 2003.
Smithius, Renate. "Preaching to his Daughter: Jacob Anatoli's Goad for Students (Malmad ha-talmidim)." In *Jewish Education from Antiquity to the Middle Ages: Studies in Honour of*

Philip S. Alexander, ed. George J. Brooke and Renate Smithius, 341–397. Ancient Judaism and Early Christianity 100. Leiden: Brill, 2017.

Soloveitchik, Haym. "A Note on the Penetration of Roman Law in Provence." *Tijdschrift voor Rechtsgeschiednis* 40 (1972): 227–229.

—. "Can Halakhic Texts Talk History." *AJS Review* 3 (1978): 153–196.

—. *Collected Essays.* 2 vols. Oxford: Littman Library of Jewish Civilization. 2013–2014.

—. "Jewish and Provençal Law: A Study in Interaction." In *Mélanges Roger Aubenas*, 711–723. Montpellier: Faculté de droit et des sciences économiques de Montpellier, 1974.

—. "Rabad of Posquieres: A Programmatic Essay." In *Studies in the History of Jewish Society in the Middle Ages and in the Modern Period*, ed. Immanuel Etkes and Yosef Salmon, 7–40. Jerusalem: Magnes Press, 1980.

—. "Three Themes in the Sefer Ḥasidim." *AJS Review* 1 (1976): 311–357.

—. *The Use of Responsa as an Historical Source.* Jerusalem: Shazar Institute, 1990. Hebrew.

Sparks, Chris. *Heresy, Inquisition and Life Cycle in Medieval Languedoc.* Heresy and Inquisition in the Middle Ages 3. Woodbridge: York Medieval Press, 2014.

Spufford, Peter. *Handbook of Medieval Exchange.* Royal Historical Society Guides and Handbooks 13. London: Royal Historical Society, 1986.

Stampfer, Shaul. *Families, Rabbis and Education: Traditional Jewish Society in Nineteenth-Century Eastern Europe.* Oxford: Littman Library of Jewish Civilization, 2010.

Steiner, Richard C. "Kol Nidre: Past, Present and Future." *Jewish Studies Internet Journal* 12 (2013): 1–46. https://jewish-faculty.biu.ac.il/files/jewish-faculty/shared/JSIJ12/steiner.pdf.

Steinschneider, Moritz. *Hebrew Translations of the Middle Ages and the Jews as Transmitters.* Ed. Charles H. Manekin, Y. Tzvi Langermann and Hans Hinrich Biesterfeldt. Amsterdam Studies in Jewish Philosophy 16. Dordrecht: Springer, 2013.

Stern, Gregg. "What Divided the Moderate Maimonidean Scholars of Southern France in 1305?" In *Be'erot Yitzhak: Studies in Memory of Isadore Twersky*, ed. Jay M. Harris, 347–376. Cambridge, MA: Harvard University Press, 2005.

—. *Philosophy and Rabbinic Culture: Jewish Interpretation and Controversy in Medieval Languedoc.* London: Routledge, 2009.

Strashun, Matityahu. "Mikhtav ʿal devar R. Shem Tov baʿal ha-ʾemunotʾ (Letter about Rabbi Shem Tov, author of Sefer ha-Emunot)." *Pirḥe Ẓafun* 1 (1841): 46–48.

Strayer, Joseph R. *Les gens de justice du Languedoc sous Philippe le Bel.* Études d'histoire méridionale 5. Toulouse: Association Marc Bloch, 1970.

—. *The Albigensian Crusades.* New York: Dial Press, 1971.

Sussmann, Yaacov. "Rabad on Shekalim? A Bibliographical and Historical Riddle." In *Me'ah She'arim: Studies in Medieval Jewish Spiritual Life in Memory of Isadore Twersky*, ed. Ezra Fleischer et al., 131–170. Jerusalem: Magnes Press, 2001. Hebrew.

Talmage, Frank. *Apples of Gold in Settings of Silver: Studies in Medieval Jewish Exegesis and Polemics.* Ed. Barry Dov Walfish. Papers in Mediaeval Studies 14. Toronto: Pontifical Institute of Mediaeval Studies, 1999.

—. *David Kimhi: The Man and the Commentaries.* Harvard Judaic Monographs 1. Cambridge, MA: Harvard University Press, 1975.

Tanenbaum, Adena. "Arrogance, Bad Form, and Curricular Narrowness: Belletristic Critiques of Rabbinic Culture from Medieval Spain and Provence." In *Rabbinic Culture and Its Critics: Jewish Authority, Dissent, and Heresy in Medieval and Early Modern Times*, ed. Daniel Frank and Matt Goldish, 57–81. Detroit: Wayne State University Press, 2008.

Ta-Shma, Israel M. *The Early Ashkenazic Prayer: Literary and Historical Aspects.* Jerusalem: Magnes Press, 2003. Hebrew.

—. *Early Franco-German Ritual and Custom.* Jerusalem: Magnes Press, 1992. Hebrew.

—. *Rabbi Zeraḥiah ha-Levi ba'al ha-Ma'or u-vene ḥugo: Le-toldot ha-sifrut ha-rabanit be-Provans.* Jerusalem: Mossad Harav Kook, 1992.

—. *Ritual, Custom and Reality in Franco-Germany, 1000–1350.* Jerusalem: Magnes Press, 1996. Hebrew.

—. *Studies in Medieval Rabbinic Literature.* 4 vols. Jerusalem: Bialik Institute, 2004–2010. Hebrew.

Terris, Jules de. *Les évêques de Carpentras: Étude historique.* Avignon: Seguin Frères, 1886.

Theis, Valérie. *Le gouvernement pontifical du Comtat Venaissin.* Collection de l'École française de Rome 464. Rome: École française de Rome, 2012.

Toch, Michael. *The Economic History of European Jews: Late Antiquity and Early Middle Ages.* Études sur le judaïsme médiéval 56. Leiden: Brill, 2013.

Touati, Charles. "Le problème du Kol Nidrey et le responsum inédit de Gersonide (Lévi ben Gershom)." *Revue des études juives* 154 (1995): 327–342.

Toukabri, Hmida. *Satisfaire le ciel et la terre: Les fondations pieuses dans le judaïsme et dans l'islam au moyen âge.* Bibliothèque d'études juives 44. Paris: Honoré Champion, 2011.

Turlan, Juliette M. "Recherches sur le mariage dans la pratique coutumière (XIIe–XVIe s.)." *Revue historique de droit français et étranger*, 4e sér., 34 (1957): 477–528.

Twersky, Isadore. *Introduction to the Code of Maimonides (Mishneh Torah).* Yale Judaica Series 22. New Haven: Yale University Press, 1980.

—. *Rabad of Posquières: A Twelfth-Century Talmudist.* Cambridge, MA: Harvard University Press, 1962; 2nd ed., Philadelphia: Jewish Publication Society of America, 1980.

Urbach, Efraim Elimelech. "Rabbi Menahem ha-Meiri's Theory of Tolerance: Its Origin and Limits." In *Studies in the History of Jewish Society in the Middle Ages and in the Modern Period Presented to Professor Jacob Katz on his Seventy-Fifth Birthday*, ed. Immanuel Etkes and Yosef Salmon, 34–44. Jerusalem: Magnes Press, 1980. Hebrew. Reprinted in *Studies in Judaica*, ed. Moshe D. Herr and Jonah Fraenkel, 366–376. Jerusalem: Magnes Press, 1998.

—. *The Tosaphists: Their History, Writings and Methods.* 4th ed. 2 vols. Jerusalem: Bialik Institute, 1980. Hebrew.

Valenzuela-Lamas, Silvia. "Shechita and Kashrut: Identifying Jewish Populations through Zooarcheology and Taphonomy: Two Examples from Medieval Catalonia (North-Eastern Spain)." *Quaternary International* 330 (2014): 109–117.

Venetianer, Ludwig. *Das Buch der Grade von Schemtob b. Joseph ibn Falaquera.* Berlin: Calvary, 1894.

Verger, Jacques. *Men of Learning in Europe at the End of the Middle Ages.* Trans. Lisa Neal and Steven Rendall. Notre Dame: University of Notre Dame Press, 2000.

Warburg, A. Yehuda. "The Propriety of a Conditional Divorce." *Tradition* 47 (2014): 31–56.

Wei, Ian P. *Intellectual Culture in Medieval Paris: Theologians and the University, c. 1100–1330*. Cambridge: Cambridge University Press, 2012.

Weil, Gérard E. "Enquêtes et chantiers: Tallard et Espinasses." *Provence Historique* 32 (1982): 437–446.

—. *La Bibliothèque de Gersonide d'après son catalogue autographe*. Ed. Frédéric Chartrain. Leuven: Peeters, 1991.

—. "Symilon de Lambesc Courrier du Dauphin, Symilon d'Hyères Assassiné au Conil du Castelet en 1340 & les rabbins de Haute-Provence." In *Les juifs dans la Méditerranée, médiévale et moderne*. 25–52. Cahiers de la Méditerranée: Collection de la Revue des études juives 10. Nice: Université de Nice, 1986.

Welkenhuysen, Andries. "La peste en Avignon (1348) décrite par un témoin oculaire, Louis Sanctus de Beringen." In *Pascua Mediaevalia: Studies voor Prof. Dr. J.M. de Smet*, ed. R. Lievens, E. van Mingroot and W. Verbeke, 452–492. Mediaevalia Lovaniensia, ser. 1, 10. Leuven: Universitaire pers Leuven, 1983.

Wernham, Monique. *La communauté juive de Salon-de-Provence d'aprés les actes notariés 1391–1435*. Studies and Texts 82. Toronto: Pontifical Institute of Mediaeval Studies, 1987.

Wieben, Corinne. "Unwilling Grooms in Fourteenth-Century Lucca." *Journal of Family History* 40 (2015): 263–276.

Wieder, Naphtali. *The Formation of Jewish Liturgy in the East and the West: A Collection of Essays*. Jerusalem: Ben Zvi Institute, 1998. Hebrew.

Winroth, Anders. "The Legal Revolution of the Twelfth Century." In *European Transformations: The Long Twelfth Century*, ed. Thomas F.X. Noble and John Van Engen, 338–353. Notre Dame: University of Notre Dame Press, 2012.

Woolf, Jeffrey R. *The Fabric of Religious Life in Medieval Ashkenaz (1000–1300)*. Leiden: Brill, 2015.

—. "French Halakhic Tradition in the Late Middle Ages." *Jewish History* 27 (2013): 1–20.

—. "Methodological Reflections on the Study of Halakhah." *European Association for Jewish Studies Newsletter* 11 (2001): 9–14.

Yahalom, Shalem. *Between Gerona and Narbonne: Nahmanides' Literary Sources*. Jerusalem: Ben Zvi Institute, 2012. Hebrew.

—. "On the Place of Hasagot ha-Rabad in the Literature of the Rishonim." In *Ta Shma: Studies in Judaica in Memory of Israel M. Ta-Shma*, ed. Avraham (Rami) Reiner et al., 443–465. 2 vols. Alon Shevut: Tevunot, 2011. Hebrew.

Zalcman, Lawrence. "Christians, *Noṣerim* and Nebuchadnezzar's Daughter." *Jewish Quarterly Review* 81 (1991): 411–426.

Zimmer, Yitshak (Eric). *Olam ke-minhago noheg: Perakim be-toldot ha-minhagim, hilkhotehem, ve-gilgulehem* (Society and Customs: Studies in the History and Metamorphosis of Jewish Customs). Jerusalem: Shazar Center for the History of Israel, 1996.

Zinder, Ariel. "'There they stand at midnight, time and again': Seliḥot for Repentance Nights by Yitzḥak ibn Giyyat." PhD diss., Hebrew University, 2014. Hebrew.

Zohar, Zvi. "Teleological Decision-Making in Halakhah: Empirical Examples and General Principles." *Jewish Law Association Studies* 22 (2012): 331–362.

Zonta, Mauro. "Medieval Hebrew Translations of Philosophical and Scientific Texts: A

Chronological Table." In *Science in Medieval Jewish Cultures*, ed. Gad Freudenthal, 17–73. Cambridge: Cambridge University Press, 2011.

Zunz, Leopold. *Gesammelte Schriften*. Berlin: Gerschel, 1876.

—. *Literaturgeschichte der synagogalen poesie*. Berlin: Gerschel, 1865.

—. *Namen der Juden*. Leipzig: Fort, 1837.

—. "Ritus der Synagoge von Avignon." *Allgemeine Zeitung fur Judentums* 144,147, 151 (1838); 3, 12, 18, 20, 21, 30, 72, 83, 89, 103 (1839); 11 (1840).

—. *Zur Geschichte und Literatur*. Berlin: Veit, 1845.

Index